I'm Every Woman

LONNAE O'NEAL PARKER

I'm Every Woman

Remixed Stories of Marriage, Motherhood, and Work

Amistad

An Imprint of *HarperCollins*Publishers

HarperCollins books may be purchased for educational, business, or sales promotional use. For information, please write: Special Markets Department, HarperCollins Publishers, 10 East 53rd Street, New York, NY 10022.

FIRST EDITION

Design by Katy Reigel

Printed on acid-free paper

Library of Congress Cataloging-in-Publication Data

Parker, Lonnae O'Neal.
    I'm every woman : remixed stories of marriage, motherhood, and work /
Lonnae O'Neal Parker.—1st ed.
        p.   cm.
    ISBN 10: 0-06-059292-3 (alk. paper)
    ISBN 13: 978-0-06-059292-9
        1. African American women. 2. Women, Black. 3. Marriage. 4. Motherhood.
    5. Women—Employment. I. Title.

E185.86+
305.48'896073'0092—dc22
    [B]   2005041237

05   06   07   08   09   BVG/RRD   10   9   8   7   6   5   4   3   2   1

For Momma, with love. Now I understand
For Momma Susie and Grandma Mable, who speak to me
For Betty Powers, Sarah Gudger, and Jenny Proctor,
the slave women who lived to tell about it
And for all the black women whose way I try to walk

Acknowledgments

This book was born around the dining room table of my dear friends, Liana and Jabari Asim, where many are nourished. I used to take pride in being a writer with book potential. It was the Asimteam who turned that potential energy kinetic.

Liana, thank you for your inspired midwifery. For sustaining phone calls, for ideas brimming with wisdom and intelligence, and, most definitely, for that weekend retreat when I despaired. You are a gift to my life and that of my family. Thank you to Jabari, my *Washington Post* colleague, for introducing me to that little man at Chehaw Station who requires that our work possess an extra level of research and commitment. You really do have an answer for everything. Your intellectual rigor and brilliance have helped light some of my darkest writing places.

Thank you to my editor, Dawn L. Davis, who got it from the moment I sat down—who has a knack for getting it. It was so affirming to share late night e-mails when the women's work seemed endless. I am privileged to have worked with you on this project. (Sorry about that whole *voodoo doll* thing. The writing can make you crazy.) Thank you to my agent, Joy Harris. You have wonderful instincts and your expert touch enabled me to grow into this project. I love working with you. Stacey Barney, thank you for your keen insights and your ear for language. I have so appreciated being able to call you for help and, of course, the occasional primal scream.

Thank you to my former boss, Eugene Robinson, for talking to me about books until I was writing one of my own, then giving me the time to do it. Even though you skipped over the hellish parts, I'm not mad, homey. A heartfelt thanks to my current boss, Deborah Heard. Your sustained, thoughtful attention helped turn me into a writer and the chair in your office has been one of the best parts of my career. Thank you for allowing me to grow.

Thank you, Sydney Trent. I am so grateful for all you did. You went above and beyond the call and I don't know that I could have gotten through this without your editing eyes. Thank you, Lynn Medford. You are my Wilson, (WILSON! like from the movie, *Castaway*) and I took enormous comfort in the fact that you were just a few clicks away.

Thank you, Donna Britt and Jo-Ann Armao, who first gave me the space to write.

A hearty thank you to Professor Bart Landry. Your book, *Black Working Wives,* gave me the theoretical clarity I needed and your patient explanations greatly aided my understanding and writing. Thank you, Professor Adele Logan Alexander, for giving me a more vivid and detailed understanding of the lives of black women. Thank you, Valerie Boyd, for your television expertise. Thank you, Ericka King, for all your research assistance.

Thank you to my *girls*! I love you! Your friendship is one of my greatest blessings and this book is only the latest thing I couldn't have done without you. Thank you, Terina Winfrey, for your weekly calls. They were such a perfect touch! And knowing you'd be checking in helped me stay calm and get through the work one chapter at a time. Thank you, Shonda Sims. Your calls and enthusiasm and long talks over shared mother-of-three moments inspired me. Your excitement was contagious and always let me know I was on the right track. Thank you, Julie Stanton, for your wisdom and advice. I love your ability to see things clearly and I've had a whole vicarious life through your travels. Lafayetta Boone, thank you for your genorosity, constant encouragement, and affirming gifts of soul food. They kept me feeling well loved and well fed, which helped me keep going. Thank you, Dana McCurry, for being right there at every stage with just the right take on things. Your thoughtfulness has meant the world and helped me draw strength when the way got rough. Thank you, Stephanie Crockett, for knowing what I needed to write and giving it to me. What a gift! Thank you for understanding the work the way a writer would. Some of my prettiest words are yours. Join me in this place.

Thank you, Rhome Anderson. You always said I should write a book. Thank you for reading and for informing my perspective. Your intelligence and hip-hop artistry lifts me. Thank you for continuing to break bread Sunday afternoons at the Parkers'. Aaron McGruder, thank you for making me understand how to do the work, and how important it is. I truly miss you on this side of the world.

Thank you to my *Washington Post* colleagues past and present who encouraged me and helped inform my perspective: Deneen Brown, Lisa Frazier Page, Yolanda Woodlee, Tom Shroder, Marcia Davis, Natalie Hopkinson, Mae Israel, Michelle Singletary, Rita Kempley, Vanessa Williams, Esther Iverem, Teresa Wiltz, Jennifer Frey, Ann Gerhart, Krissah Williams, Ovetta Wiggins, Tracey Reeves,

Nancy Trejos, Claudia Levy, Leslie Morgan-Steiner, Julie Tate, Jacqueline Trescott, Mary Lischer, and Lynne Duke. Thank you, Kevin Merida, Doug Worthy, Michael Fletcher, Darryl Fears, Keith Alexander, Justin Blum, Stephen A. Crockett, Jr., Courtland Milloy, and, certainly, Hamil Harris. Thank you, Wil Haygood, who told me book writing was hard lonely work, and it was, but less so with his encouragement. Thank you also to Stephen Hunter who, of course, likened the work to fighting a long battle and helped me understand how to show up at the computer every day. Thank you Marvin Joseph for making me look good.

Thank you to my fellow journalism colleagues and travelers, De-Wayne Wickham, David Person, and Betty Bayé. Your support has meant a great deal to me.

Thank you to family friends: J.R. and LaFonda Fenwick, Thomas Johnson and Ebony Boulware-Johnson, Brian and Elanna Gilmore, Leo and Cathi Givs, Keith Boone, Tynesia Hand-Smith, Yelberton Watkins, Alicia Miller, Lois Peck, Jayne Seidman, Joby DuPree, Angie Fox and the Social Butterflies, Kim Alfonso and the Butterflies, the Sojourners.

Thanks to Meri and Shante at Merle Norman. All that eyebrow therapy helped me through.

Thank you, thank you to Monique Greenwood and Brian Evans, for hosting me at Akwaaba DC. Your writer's retreat restored me and gave me a quiet place to scratch out my thoughts.

Thank you, Bridget Warren, for your guidance and support through the years.

Thank you, Ben Ellis, for giving us better tools.

Dona Patti, gracias por toda su ayuda con la casa y especialmente con los niños. Adoramos que seas parte de nuestras vidas y no puedo imaginar este libro sin ti. Me alegra saber que podemos cuidar de nuestras respectivas familias.

Finally, thank you to my family who gave me everything I needed to write and more. Thank you, Joel for all your cards. Thanks, Brandon, Ryan, Darryl, and Alex, I love you guys. Thanks for the memories: Uncle Ronnie and Aunt Carolyn, Traci, Ronald, Amber, Cousin David, Aunt Jackie, Uncle Al and Aunt Dorothy, Uncle Dave, Julia "Cee-Cee," and Marcus B.

Thank you to Tim and Joye, Robin and Robert. Thank you, Ruth "Shaggy" and Tom "Peanuts," for your gifts of music and reunion.

Thanks, Cousin Kim. You are my little sister and I'm glad we're walking this way together. Thank you, Brittany for all your help. I am thrilled that you are in our lives and not just because I love to keep a relative in the basement.

Big hugs and thank yous to my mother-in-law, Evelyn Parker. We are so blessed to have you close. Thank you for always being there.

Thank you, Charles Allen O'Neal, I hope one day you find your way back.

Lisa, thank you so much for staying up and letting me read to you. There's little that's more special than late night talks with your sister. I love you and thank you for always looking out for me.

Thank you to my darling children. I love you always. Sydney, thank you for your help with your sister and brother and for stacking my books and papers. I know you wanted this book to be entitled *Sydney and the Others* and I'm sorry it didn't work out. Why don't you save that for your special book? Savannah, thank you for your smarts and funny jokes and letting me rub your back. You always give Mommy good things to say. Satchel, thank you for twisting my cell phone apart. I know you just wanted to free me from outside distractions. And when you plucked the "I" off my computer keyboard I realize you were just trying to remind me it's not all about me.

Thank you, Ralph. Sonnets of love to you. You held it all down, just like you always do, and gave me room write, even when you didn't have room to spare. Thank you for listening to all my rewrites. Your support has meant the world to me and the kids and we are so lucky to have you.

Momma, thank you for making this book happen; for your stories and phone calls and all your support. You gave me more will. Thank you for teaching me about how best to love daughters and being fiercely in my corner. I love you so.

Finally, to Lamis Jarrar. All my successes are yours. Thank you for doing the work with me. It's the only reason I can write. You are my other mother and I owe you my world. I love you always.

I have undoubtedly forgotten someone whose support has meant a great deal to me. Please forgive me and know that you are also appreciated.

Contents

Introduction

In my high school chemistry class, all the black girls used to sit at neighboring tables paying scant attention to talk of valence, molarity, and atomic half-lives. During lectures, we often remained engrossed in conversation, except for every so often when one of us would take a break from the group affirmations to answer a question or join in the larger class discussion. We doubted that advanced chemistry ultimately had a great deal to do with our hopes and aspirations, but we were well-versed in the ways of two worlds. We knew the importance of lifting our voices on our final grades, and we understood the value, subtle and manifest, of going on the record with our insights.

I was reminded of the duality of those times when a friend asked why I wrote this book. It is, in part, a response, I told her. An attempt to raise my hand to say, *Excuse me, I'd like to offer a little different take on motherhood methods or contemporary child equations.*

For years I've listened to the din of modern womanhood in the larger classroom of my peers. I've ducked the exploding salvos and sidestepped buried land mines that have torn into women from both sides of the mommy and culture wars. I've watched from a safe distance, keeping counsel with other black women with long histories and instructive family narratives to sustain us as we struggle, not with each other, but to nurture our families, agitate for our communities, and keep our eyebrows arched and lovely. It is consuming work with its own sets of challenges and rewards that can keep us too busy to weigh in with observations and lessons learned, especially since no one is asking us.

If you do a search for *working mothers* at Border's Books online, you'll get more than 750 hits. Change that to *black working mothers* and you get seven. The same online search at Barnes and Noble only gives you 195 *black working mother* titles, many of which simply feature the word *black,* while the total for *working mothers* is nearly 3,500 (although many of these also merely feature the words *working mother* or *mother* and may not be directly related to the subject of working mothers). It is ironic that the voices of black women have not penetrated media and popular culture discussions of family and work/life balance in a more meaningful way. After all, significant numbers of middle-class black women have been struggling to have it all since before their mainstream counterparts even won the vote. Especially in cities, a majority of black women have worked outside the home and raised families for more than one hundred years. Nationally, a majority of married, middle-class black women— women who could have chosen to stay home—have been in the labor force since the mid-1950s. Their married, middle-class white counterparts reached the same status nearly twenty years later.

It is that history, and our own frequent insularity, that helps explain why I didn't realize there existed a culture of guilt in motherhood or that some women felt they had to choose between work and family until I was in my mid-twenties. It's why recently, when I told a good friend, an award-winning former journalist who's raising an eleven-year-old daughter, about another "mommy wars" book just out, she asked, "What's that?," having never heard the term or registered the media-fueled at-home- versus at-work-mom conflict.

I became familiar with the term only after writing a couple of work and family articles for the *Washington Post*. Some of the hostile letters that came back spoke to a reality so divorced from own that they gave me the surreal urge to do a microphone check; to tap my fingers urgently against the national collective conscious and say, "Hello, is this thing on?" They let me know that despite enormous strides and several very high-profile black women on our political and cultural stages, some of our most vital stories have not been heard, and our most enduring parts are yet unseen.

Because my pop-culture references go way back, I was reminded of Burt Campbell (actor Richard Mulligan) on the controversial ABC television series *Soap,* which aired for four years beginning in 1977. Even though everyone could plainly see him, Burt thought he could make himself invisible with a snap of his fingers. Sometimes I click my fingers against my computer keys and I, too, feel myself disappear—my words and history consigned to our great national nowhere where differences can't be contemplated and amnesia is air.

Because I am a student of literature, I was reminded of the nameless protagonist in Ralph Ellison's classic 1952 novel, *Invisible Man*. "I am an invisible man," Ellison writes in the prologue. "When they approach me they see only my surroundings, themselves, or figments of their imagination—indeed, everything and anything except me." But because I am a child of hip-hop, I can choose to deny negation like MC Lyte, "Never underestimate Lyte the Emcee; I am a rapper who is here to make the things the way they're meant to be." I can layer my truth like the bodies of African women, tight-packed below the decks for the trip into slavery, setting it to a rhythm to try to move the crowd. And I can even read from my own sheet music.

When my mother was a girl, black women, a plurality of whom worked as domestics or whose cooking and cleaning labors were domestic derivatives, made about twenty-three cents on the dollar. It was the kind of oppressive reality against which even the loftiest notions of personal initiative were often futile. It made for such economic insecurity that tough family times, personal shortcomings, limited access to quality education, or even home mortgages were often sealants. It is the interplay of these kinds of factors that can lead to bad outcomes for black women that echo through generations. But this is not a book about any of that. Those echoes receive plenty of attention in Metro newscasts and public policy debates where humanity and history are sometimes given short shrift.

If this book is, in part, a response, it is in greater part a celebration. It is memoir and history; an assembly of voices and perspectives and names of women you might not know but whose struggles presaged modern womanhood and whose head start on questions of how *does* she do it offers insights, both sublime and waaay over the top. It is many of these voices that steady me on my feet when the hour is late, the woman's work is endless, and sleep is a dream.

In the late nineteenth century, women's rights pioneer Susan B. Anthony counseled black journalist and activist Ida B. Wells not to have children, warning that they would force her attentions from her writing and anti-lynching crusade. Wells ignored her advice, instead often nursing her two sons on the train en route to public-speaking engagements. Wells's example is useful when I try to retrofit my own schedule around the care and demands of a husband and three children. But while Wells's example is powerful, it is more than a century old and in order to use it properly, it needs to be remixed.

Do you remember the scene from the movie *The Matrix* where Neo (Keanu Reeves) goes to visit the mystic Oracle and finds a young telekinetic bending spoons? "Do not try to bend the spoon, that is impossible," the child tells Neo. "Instead only try to realize the truth: There is no spoon. Then you'll see it is not the spoon that bends, it is only yourself."

The history of black women, the stories of my grandmothers and mother, lets me know there is no magic pill to conjure time, and we can't go around shaking a stick at our lives to stop everybody from tugging on us. Sometimes we can't alter a physical reality, but we can bend our minds. We make our choices, and whenever possible we choose joy, mindful that just having options is, in itself, a luxury and such an amazing grace.

When I tell myself I'm tired after everything I have to do as a wife and mother and reporter, Ida B. Wells tells me, *yes, well, you're not the first woman to be tired* and her example gives me heart. Or I visit a *Washington Post* colleague and read the Arabic proverb that scrolls across his computer screen: "Dwell not on thy weariness, thy strength shall be according to the measure of thy desire," and that speaks to me in the way that voices not often heard sometimes do.

Which is why I thought it was time to for me to speak up.

I don't imagine my voice can fill the gap. The gap is bigger than me and older than me, shaped by long history and powerful forces and filling it requires a chorus. Instead, I merely hope to be part of what will be an ongoing effort to reclaim a space for black women's experiences. I realize it takes humility to listen to other people's stories, but I believe that perhaps we are in a good place for that to happen.

A good friend recently called to tell me a story about her neighbor and the neighbor's friend, both white women, gushing over the 1995 Maya Angelou poem *Phenomenal Women*. They had discovered it for the first time and vowed to pass it on since it spoke to them and reminded them of so many other women they knew. My friend also marveled that she had recently heard actress and talk-show host Kelly Ripa remark that if she could have the perfect body, it would be Halle Berry's. Even a generation ago, it would have been impossible to imagine this space. It's black women who've come a long way, baby—who've already been wherever it is you are. You won't find women who've been more tired, heart-broken, and oppressed—or more joyful, triumphant, and accom-plished. That's the thing about being the oldest women to walk the planet; there is more time for the universe to let you in on a few secrets.

Maybe that's why when a record company executive balked at star songstress Chaka Khan's pregnancy in the early 1970s, accord-ing to her memoir *Through the Fire,* she was able to tell him, "I'm gonna have babies and be a star—with you or without you. How 'bout that?" Maybe it's why she predated the celebrity trend of cele-brating her pregnant belly in short tops and low-cut pants by about thirty years and why she kept performing in low-cut pants, even when they revealed her C-section scar. Perhaps it is why her 1978 recording of the Nick Ashford and Valerie Simpson song, *I'm Every Woman,* rings and reminds and resonates so loudly for so many and why journalist and author Mark Anthony Neal maintains there's such special affection for her by the hip-hop generation.

Sometimes, when I'm writing late, when it's the early morning and I've had a full day behind me with a full day up ahead, I fanta-size about a simpler life. But mostly, I do not waste my time pon-dering irreducibles. Instead, I bend my mind. I remind myself of other women's stories of love and pain and sacrifice.

I remind myself who I am, where I came from. And that puts it all in perspective.

I

It's All in Me

Anything you want done baby,
I'll do it naturally . . .

CHAKA KHAN

NOT LONG AGO, my husband, Ralph, and I were visiting good friends, a college buddy of Ralph's and his new wife, when they decided to break out their wedding DVD from the year before. We eagerly gathered around their family room television as they cued the disc. This should be delightful, I thought, because I had had more fun at Thomas and Ebony's wedding, on a small island off the coast of North Carolina, than any I'd ever been to.

The reception was every bit as raucous as I remembered. Ebony's father boogied down a makeshift Soul Train line. The groom, my husband, and all the other brothers from their Omega Psi Phi fraternity performed their Nasty Que Dog hops with the same enthusiasm (if not elevation) as their undergraduate days at Duke.

And then, caught on tape, there I was along with two other partygoers, dancing onstage with the lead singer from the band. He was shirtless under his shiny dark suit, like Butch Lewis at those old Sphinx Brother's prizefights you used to be able to catch on network television. Sweat dripped from his forehead and ran down his chest. The brother was hot, and we were doing our best to mop up after him.

The three of us were professional women—an obstetrician with a thriving private practice, a financial analyst for a Fortune 500 company, and me, a reporter for a major metropolitan newspaper. Except that night, we were more like Oaktown 357. We fanned the singer's forehead. We blew deep, cooling breaths on his face and we wiggled him from behind as the video rolled, my husband snapped photos, and the band played on.

In that moment captured for posterity, it didn't seem to matter that all of us had reached a certain status in our lives. That we had three husbands and nine children and performed more than 120 hours a week of highly compensated work between us.

Of course, come to think of it, perhaps that is precisely why we danced with such abandon and clapped our hands with so much joy.

My Lord, who the ones that don't know why the caged bird sings?

Later in the video, the camera caught me doing a solo. By that time, it had begun to rain heavily. The warm, humid air mixed with the languid moves of a couple of hundred dancing black people to make my hair 1982-big just in time for my rendition of "We Are Family." I mouthed the words and pointed to all the wine-drinking women I had come to care for so deeply that weekend. Like I said, it was a real good time.

And watching that video I was transported to another time. A mid-1970s time when I was a little girl and the whole world was the segregated South Side of Chicago. There is no discernible occasion to those old videos. Just my parents and grandparents, neighbors and cousins, loud-talking, hard-drinking, and card-playing; celebrating being together or fighting because they're in too close. Hammy children, shooed from the presence of "grown folks," dart in and out of focus, risking censure or swatting, to be on film. They are determinedly festive moments sandwiched between lives of drama and work. Moments where colored people aggressively snatched joy because tomorrow was not promised and because, looky there, my daddy, Lonnie Gerald, had bought himself a reel-to-reel.

Sometimes, in those old videos, the camera falls on my mother, Elizabeth, known to everybody as Betty Lou in the small southern Illinois town of Centralia where her beauty was legend. There's Momma, Lena Horne–lovely, but with a harder life. A schoolteacher, mother of three, wife of my bright, charismatic, alcoholic daddy. On video, it's like Momma has gotten word that happily ever after may not be going her way; that the promise of an easy street might be the biggest beauty myth of all, but she's got years to go before she knows it for sure. With some of that life showing through, Momma, who looks like she's had a couple of beers, has also got a couple of songs. A few sashays for the camera and a little bit of strut, to remind somebody or maybe just herself that she is, after all, a glorious creature. Momma smiles and laughs and puckers her lips.

Seeing myself on video, I am reminded of those images of my mother from so long ago. Of the ways our lives have converged and how they've separated. Of when we've struggled and where we've triumphed. And I am deeply affected to realize that both of our moves have been captured on tape.

Earlier that weekend, before that wedding video was shot, my husband, Ralph, and I were on a ferry on our way to the island where the festivities were being held. We sat next to a white couple. The wife and Ebony were friends from Johns Hopkins where both were doctors, and we started talking about kids. I had left my three in the care of my sister an hour outside Raleigh, North Carolina. At

the time, my youngest was less than two months old and I watched
the woman, in particular, try to wrap her mind around how I could
stand being parted from my newborn son.

She couldn't imagine leaving her kids so young, she told me.
Well, it's my third, I said nonchalantly. She had three kids too, but
she breastfed, she persisted. Right then I could see I was going to
have to give that white woman a bit of sustained attention. I looked
at her squarely and smiled.

Don't get it twisted, I thought to myself.

It took six months before I left the house after my first daughter
was born, and that was just to attend an infant CPR class. I left my
second daughter with my husband and live-in nineteen-year-old
cousin for a spa weekend when she was eight weeks, but I breastfed
all three of my children (who I had without epidurals) for a year. I
volunteer in my children's classes; I bake cupcakes for birthday
treats and brownies from scratch for school bus drivers, and I'm not
a woman who likes to bake.

I explained to the woman on the ferry that my sister loves me,
she loves my children, and she would care for them tenderly until I
returned. Meanwhile, I needed some time to see friends, time to let
my husband rub my back where it ached, time to dress lovely and
dab perfume at my pulse points and on the insides of my thighs.

Momma just need to back that thing up, I thought about telling
her, but I did not. I'm not sure if she would have understood that
the things that I know seem as old as black women in the world.
That if I don't insist on taking my own moments, no one in my life
is going to hand them over.

Like most of the postmodern, postfeminist, post–civil rights
women I know, mine is an ambitiously busy life. It is crowded with
career and family; freighted with history and culture. Sometimes
after work, I hang in the driveway of my suburban Washington,

D.C., home unable to break away from National Public Radio's "All Things Considered." Maybe I'll listen to Pachelbel's Canon in D and remember romantic old commercials for L'Air du Temps perfume. Or perhaps I'll pop in a CD of Eric B. and Rakim's greatest hits and spend a few minutes with my old friend hip-hop—"I got soul (you got it!) / That's why I came / to teach those who can't say my name." Sometimes I'll linger in my car with the radio on because driving back and forth to my job as a reporter for the *Washington Post* might be the only alone time I'll get all day.

There are days when I barely break the threshold of my door before my children pounce on me. My ten-year-old daughter, Sydney, wants her party invitations sent, wants to tell me "a new episode of *That's So Raven* is coming on at seven, six central," wants me to take her to the store or buy her sugarless gum or help her with long division. My six-year-old daughter, Savannah, wants me to braid her hair, wants to know if next year I will think about buying her some high-heeled boots like Alexis, wants me to pick her up because her "feet feel weak." And, my two-year-old son, Satchel, just wants to wrap himself twice around my legs and run sticky, insistent fingers through my hair.

Under the unyielding pressure of deadline, with sources eluding me, editors bearing down on me, children clamoring for me, and a husband who needs to see me so we can "you know, reconnect," there are some days when I am unable to hear myself think. Mornings when we're out of hair grease and rice milk and I've agreed to volunteer at the kids' school before I'm supposed to interview officials at the Cuban Interest Section. Evenings when I hurl from ballet to gymnastics to classical piano lessons and long to simply come home and have sleep for dinner. Some weeks I scarcely have a moment to peek in the ladies' room mirror to make sure my eyebrows still maintain their well-defined arch.

There are times when having it all can seem like just *a little too much*.

It is during these moments that the blackest of voices comes to me. "No'm I nebbah knowed whut it wah t' rest. I jes wok all de time f'om maunin' till late at night." The words of Sarah Gudger, in *Unchained Memories: Readings from the Slave Narratives*, stay on my mind. They work their way into old parts of my soul, speaking in tongues, stiffening my spine across oceans of time. And from the R & B classics section midway down my rack of CDs, these old souls are joined by other more modern voices, helping me to remember who I am.

"I'm every woman, it's all in me." And I smile and nod and sing along with the chorus.

For me, that song is just one more tool I use to navigate my space. To cheer myself on. To create what I like to call my Lonnaeness, because black women have always had to fashion our own mythology.

Modernist British writer Virginia Woolf and my Aunt Jackie, an agoraphobic who used to entertain in silk lounging outfits and sue people for a living, have both made me understand that a woman's got to find a room of her own. So I've created a room in my house where the *New Yorker* shares shelf space with a picture of me hugged up on rapper LL Cool J. It is a place that features a poster from the *Boondocks* comic strip, which has challenged the sexual objectification of black women, and a video about *The Life and Times of Sara Baartman, the Hottentot Venus*, the young South African tribeswoman who in the early nineteenth century was exhibited naked in a cage in European capitals. It is both a place to remind me that struggle is constant, and a room to look out over riotous leaves fallen from old trees, and the delighted children who gather them in piles and know that my life has been touched by a full measure of grace.

I've also learned to find that kind of place in books and music and movement. To pay attention to distant psychic recesses where the long dead visit me to whisper their secrets. And, of course, I've found it in memory and reruns from old television shows. As far back as I can remember, my earliest prayers and meditations were shaped by popular culture. Because the little O'Neal kids had a color TV all our own.

When I was a child, I wanted to be good and adventurous like the cartoon character Speed Racer, the hero. Speed's girl was cute, but I couldn't abide Trixie because she didn't have any tricks at all. She never got to drive. And riding shotgun was out. Because there never has been enough light for me to bask in reflected glory. I needed my own special powers like Elizabeth Montgomery in *Bewitched,* or Barbara Eden in *I Dream of Jeannie.* Like those women, I wanted to move and conjure and bend things with my mind. And like them I wanted to be beautiful. Because I had a momma who I've never been able to touch. Because there's always a song about the beautiful ones. Of course there were also those who were not beautiful but acted like they were and often that seemed to work just as well. I wanted to be good, but also a little bad, like Pam Grier in *Friday Foster,* even though I only ever saw her on posters or in *Ebony* or *Jet.* We had to duck down in the back of the station wagon at Chicago's Halsted Outdoor Drive-In because the middle-class O'Neal children were not allowed to watch anything restricted—leastways not on screen. Later, I wanted to be bad like Vanity and Apollonia, because some nasty girls were just nasty, but they were the nasty girls who all the brothers loved.

I wanted to be like Melissa Gilbert, Laura Ingalls Wilder, aka

"Half-Pint" on *Little House on the Prairie*, because she loved to read. Because she was smart and just, and that seemed to bring a certain order to her world. Then I wanted to be Kelly, from *Charlie's Angels,* because she was radiant and self-possessed, with a clear moral code plus amazing karate kicks. When I was a schoolgirl, my girlfriends and I pretended we were Charlie's Angels, tying sweaters around our heads to make-believe our long, flowing hair was "down," and I was always Kelly. I had to be Jaclyn Smith because even as fantasy, Farrah Fawcett was just too over the top for little girls growing up on the dark side of Chicago.

I remember clearly the day many of my fantasies seemed to converge with an actual career path. It was after my sister Lisa, four years ahead of me in school and always beyond me in deliberation and authority, told me she was going to college to major in journalism. It was her junior year in high school and she had just heard a white woman at a career fair talk about traveling and meeting exciting people and writing for a newspaper. By that time, we were a few years suburban, having moved to Hazel Crest from the South Side, where the notion of being a reporter was like a winter ski vacation, so far outside the known parameters of our world it was neither contemplated nor missed.

But as I listened to my sister talk, a blueprint for a future Lonnae took root in my mind. My grandparents went straight from childhood to work. My paternal grandmother, Momma Susie, known as "Baby" to most in that small southern Illinois town of Centralia, was the only one to finish high school. She cried hard and married young because there was no money for college. (Always a standout in math, she later loan-sharked in her pajamas from a wingback chair in her family room.) My graduate-degreed parents were teachers and administrators, and my sister wound up following in their path, but even when I didn't write a thing, when I wouldn't open my mouth and couldn't hear my voice, I have always been a woman with stories to tell. The first afternoon I ever heard the word "journalism," I knew I was onto something. Though I did not know the details, the Watergate scandal had given the profession an air of purpose and nobility and I had the profound sense that journalists served the greater good (like *Police Woman* and *Get Christie Love*).

Of course on that day, I gave only small, spare thoughts to sparkling prose or public accountability. Instead I saw myself holding a notepad, flashing a press pass, and being ushered backstage. I was thinking of Noel Neill, Lois Lane, in reruns of the black-and-white serial *The Adventures of Superman*. I was thinking of glamour, do-gooder adventure and romance in the arms of a superman. And I was thinking of how very, very cute I would look wearing slim skirt suits and pillbox hats to work. Growing up, there was never any question that I would go to college and then go to work. It wasn't until I was an adult that I even understood that some women considered paid, outside-the-home work optional. Because for the black women in my world, work wasn't an option at all.

I never woke to a house where my mother was still sleeping. I can't recall a single pair of her pajamas. Mothers, it seemed, always came dressed and ready. And that seemed truer of my mother, Betty Lou, than anyone I can remember. Momma moved to Chicago as a young wife and mother and, after college, began working as a teacher in the Chicago public schools, where she remained, day in and day out, for more than three decades.

In my mother's world, there was no staying home and taking care of your kids. If you stayed home, you were taking care of your kids and a bunch of other people's kids as well. Momma was an educated professional who, after eight-hour workdays, fixed dinner and did dishes in high heels and makeup because although she was tired (black women have always worked tired), the cryin' shame was to just let yourself go. Momma watched television too; she saw images of white women, who worked solely to make their homes comfortable for their husbands and children, but none of that had anything to do with her or the people she knew. For practical reasons and reasons that stretched beyond recall, on the South Side, and other black places, the Brady Bunch rules just didn't apply. Black women and field work and house work and paid-outside-the-house work simply go too far back.

Not long ago, I found an illustration of that point at an antique store in West Virginia. I was rifling through a crate of old magazines when a 1903 cover of the *Saturday Evening Post* made me linger. It was a drawing of black sharecroppers picking cotton. One woman was standing straight with a hand wiping her brow just underneath the place where her handkerchief met her head. Her other hand was pressed into the small of her back and she was closing her eyes against the midday sun. Standing in that antique store, as I studied the picture, it seemed that I could feel the hurt deep in that black woman's back, and maybe in her soul as well. "Bone memory" is what journalist Rohan Preston calls it. It's the history and culture that we know, that's all curled up inside us, that can't be explained. "Rise to be born with me, brother. I come to speak through your dead mouth," is how Nobel Prize–winning Chilean poet Pablo Neruda put it.

The same year that cover ran, the Victorian era, with its romanticized notions of home and hearth, was winding down in the United States. For nearly a century, white society had been entrenched in the cult of domesticity, with strict social norms teaching middle-class white women and strivers that they ought not to furrow their brows with worldly or unpleasant thoughts. They taught white women that the work of a proper wife and mother, the highest (and only) role they could aspire to, was to keep her home lovely with knowledge of floral languages and handmade offerings of wifely creativity. Victorian-era literature warned against harsh words, corporal punishment, and subversive challenges to a husband's natural authority. It elevated white women's status at the same time it undercut their freedom of movement, assembly, ambition, and thought.

An excerpt from the 1903 publication *Correct Social Usage: A Course of Instruction in Good Form, Style and Deportment* admonished that a young rural woman had to make allowances for place. That she mustn't "feel above" hired men who couldn't distinguish between an oyster fork and a fish fork. And she ought not doubt her own mother's breeding for being unfamiliar with rosewater and oil soaps. I search the text in vain for how that young Victorian woman, kind and generous of spirit, is supposed to feel about that sister wiping the sweat off her head in those nearby cotton fields— if her Christianity and good breeding ever compel her to offer water, a kind word, or an extra set of hands to lighten a black woman's load.

And (in a distinct and bitter bone memory) I guess the world just would have come to an end if she had gotten her own ass out there and picked cotton.

The year 1903 was also the year W. E. B. Du Bois wrote *The Souls of Black Folks* and spoke of double consciousness; of ever feeling the "twoness" of being black and American, of being able to see yourself through the eyes of your oppressor. I imagine those sisters in the cotton fields could feel it—triple consciousness, they might even have called it, feeling the profound separateness of both their race and their gender.

Just like those black women a century earlier, in my colored-only world, my momma worked, my aunts worked, all the women on our block in Chicago worked. During the decade when Betty

Friedan wrote, in her book *The Feminine Mystique*, that vaguely discontented white women were asking themselves "Is this all?" some of the most intensely feminine women I've ever known were, like their mothers and grandmothers before them, telling themselves, "Lord, *chile,* I can't take no more." When we moved to the integrated suburbs of Chicago in the late 1970s, virtually all those black women worked as well. But enormous strides in education and racial parity had been made so that while some of them merely had jobs, most were able to dream of careers for their daughters. That they dreamed of families for them as well went without saying. So prevalent, so expected, so much like air was the notion of getting out of the house and hitting it every day, I was in college before I realized that some women considered working to be an option. And I was a twenty-four-year-old sales aide in the advertising department of the *Washington Post* the first time I heard from a white female colleague that some mothers felt guilty for working. I remember being surprised at so foreign a concept—something I had never heard in all the conversations with all the black women I had ever known.

I'm not a combatant in the mommy wars—a narrowly fought conflict that holds to a strict work-family divide and lays claim to an idealized mantle of ultra-fulfilled supermotherhood. I'm not a general, a foot soldier, a victim, or a victor. I'm not even a conscientious objector. I'm more like a neutral observer, or better yet, a foreign correspondent, fairly well versed on the issues, aware that both sides care deeply about their positions, but rarely feeling personally touched by their battles.

I once wrote a Mother's Day piece for the *Washington Post* magazine called "The Donna Reed Syndrome," about taking a year's leave of absence from the paper to freelance and travel, and my subsequent decision to return to my career. I was surprised at the letters that came back. There were women who took my choice as a personal indictment against them. "I suppose Lonnae O'Neal Parker would think I'm pathetic—I have stayed at home since the birth of my son three years ago," wrote one woman, and I clearly remember my reaction—about how I wasn't thinking of that woman at all.

What I was thinking about then, and continue to do so, are all the people who sacrificed their talents and the upside of their heads so that I could be in a position to be a reporter. I recalled the brother, a good friend, who once reminded me that since I had a voice, I had a serious responsibility to raise it. I remembered how a story I wrote about two black children who suffocated while playing inside an abandoned car because their southeast Washington neighborhood lacked a playground prompted one organization to call and say they were moved to build a playground for other southeast Washington children.

I think about all the black lilies of the field who stood up straight against the ache in their back and the broken ones who never could. I was thinking how I can't ever recall a conversation with a black woman who asked me why I worked, and when I hear of a black woman who doesn't, I'm glad she's got a man who's earning money and willing to give her the opportunity to nurture her own family because the historical significance of her position is profound. I think about how if that helps her to raise sane, righteous kids, then more power to her, because that means we're all going to be better off.

Like that Victorian woman a hundred years ago, it seems, few of the combatants and cultural arbiters in the mommy wars see me in three full dimensions—to the extent that they see me at all. They seem not to realize that women of color might have different imperatives, a different history, different sets of assumptions, not to mention a few cousins, who might need a helping hand to make it into the middle class. I find myself deeply unmoved by people who are unable to look outside of themselves or pick up lessons from other histories and cultures. And I cannot imagine an existence unable to remember rapture or pain in bone memories of its own. Understand, it's not that I think that black women have all the answers— only that we have struggled with the questions longer and that sometimes our tool sets are more expansive. I am clear that in all cultures there are other committed women who deeply believe they must stand on one or another side of a work-family divide and agitate in order to create a better world for their children. And really, I can dig it. I'm actually quite grateful that I can skim some of their best parts off the top. But these women must never, ever try to give me any of their excess baggage.

Because I'm not even remotely in a place where I will accept it.

I give a nod to all those women who have walked my way, carrying heavier burdens than I could stand with more grace than I could muster, and I sense a truth, layered like a shadow across black skin. Every hip must sway, every tongue got to confess. Out of respect for those who bowed until broken, the rest of us have got to work, have got to advance the ball just a little, and find time to celebrate our gifts of joy and humor and sensuality. That just on GP, on general principle, black women with wings must necessarily soar, even if it's just to show other folks how it's done.

The other day, I saw a television feature on Audrey Hepburn and called my ten-year-old in to watch. With her elegance and self-possession Hepburn always speaks to me—always sets my mind to contemplating cigarette pants and ballerina flats. Good taste is timeless, I tell my daughter Sydney, and I try to get her to appreciate the glamour and sophistication of old Hollywood. Of course since glamorous old Hollywood wasn't keen on black folks, I also let my daughter in on another secret.

Always write yourself into the script.

I once heard Hepburn reciting a poem, "Time Tested Beauty Tips" by writer and television host Sam Levenson, said to be her favorite, and the beauty of her recitation has stayed with me for years.

> For attractive lips, speak words of kindness.
> For lovely eyes, seek out the good in people.
> For a slim figure, share your food with the hungry.

I feel all of that humanity. But in keeping with my postmodern, postfeminist, post–civil rights reality, I've had to recast it a bit. Here's the remix.

> For being in possession of every single right Fannie Lou Hamer fought for without being forcibly sterilized or beaten until your fingers won't bend like Fannie Lou Hamer, speak up, even when it hurts.
>
> For children who are yours to keep, who no one wrestles from your arms, sells, or whips while you are made to watch, for children who come home at the end of every day, do some work on behalf of someone else's child.
>
> For having all your faculties, for never having been locked inside the Maryland Hospital for the Negro Insane, put your mind to work on the pressing issues of the day.
>
> For Gary Dourdan on *CSI* and Morris Chestnut in *The Best Man,* thank God for the beauty of black men and then hold the beautiful and ugly alike to account.
>
> For every single rhythm in your life, dance with raucous abandon or in small well-choreographed steps, just to show the universe that you know what to do with the gift of joy.

My models are disparate and my lessons come from unlikely places, but I am a child of hip-hop and a direct descendant of jazz. Freed from lunch-counter racism but charged by lived history, I am educated and entitled and free to sample, to construct a me and a life and a vision of my world and an arc to my day in a way that my mother and my grandmothers never could.

So then it is deep in the tradition of black women, tasked with serious purpose but able to take time for sublime pursuits in the midst of their hardest work, and in the partial aesthetic of slim white girls, whom the larger culture rewards with roses and love, that I have styled myself.

I am every woman. And I have sampled heavily to come up with my sound.

Carrying Your Burden
in the Heat of the Day

De nigger woman is de mule uh de
world so fur as Ah can see. Ah been
prayin' fuh it tuh be different wid you.
Lawd, Lawd, Lawd!

ZORA NEALE HURSTON,
*Their Eyes Were
Watching God*

I REMEMBER THE DAY the first slave woman came to me.

I was in Guatemala doing a Spanish immersion program with my then seven-year-old daughter Sydney. It was my second trip to the country and I brought my first grader because by that time, my husband and I could afford to buy her just about anything she might want. And she had come to want a great deal.

"Brittany has a radio and a CD player and a VCR and a TV and a telephone in her room, and she's only six. When can I get my own telephone, Mommy?" Sydney wanted to know. I took her to Central America to learn Spanish and to put her eyes on something different. To show her a hunger that reached beyond material things.

During the day she went to bilingual school and I took Spanish classes. On weekends, we roamed the centuries-old ruins of the ancient capital city of Antigua. I talked about the legacy of colonialism to try to help explain the grinding poverty of the indigenous women in the park. And I took that opportunity to talk to her about slavery. Oppression had happened to people all over the world, I told her. Although slavery happened to black people, it was not because there was something wrong with their blackness. Late at night, we each wrote in our journals, and for hours, whenever I was alone, I read a series of slave narratives collected as part of the Federal Writers' Project in the late 1930s.

"What fo' yous wants dis old nigger's story 'bout old slave'y days?" the old woman, Betty Powers, asked me directly as if time weren't stretched out like the arms of Jesus between us. "T'aint worth anything."

I read about children flogged with leather straps for crying too hard when their mommas were sold. I read about women who worked from dark morning to dark night, then stayed up to spin their quota of cloth so they wouldn't get beaten. I read about women who left the fields to have their babies, but had to be back picking cotton the next day. I read some stories my head refused to hold, but it was the words of the old slave woman Jenny Proctor that managed to linger on my mind.

She told of being a young girl and of trying to keep house for the Ole Miss. Of one day finding a biscuit in the kitchen.

I finds a biscuit and I's so hungry I et it, 'cause we nev'r see sich a thing as a biscuit. When I et dat biscuit and she comes in and say, "Whar dat biscuit?" I say, "Miss, I et it 'cause I's so hungry." Den she grab dat broom and start to beatin' me over de head wid it and callin' me low-down nigger. I guess I jes' clean lost my head 'cause I know'd better den to fight her if I knowed anythin' 'tall. But I start to fight her and de driver he comes in and he grabs me and starts beatin' me wid dat cat-o-nine-tails. He beats me 'til I fall to de floor nearly dead. He cut my back all to pieces, den dey rubs salt in de cuts for mo' punishment.

When Ole Marster come to de house, he say, "What you beat dat nigger like dat for?" And de driver tells him why and he say, "She can't work now for a week. She pay for several biscuits in dat time."

I still got dem scars on my olde back right now, jes' like my grandmother have when she die and I's a-carryin' mine right on to the grave jes' like she did.

Thinking about Sister Proctor, her biscuit and her scars, put me on my knees and made me rock back and forth, keening from deep, painful things. I asked God, I asked the universe, I asked all the names I knew to ask if I could somehow wash that old slave woman's feet. I prayed to rub some of the mud and the affliction from the hard parts of her soles, and I ached in memory of all the black women and all their black sorrows both time and I had forgotten.

But if it was the slave woman's suffering that put me on my knees, it was her living to tell about it that straightened me up, that even now helps me to understand the very serious business of keep on keepin' on. (Like Gladys Knight before me, *I've really got to use, my imagination.*) Whenever I'm in a bad way, Miss Jenny Proctor always sticks a knee in my back and squares up my shoulders.

A couple of years later, as part of an article I was working on, someone sent me the companion book to the 2002 HBO documentary *Unchained Memories, Readings from the Slave Narratives.* It came with a picture of Sarah Gudger:

> No'm, I nebbah knowed whut it wah t' rest. I jes wok all de time f'om mawnin' till late at night. I had t'do ebbgathin' dey wah t'do on de outside. Wok in de field, chop wood, hoe cawn, till sometime I feels lak mah back sholy break.
>
> Lawdy, honey, yo' cain't know whut a time I had.

Some people paste pictures from when they were fat to their refrigerator doors as a reminder not to overeat. I keep a picture of Sarah Gudger in my study on my wall to remind me of something else.

In the picture, she isn't looking my way. She's staring far off and I don't know if she's able to see me in that distant place that holds her eyes. I don't know if she's even able to imagine me in my study, with a woman to watch my kids, surrounded by books, writing for one of the most highly regarded newspapers in the world, but every day I imagine her. She gets loud in her silence. She lets me fuss a little, but mocks me if I complain too much about how *hard* it all is. She tells me stories about black women who labored right to the edge of human endurance, who worked like animals for other people. Then she demands to know how hard I'm willing to work for my own.

When the slave women come to me, they don't travel through time bringing kind words and a gentle spirit. They bring salt and vinegar and gnarled black fingers to poke at my sides until I get out of bed. They take me to work when I don't want to go and make me tend children I wish were asleep. They remind me, Miss Free Woman of Color, that they didn't keep living when dying would have been so much more merciful just so I could look cute or shop at Nordstrom's. They remind me that it is my turn to carry the weight.

And of course there is always something there to remind me of how heavy that weight has been.

Several years ago, I saw a photo from *Without Sanctuary,* the exhibit of pictures, postcards, and memorabilia from the estimated 4,743 lynchings between 1882 and 1968 (nearly 75 percent of those victims were black). I think of that exhibit whenever our national conversation turns to talk of terrorism. In the photo, you can just make out the flowers on Laura Nelson's dress as she hangs from a bridge a few feet from the fourteen-year-old son whose life she tried to save in Okemah, Oklahoma, in 1911. By that time, the promise of Emancipation and Reconstruction had long given way to violent Southern backlash and Northern appeasement and, in the 1896 case *Plessy v. Ferguson,* to the Supreme Court ruling that allowed states to legalize segregation—to a period of oppression often called the nadir of modern black history.

After the Civil War four million former slaves likely imagined the darkest times were behind them and they were finally on their way to realizing full American citizenship. The roughly two million black women, 95 percent of whom lived in the rural South, were poised to finally make decisions about how to organize their lives and their households. And, they had hoped, their work.

They had emerged from more than two centuries as bondswomen with a number of strengths. The slave community had developed "an ethos of mutuality." Since they lived under the constant threat that the most important people in their lives could be forever sold away, slaves learned how to form and reform bonds of community and family. They learned to rely on themselves, insofar as possible, for care, self-affirmation, and resistance. They learned families didn't have to be kin, and a community, whose ranks were closed to a hostile world, had to be counted on to administer to the most pressing and the most basic collective needs.

Noting these traits in her book *Labor of Love, Labor of Sorrow*, historian Jacqueline Jones quotes a former white woman slave-holder's evident irritation that some blacks who weren't able to work were still able to eat, saying "it is a well-known fact that you can't starve a negro," because even when it meant added hard-ship, the community wouldn't allow one of its own to go hungry. Another strength could be found in the relative gender equality of women. Contrary to the stereotype of a slave matriarchy, the black family emerged from slavery with a much more equal balance of power between the sexes than what existed among whites. It was something historians now concede that actually approached "a healthy sexual equality," Jacqueline Jones writes, owing to the labor and economic contributions black women had always made to the family.

Finally, during slavery, labor had been gender-blind, with women doing men's work in the fields and women's work at home. And because the bodies of slave women had not been their own, any attempt at virtue or chastity had interfered with property rela-tions on the plantation.

> The contrasting contexts of black and white women's lives called for different, even opposite responses. While submis-siveness and passivity brought protection to the white mis-tress, these characteristics merely exposed black women to sexual and economic exploitation. Black women, therefore, had to develop strength rather than glory in fragility, and had to be active and assertive rather than passive and submissive,

wrote sociologist Bart Landry in his book *Black Working Wives, Pioneers of the American Family Revolution.*

And the universe whispered, *Speak up, sister, because no one else is going to save you.*

After Emancipation, now free to redefine their roles, it turns out most rural black women also tried to adopt a cult of domesticity—to confine their work to the care of their husbands and children. This, of course, incensed white planters with fields to cultivate. Landry writes:

> All across the South, planters complained about the refusal of black wives to work. "The women," one lamented, "say that they never mean to do any more outdoor work, that white men support their wives and they mean that their husbands shall support them." This was not a decision made by wives alone. Planters frequently acknowledged the role of the husbands in keeping their wives at home. One Boston cotton broker noted that planters hiring twenty hands, have to support on an average twenty-five to thirty negro women and children *in idleness*, as the freedmen will not permit their wives and children to work in the fields.

Their brief interlude with domesticity was doomed, however. After the Civil War, the priority for white politicians and plantation owners in both the North and the South was to rebuild the cotton economy. In 1865 President Andrew Johnson enacted the first Black Codes—laws applied to the southern states that curtailed the personal and political rights of the newly freed slaves. These codes mark the beginning of the Jim Crow segregation laws. The thrust of the Black Codes was to control the labor of blacks, including black women and children, to keep them tied to the land in servitude as sharecroppers. Black women were forced from their homes and back into the fields. In *A Short History of Reconstruction,* Eric Foner writes that Louisiana and Texas, among others, enacted codes with provisions mandating that work contracts "embrace the labor of all the members of the family able to work." This made it *illegal* for black women to stay home and make tinctures of roses, decorate their parlors, or even just care for their husbands and children who were still sometimes forcibly removed due to laws allowing them to be apprenticed, ostensibly for their own good, as workers for white farmers.

Historians talk about planters sending around riders to try to force black wives into the fields. "These planters complained about black women and not having a sufficient workforce, calling them lazy and ridiculing them for playing the lady," says Landry. Additionally, since small farming was so labor-intensive, and sharecropping so exploitative, it usually required the work of all family members just to survive. "Thus in 1870, when over 40 percent of black married women reported jobs to census takers, most as field laborers, 98.4 percent of rural white wives reported that they were 'keeping house.'"

The stultifying hardship of living hand to mouth, combined with a dramatic increase in white mob violence against the newly freed black families caused many southern blacks to migrate. They moved from the fields and plantations to small southern cities, then to larger southern cities and border states, and finally to the factories of the North. This movement, known as the Great Migration, great accelerated with the advent of World War I. In the cities, black women's wages became even more crucial to the survival of their families. But the majority of married black women were locked out of clerical work and all but the most menial, low-paid factory work, often in dangerous and segregated conditions, so they worked as domestics, unlike their married white working-class counterparts, who more often sent children out to work so the family could conform to the middle-class cult of domesticity.

During the 1930s, when significant federal legislation dealing with minimum wages, maximum hours, and Social Security and unemployment compensation was enacted, only 10 percent of black women were directly affected: agricultural and domestic labor was specifically exempt from the legislation, and these were the areas where nine out of ten black women worked. Their exploitation continued, only minimally abated.

They took in laundry. They lived as domestics with white families or, especially if they were married with their own families, they lived out, putting in fourteen-hour days for the mistress, but whenever possible, insisting on a few hours to take care of their own homes and families before daybreak or after dark.

For these families, child care was left to relatives and neighbors, or children were left to fend for themselves. Jacqueline Jones writes:

It was not until the end of the day that she had any time to spend with her own children, and then only if she could locate them quickly. At times a woman would have to scour the community for little ones who had gotten lost or fallen asleep in some tucked-away nook or cranny. Once recovered, they were bound to be cranky, tired, and hungry. A mother had to squeeze whatever attention and affection she could find time to give her children into these late-night hours and her day off. Yet their welfare remained a constant preoccupation with her as she fed, diapered, and amused white babies.

Apparently, according to Jones, this sometimes caused black domestics to iron-burn the mistress's clothes and clog up her stove so that it broke down more often than it should.

But while there have always been a sizable number of rural and urban working-class black women who may have desired something more Victorian, but labored outside the home because of economic necessity, it is the work of middle-class black women, women with choices, who historically presented the most dramatic departure from the mainstream cultural norms.

The black middle class grew largely out of the half-million total free black population that predated the Civil War. Free blacks were scattered throughout the country but more often in cities where the men were professionals or skilled craftsmen and the women were dressmakers and domestic workers. In the North, middle-class black women often got an education, were active in the abolitionist movement, and worked most especially as teachers. These free blacks didn't see themselves as free from hard work, but rather as free to use their energies and talents on behalf of their own households and communities.

In that post-Emancipation period of vulnerability, the rising middle class of the late nineteenth and early twentieth century began to mobilize in earnest, continuing in the black woman's tradition of making civil rights—indistinguishable from women's rights—the focus of their labor. (This was a tradition that could be seen as far back as Maria Stewart, the nation's first female public speaker, black or white. She decried both the evils of slavery and waiting on men to fix things; Harriet Tubman, the gun-toting "black Moses" and Union spy who led some three hundred slaves through the underground railroad to freedom; and Sojourner Truth, who gave eloquent speeches on women who bore the pain of heavy loads.)

Because black women had been excluded from the cult of domesticity, free black middle-class women had no restrictions on how broadly they could define their roles. And they determined that those roles must necessarily include not only family and motherhood but also career and community activity. Slavery had taught them that the community was more vital than the self, that blacks were linked by a common destiny, and that the needs were too pressing and the work too hard to leave to black men alone.

Historian Shirley Carlson writes about the differing perceptions of the "ideal woman" in black and white communities during the late Victorian era.

The black community's appreciation for and development of the feminine intellect contrasted sharply with the views of the larger society. In the latter, intelligence was regarded as a masculine quality that would "defeminize" women. The ideal white woman, being married, confined herself almost exclusively to the private domain of the household. She was demure, perhaps even self-effacing. She often deferred to her husband's presumably superior judgment, rather than formulating her own views and vocally expressing them, as black women often did. A woman in the larger society might skillfully manipulate her husband for her own purposes, but she was not supposed to confront or challenge him directly. Black women were often direct, and frequently won community approval for this quality, especially when such a characteristic was directed toward achieving racial uplift. . . . The ideal black woman's domain, then, was both the private and public spheres. She was wife and mother, but she could also assume other roles, such as schoolteacher, social activist, or businesswoman, among others.

White women had done yeomen's work in the service of charity, abolition, and suffrage movements, but they often had to justify that work as an extension of their natural caretaker roles within the home. (Additionally, during the march toward women's suffrage, many of the titans of that movement chose a policy of "expediency," if not outright racism, making the point that the white women's vote could counter the influence from men of the "lower races.")

After the Civil War, activist black women often formed clubs to continue their struggles for racial uplift—access to education and health care, antilynching crusades, and women's equality. What you had, says Landry, were middle-class black women who championed a "threefold commitment to family, career and social movements." In so doing, he argues, they offer a different version of "true womanhood," one that many white women eventually adopted in the 1960s and 1970s.

Still, it wasn't until the Civil Rights Act of 1964 and other gains of the 1960s that large numbers of black women were able to move out of the rigid racial and gender tracts that had defined their labor since Emancipation. For the first time, large numbers of black women who had been cleaning women, custodians, cafeteria workers, and hospital orderlies moved into clerical work or became telephone operators and department store clerks. They entered textile factories in the South (even though, as Jacqueline Jones points out, by the 1970s Southern textiles had begun to fail). More black women were able to avail themselves of increased educational opportunities and secure higher-paying, more prestigious jobs in business, communications, and academia, thus fostering increased mobility. But a large percentage remained mired in impoverished communities with poor schools and low-paying jobs, making for the wide divergence in the black women's work story that continues today. While 14 percent of working black women fall below the poverty line, 24 percent of black women occupy the professional-managerial class. According to a spring 2005 Census Bureau report, college-educated black women actually earn slightly more than their white, college-educated counterparts.

(A brief overview of modern women's work history: In 1970, more than 70 percent of married black middle-class women and nearly 45 percent of married black working-class women were in the labor force. The numbers for white married middle- and working-class women in the labor force had been steadily increasing from the 1930s when economic hardship forced white wives to enter the labor force in significant numbers. The modern women's rights movement of the 1960s accelerated that trend. In 1970, 48 percent of white middle-class and 32 percent of white working-class wives were in the labor force. By 1990, the numbers were much more equivalent with nearly 85 percent of black married middle-class women in the labor force, along with about 70 percent of white married middle-class women. The same year, while nearly 60 percent of married black working-class women were in the labor force, nearly 50 percent of white married working-class women were in the labor force as well. By 2002, 63 percent of employed black women age sixteen and over held middle-class jobs. For white women sixteen and older, that figure was 74 percent.)

One of the women who championed black women's "threefold commitment" was journalist Ida B. Wells.

Growing up, I knew the name Ida B. Wells (who became Ida B. Wells-Barnett after she married) only as the name of a housing project in Chicago. In fact, so common was this frame of reference, when I was a student at Southern Illinois University in Carbondale, some of the other black students rechristened our dormitory, Schneider, Schnida B. Wells, in recognition of what felt like a deliberate effort to concentrate all the black students on the east side of campus. It was only after I was grown, after I began looking into the work history of black women, that I truly discovered this tiny black woman who had sued the Chesapeake & Ohio Railway after she was dragged from the first-class section of a train bound for her home in Memphis in 1884. She won the case, but with segregation heading toward entrenched law, the Tennessee Supreme Court overturned the ruling.

Wells was born in Mississippi, but when she was sixteen, her parents died of yellow fever and she assumed the care of her five siblings, moving in with relatives in Memphis. She was a teacher at the time of the railroad incident, and later began writing a column that was picked up by black newspapers around the country. She distinguished herself with muckraking journalism critical of both black leadership and increasing white oppression. But it was the 1892 lynching of close friend and storeowner, Thomas Moss, and two other men, that gave Wells (along with another daughter of Memphis, Mary Church Terrell) the crusade she would wage the rest of her life. Moss and two friends were owners of a grocery store that successfully competed with a white Memphis grocery. Eventually, a white mob attacked Moss's store and three whites were shot (they recovered). Later, Moss and his partners were lynched and their store looted.

Wells began her campaign against lynching with scathing editorials and, later, sharp reporting (she gathered details on 728 lynchings against not only men but women and children as well) that challenged the notion that blacks were primarily lynched because of attacks against white women; only one-third of the men had even been accused of rape, and many of those accusations were specious. Instead, Wells linked lynching to racism and patriarchy, and exposed its economic underpinnings by finding it was frequently blacks with property who were attacked and afterward their small businesses were looted or shut down. She contended it was a form of extralegal terror designed to augment the power of white men, as well as to perpetuate myths about the nature of white womanhood and black male sexuality. After one such editorial, suggesting that sometimes white women engaged in voluntary unions with black men, her office was ransacked and she was banned from the South upon threat of death.

She relocated to Chicago, and when she lacked funds to publish her findings, fellow black women activists staged a fund-raiser. As Paula Giddings details in the book *When and Where I Enter*,

> Wells' pen name, Iola, was spelled out in electric lights across the dais. The printed programs were miniature prototypes of the *Memphis Free Speech*. Soul-stirring music was interspersed with uplifting speeches. Five hundred dollars was collected for the booklet, which Wells dedicated "To the Afro-American women . . . whose race love, earnest zeal and un-selfish effort made possible this publication."

I am a black woman journalist, but I did not learn Wells' history as a student in journalism school. Neither did I learn about the president of the Missouri Press Association, James W. Jacks. Shortly before the turn of the twentieth century, Jacks, furious that anti-lynching activists like Wells continually called attention to the on-going sexual exploitation of black women and girls by white men, penned a letter in which he alleged that the "Negroes in this country were wholly devoid of morality, the women were prostitutes, and all were natural thieves and liars."

With that charge, middle-class black women begin to see themselves as saviors of the race, tasked with the grave responsibility of disproving the white stereotypes that victimized their families. So great was the black women's fury at the letter that representatives from clubs around the country met and organized the National Association of Colored Women in 1896, adopting the motto "Lifting As We Climb."

One of the organization's founders was Mary Church Terrell. Lynching victim Thomas Moss had been at Terrell's wedding. In 1916 Terrell gave a speech on "The Modern Woman" to a packed church audience in Charleston. The tenor of the evening was recalled by activist Mamie Garvin Fields. Deborah Gray White recounts it in *Too Heavy a Load:*

> According to Fields, Terrell spoke not only about the modern woman, but in her pink evening dress and long white gloves, with her hair beautifully done, "she was that Modern woman." Fields marveled at Terrell's graceful walk to the platform and the way she projected her voice out across the huge crowd. "We have our own lives to lead," she told them. "We are daughters, sisters, mothers, and wives. We must care for ourselves and rear our families, like all women." Going on, she spoke of the special mission of the educated black woman. "We have to do more than other women. Those of us fortunate enough to have education must share it with the less fortunate of our race. We must go into our communities and improve them; we must go out into the nation and change it."

It can seem ironic that Terrell and many of her club-women contemporaries could, and often did, pass for white, especially when traveling; that such ardent race women had to sometimes set their heavy things down or rest their eyes for a moment. It is for me another complexity to ponder, a way to give myself permission to chill, to gather myself, and an impetus to keep striving.

Mary Church Terrell and Ida B. Wells-Barnett were both married with children. They were dedicated and charged with history and purpose, but they were not superwomen and there never has been a magic pill to balance out women's lives and keep shadows from falling into days that cry out for a few hours more. They and other activist women often complained about too much to do, too many hands tugging at their skirts, and always too little time. According to White, Terrell, who was "torn between the financial contribution she felt she should make to her household, the service she thought was her duty to perform for black women, and the desire to be home with her daughter," tried to work out of her own home, although that proved difficult since so much of her work was public speaking.

Suffragette Susan B. Anthony, who remained single, counseled Wells-Barnett to do the same. She said marriage and children would take too much from her work. Instead, Wells-Barnett nursed her two sons, taking them with her on trains on the way to her lectures. In the end, says White, "club work and anti-lynching race work tugged at her as hard as the needs of her sons. Like Terrell, she simply learned to live with her ambivalence."

I will stumble if I try to list the litany of black women in whose tradition I find inspiration and, often, a self-correcting mechanism that saves me from my whines. If I could sound a perfect note when life comes back around, I would sing of "Strange Fruit" with Billie Holiday and hum along with Bessie Smith's "Wash Woman Blues." I would wax poetic about the presidency with Ms. Shirley Chisholm—unbought and unbossed—and powwow on power to the people with Professor Angela Davis. I would celebrate the percussive persuasion of Mary Frances Berry and Mary McLeod Bethune. I would speak loudly of women whose names we don't know, because there is breath and memory and power in the words,

words like those of the seventy-two-year-old washerwoman during the 1955 Montgomery, Alabama, bus boycott who said, "My feets is tired but my soul is at rest."

I do not pretend to have these women's mettle or humility or seriousness of purpose. I just know the thought of them keeps me up late writing when I'd rather be asleep.

In 1916, Mary Church Terrell ended her speech on a sticky night in Charleston with a question for the hushed crowd of clubwomen and washerwomen and teachers; a question for the crowd of black women with hopes for their daughters and their daughters' daughters, and, I believe, distant hopes for Lonnae O'Neal Parker to go along with the question that moves me still.

"Who of you know how to carry your burden in the heat of the day?"

Tending to
Our Mothers' Gardens

She had nothing to fall back on; not
maleness, not whiteness, not ladyhood,
not anything. And out of the profound
desolation of her reality she may well
have invented herself.

TONI MORRISON

THEY SAY MY GREAT-GRANDMOTHER, Jessie Mae, left that
white man there in the windowsill, dead where she shot him.

It was the early 1920s in Macomb, Mississippi, and the white
man, reduced in family lore to Jim Crow anonymity, had been
coming in after her. He had been by her house earlier in the day,
making crude sexual references. Later, had come back knocking on
the door, and when she wouldn't let him in, had started through the
window, all the while talking about all the things he was going to do
to her. Things, apparently, that she did not want done. So she
picked up a .38-caliber Smith & Wesson and killed him as he straddled the sill.

And since it was the early 1920s in Macomb, Mississippi—since fifty blacks had been lynched in the state between 1918 and 1923, five of them women—her close family acted fast. They took Jessie Mae one way, and my grandfather Lonnie and his twin brother Larry another, spiriting the family out of town before dawn could break over another Mississippi burning. Jessie Mae joined her husband, Alexander, in Illinois, but Lonnie and Larry didn't rejoin their parents until nearly a dozen years later. And that's how my grandfather, "Papa Lonnie," a man most called "Chef," came to live in Centralia, Illinois. How he sometimes came to pull out that old Smith & Wesson gun, showing it off for family and friends. (Years later, money would change hands, and Jessie Mae was allowed to return to Macomb, where she died, or so the story goes.)

In Centralia, Papa Lonnie met and married my grandmother, Momma Susie, one of eight poor but beautiful children of Charlie and Minnie Bibb, when she was eighteen. The couple owned a restaurant-tavern called O'Neal's Place, but everybody called it the Confectionary. It was a place to celebrate colored people with smoked and smothered and deep-fried offerings. A place of chicken dumplings and rib-tip sandwiches, Jack Daniel's on the shelf and the Temptations on the jukebox. A place where every day, a woman came around with a tip board and even small kids could gamble if somebody spotted us a dollar. The Confectionary was a place where a bottle of "sody" would cost you twenty-five cents, unless you were an O'Neal. Then you could go behind the counter, and, feeling all the grandness a nine-year-old could stand, get yours for free.

My grandmother had worked in the Confectionary for years, cooking and tending bar alongside my grandfather. By the time I was small, she'd cut back, only working a few hours each day, but as I got older, she stopped going to the restaurant altogether and mostly stayed home. When I was growing up, my grandparents' house was always filled with Momma Susie's homemade desserts, and thoughts of cream puffs and chocolate pies, lemon cakes and tapioca pudding, coaxed us down Illinois Interstate 57 during the last miles of those four-and-a-half-hour trips from Chicago to Centralia, where we spent the hottest weeks of every summer of my childhood.

Sweet.

Still, once you got past the baking, that whole grandmother stereotype fell completely apart.

You would be hard-pressed to find a more dour, humorless woman than my Momma Susie. Light-skinned with freckles and straight hair, I remember her putting on lipstick for a trip downtown once and transforming her mouth into this joyless red slash— very Gloria Swanson, *Sunset Boulevard*—that seemed, even to my very young eyes, eerily at odds with what lipstick was supposed to do to a face. Momma Susie would get dressed when we were very small, but as we got older, she didn't come out of her pajamas much. She passed her days in a nappy green wingback chair watching soap operas or talking on the mustard-colored phone with the cord that puddled on the kitchen floor and stretched to the nether regions of the house.

Susie—nicknamed "Baby" early on either because (a) it took a while to give her a name after she was born, or (b) because Susie was also the name of her daddy's run-around girl—was a hard-cussing woman. Frequently one or another of us nine grandkids would be looking on when she would be forced by dint of circumstance to reach deeply into her "sack full of motherfuckers" and hurl a few at somebody's head—white Jesus in the front room and velour rug of the Reverend Dr. Martin Luther King Jr. laid across the sofa notwithstanding.

My Aunt Carolyn tells a story about my cousin, Traci, coming home from a visit to Centralia and Momma Susie, and fussing at her disobedient puppy. Warning that puppy that if he disobeyed again, she was going to Beat His Ass. Once I remember my Uncle Ronnie complaining to Momma Susie that their baby daughter Amber had also picked up a few cuss words. And asking her if she could please just tone it down a little.

"Hell no," Momma Susie said. "You don't want that baby to hear me cuss, then don't bring her down here. . . .

"Shit."

My grandmother lived in a world devoid of postmodern parental ambiguity. She lived during a time when there were two sets of rules, one for kids, one for grown folks, and it wasn't for grown folks to set store by childish things. Momma Susie had made her bones and carried the aches of being poor and black and a woman and wanting college but settling for marriage to a good man who ran around, until all her disappointments had metastasized into the small bitter curses of her life. She was "Stamp Paid," like the character from Toni Morrison's *Beloved,* because she had long since taken her own measure and was clear about its worth. Momma Susie cussed out people she might have wanted to shoot so when she called somebody motherfucker, that's probably best understood as just her way of granting them a colored woman's reprieve.

While her temper was fierce, growing up I never actually saw Momma Susie hit anyone or spank any of her grandkids. Most of the terror was left to the small ugly Pekinese, Rusty, who was constantly by her side—a creature some have suggested was my grandmother's alter ego.

Rusty was small and rust-colored with that smashed-in face typical of the breed. An ugly little dog, to my young mind, and mad because he knew it—because life had dealt him a bad hand and he really wanted to be a golden retriever. He was as unfriendly an animal as my grandmother was uncompromising a woman, but Rusty leveraged his meanness, protected his turf, and lived better than a whole lot of people in Centralia.

Rusty always ate leftover bones and cuts of meat from the restaurant, and on Sundays, Momma Susie cooked him breakfast, bacon and eggs or sausages with biscuits. When Momma Susie sat in her green chair eating cream puffs, Rusty would sit at her feet eating cream puffs too, daring one of us grandkids to come close.

Summers with Momma Susie always meant weeks of delicate negotiations with Rusty. You had to get by him to get to the bathroom, but often he was not of a mind to let you pass. He'd get there first, blocking the door, looking a grandkid square in the eyes and baring those ferocious little teeth, horribly plaque-stained from too many biscuits.

Sometimes Rusty bit you and Momma Susie fussed because you didn't "get your ass out of the way." After all, he was there when we were not. And if it seems inconceivable that a grandmother, who baked from scratch, for crying out loud, and remembered every birthday with a cheery card and a crisp five-dollar bill, had a dog that might at any time without any provocation sink his small fangs into our tender brown flesh, we grandkids instead preferred to focus on the takeaway point. And the next time, we got our asses out of the way.

The fact that she had not gone to college had been one of my grandmother's greatest laments. She was smart, she always told us. Real good in math. The only one of her sisters and brothers to graduate from high school but there had been no money for college. So she raised up a family of postgraduates, seeing her sons Lonnie Gerald and Ronnie through college. She sent the grandchildren she raised through graduate and medical school and watched as the rest of us chalked up graduation after graduation.

As a child, I always listened intently when Momma Susie lectured that getting an education was the most important thing you could do. That it was far preferable to early marriage as a method of economic viability. "Go to college," she told us. "Don't get married until you're thirty and don't forget, a man will give out 'sessually' 'fore a woman will." And if my sweet-tempered Papa Lonnie was ever offended as he sat nearby while she offered her counsel, he never let on.

It was a well-known fact that Momma Susie couldn't stand white people—never had anything good to say about the effect they had had on her life. Less known was the fact that for years, every day when she packed my daddy's lunches in high school, she also packed a lunch for Daddy's white friend, Norman Schuchman, a very poor young man who mostly wouldn't have eaten otherwise. And while Momma Susie never did do funerals, she was always real broken up when somebody died. Especially if they owed her money.

Although thwarted in her educational strivings, it would be inaccurate to say that my grandmother hadn't put her math talents to work. For as long as any of us can remember, Momma Susie was an entrepreneur in the field of extremely short term loans and interest.

Night and day, people would knock on the door, or most often just walk in, since it was a small, informal town and everybody wanted to claim a special closeness with Lonnie and Baby. They'd holler loud greetings and talk about how big all we kids had gotten. They'd stand before my grandmother in her PJs in that green wingback chair. We kids would just sit on the sofa with the velvety Dr. King, watching. Or she'd call us over, and we'd have to get the comb and scratch the dandruff out of her hair.

Sometimes it would be youngsters who'd come in with a note, *Miss Susie, my momma said to give this to you,* but the pleas would always be the same. *Can I borrow something for my light bill, for my gas*

bill, for my rent. My baby needs milk, my baby needs diapers, can I
borrow $100 dollars and I'll give you $150 when I get paid on Friday.

If the terms weren't to her liking, Momma Susie would sit there, unsmiling. "No, I don't have it today," she would tell them. But if it sounded all right, she'd get up and go under the cushion of that green chair or in the cigar box in that bedroom I never, ever saw her share with my grandfather, and dig out the appropriate amount of cash. She must have had a half-dozen loans out at any given time, but I never saw her write anything down. People would pay her back in food stamps if they didn't have the cash. Or they'd just sell her $600 worth of food stamps for $300. She'd go shopping for the house or send the food stamps to her grandkids in college.

My grandmother never used any muscle. Never had any sort of tough heavy working for her. And she didn't have people who didn't pay her back. My grandparents were revered in that small town. Driven by Baby's bitter strivings and Lonnie's happy-to-be-out-of-Mississippi work ethic, they were wealthy beyond measure to much of black Centralia. A stopgap measure for invisible folks who weren't able to go to the bank and float a payday loan.

My grandfather died in 1994 and Momma Susie was alone in the house for a while before moving in with my uncle, and still a steady stream of people came by for her Godfather-like specials. She was an old woman by that time, much of her authority already slipping into legend; still, nobody ever bothered with Baby. Sometimes I think about her and I wonder, like Malcolm X wondered about West Indian Archie, a Harlem gangster with a brilliant mind for numbers, what she could have been if she hadn't started off being a poor black woman in a time and place that disregarded all three. Perhaps she would have been a lawyer or a doctor, a middle school assistant principal, the youngest director in the Sara Lee Corporation. Or maybe she would have been a reporter for the *Washington*

Post. Perhaps it's not for us grandkids—who took college for granted—to wonder. Maybe that's like wondering how my soul got over, another colored people question written in the book of life, answered in glory.

Last time I got mad at my ten-year-old, I may have told her I was going to Beat Her Ass.

I'm not proud of it. But I bet she goes to college.

My momma's people lived on the other side of town from the O'Neals. This is both a geographic and a psychic description, because in many ways my grandmother Mabel was the exact opposite of Momma Susie. I never met this grandmother. She had epilepsy and wouldn't take her medicine, said it made her woozy, so she died, lucid, years before I was born. But her stories live through Momma, and possibly through me.

Mabel Blackwell, born in 1895, ran away from her cruel, domineering father's house and married as a teen. Later, she left her first husband, moving from Centralia to Denver to stay a few years with Aunt Lucinda who understood, having herself been married and divorced five times. Aunt Lucinda had gone west, alone, as a young woman and opened and operated a boardinghouse whose secrets and adventures she took to the grave. Grandma Mabel was engaged to a man in Denver when she went with a couple of friends to see a fortune-teller. The clairvoyant told her that she hadn't met the man she was really going to marry—that she'd meet him at a wedding or a funeral. Grandma Mabel laughed her off. Later, she got word that her daddy had died. She met my grandfather, Grover Blackwell, at her daddy's funeral.

While Grover became the only black hosteler at the Illinois Central Railroad roundhouse, Grandma Mabel was one of those

Illinois clubwomen. She was active in the Ladies' Aid Society of Second Baptist Church, the Women's Christian Temperance Union, the Colored Women's Independence Club, and the American War Mothers.

She was a woman of propriety. Churchgoing and elegantly starched—always in high-heeled lace-up shoes—she hated any kind of gossip. Which is not to say she minded hearing it, just that she couldn't abide the thought of scandalous words on her family.

Neat and organized, Grandma Mabel was a woman with a plan for her days. She washed Mondays, ironed Tuesdays, Wednesday and Thursday she mended clothes or cleaned. She earned extra pin money taking in wash for white women and selling eggs outside the house. And it turns out, she earned extra money by writing fiction under a secret pen name for the kind of pulp magazines, *True Romance* and *True Confessions*, she never would allow my momma, her only daughter, to read. I've tried to find those old stories of my grandmother's, to read her yearnings and see if she's the one who gives me words, but she kept that part of herself hidden too well. "A woman's heart is a deep ocean of secrets," said the old woman Rose at the end of the movie *Titanic*. I don't know the intrigues that filled my grandmother's interior world or helped her fill her pages. I only know she was a writer, so she had secrets in spades and kept them in dark places making it so that sometimes when she was alone, she could pull the curtain back to look at them and remember, or remember to forget. I can only imagine what my grandmother's secrets might have been, but my imagination feels like a nod across generations; one of the oldest parts of a black woman's reckoning with her daughters. *I'll keep yours and you keep mine,* I imagine my grandmother would say and perhaps much later, I'll ask her.

Grandma Mabel used her extra money to buy real estate. Today,

Centralia's Blackwell Apartments stand on the site where my grandparents lived for sixty years.

Like Momma Susie, Grandma Mabel was also fixated on education and achievement. She raised three boys, her oldest, my Uncle Dave a phenom, in college by sixteen, a Ph.D. in statistics from the University of Illinois in 1941, when he was twenty-two. My Uncle Joe helped found a prestigious Cleveland law firm, and my Uncle Johnson, "Skee," stayed in Centralia, where he ran a successful trash and hauling business. His wife, Winnie, had helped lead the fight to get the public swimming pool in Centralia integrated.

When she was forty-four years old, Grandma Mabel thought she was going through menopause. Instead she was pregnant with my mother, the beautiful Betty Lou. With her three brothers grown, or nearly so, my momma, Elizabeth Louella, was often lonely. Left mostly to amuse herself or pal around with nephews her own age, she was more headstrong, more willful, than anyone thought a pretty girl should be.

I grew up listening to Momma tell stories from her childhood, parables featuring adventures and dangers from before she was ten. She was the quickest girl in her neighborhood, and one day she decided to try to outrun an oncoming cab. The driver hit the brakes and my mother narrowly missed being killed. She once thought it would be great fun for passersby to think she "started at the stomach" so she uncovered an old well and lowered herself down. She threw her arms out just in time to catch herself before falling in. Then there was that time the street had flooded badly. There wasn't another soul in sight and she decided to find out how deep the water went. She couldn't swim, but she walked until the water came just below her nose, until one more step would have taken her under, then she gingerly back-stepped her way home.

It was the 1940s and Momma was smart and imaginative and

boundless, but no one thought to channel a little colored girl's creativity and spirit. Not even Betty Lou herself. Because when you are beautiful, that's always the first card everyone plays.

As an eighteen-year-old, visiting relatives in Chicago and looking for a summer job, Momma wandered into the Johnson Publishing Company offices to see if they needed a typist. They made her a model instead. They took her picture on the spot, and one of those later became a cover of *Jet* magazine. I have pictures of her waving from the top of a float in Chicago's 1959 Bud Biliken parade. And the family has a 1959 cover from an old *Tan* magazine. Momma was the cover girl and the caption underneath read: "I Was a Teenaged Hellcat, Too Wild to Be Tamed!" My grandmother Mabel was scandalized and worried about what her society friends would think. Still, Momma saved her biggest scandal for marrying Lonnie Gerald.

My Grandmother Mabel and my father's Grandmother Minnie were friends. Momma remembers meeting Daddy when they were visiting in Chicago and she was about four or five years old. *I remember all of us kids playing up and down those steps. I remember seeing your daddy and just being bowled over even as a teeny girl. I just knew I had to have that boy.*

My parents started going together when she was fifteen. Meeting up at the movie theater or after choir practice when Mom would go to the Confectionary where Daddy was working. Daddy was a handsome, popular high school basketball and football player whose folks owned O'Neal's. Momma was beautiful Betty Lou from Southtown. It was a high school idyll. Except Daddy, like his daddy and granddaddy before him, ran around. He got another girl pregnant, and in high school, he had a son, Lance, who Momma Susie and Papa Lonnie raised.

My momma's daddy, who loved her best, might have tried to sway Momma against going steady with Daddy, but he had died when she was thirteen. He was arrested in Paducah, Kentucky, and thrown in the colored jail because they thought he was drunk. He was actually in a diabetic coma. A piece of candy would have saved his life. My Grandmother Mabel hadn't wanted my mom to marry my daddy. She said, "He'll use up all your youth and your beauty and then just toss you away like an old rag." But my momma was nineteen. *And she had to have that boy.*

She spent much of her wedding praying that nobody would speak up when the minister asked if there was any reason why these two people should not marry. They lived in Chicago as a young married couple. Momma, who had begun college at Illinois State University and finished in Chicago, began teaching school. They kept a house filled with '70s soul music, cigarette smoke and barbecue smoke, friends, family, and various passers-through: Uncle Al and Aunt Dorothy, Aunt Gladys and Uncle Dalco, Uncle Paul, Aunt Aurelia, Uncle BoBo, Aunt Rivijean, Cousin Gailey Mae, who lived with us for a time, and neighbors the Tates and Scotts and Phillipses, all party buddies of my daddy. My father was a police officer, then a schoolteacher, then the assistant principal of the largest high school in Indiana. Later my father and mother both earned master's degrees.

But close family, solid careers, and advanced degrees did little to stem the hurt that was happening in our house. When I was six months old, Momma Susie's sister, my Aunt Hilda, lost her second son, Charles. Her first son, Stevie, had been stabbed during an argument with his college roommate. Charles and Jackie, who were maybe twenty years old, were on their way home from class at the local community college when they were killed by a train at an unguarded crossing in Centralia. After their deaths, the city finally put in the signals and gates that folks had been calling for, for years. Momma Susie and Daddy decided that the couple's five-month-old son, Charles Allen, should naturally come live with us since Momma and Daddy already had a baby about the same age, me, in addition to my three-and-a-half-year-old sister, Lisa. And that's how we became Lisa, Lonnae, and Chucky, just a little too much for my high-strung mom—married to my hard-drinking, increasingly mentally unstable daddy—to handle.

When I was a small girl, I would lie in bed and take in the sounds of late Chicago nights. They were suffused with the sensuous falsetto of Al Green, who used to draw out that h in "Love and Hhhappiness," loud-talking neighbors who drank with Dad, and, into the wee hours, my parents' bitter arguing. It might have been during those early years that I first became a writer, even though I didn't know it. Even if I didn't start getting the words down on paper until twenty years later, it was then that I started to fantasize my escape, to meditate about all the things I would grow up to do and all the women that I would become. I would negotiate with God, *I promise I'll be a good girl*, to see if I couldn't quiet some of the yelling in my house and lift some of the ache up off my soul.

When I was growing up, my mother had to be at her job as a teacher in the Chicago public schools at eight-thirty but she liked to get there at eight o'clock so she could be fully prepared for her day. She'd get up at six every morning so she could have coffee and iron clothes if she needed to. She'd dress as far as her slip before waking us kids up at seven. Even though she worked full-time, like Daddy, it was always Momma's job to pull what Arlie Hochschild called *The Second Shift*, to care for the house and get us kids dressed and ready. She bathed us and picked out our clothes for school the night before. In the mornings, she fed us and made us brush our teeth. My father would already be gone to work by this time, but even if he were home, he'd maybe just tie shoes.

After we were nearly ready for school, Momma did our hair. It would regularly take twenty to thirty minutes for her to comb my sister's and my hair, but it always depended on the amount of precipitation in the air. Humidity made for stubborn kinks, and it required extra time and effort to make them lay down and be cool. These were usually the mornings that started out with tears on our part, and maybe sometimes on Momma's part as well. It wasn't until after she finished combing, until she no longer had to worry about grease and hair getting on her clothes, that Momma could get completely dressed so she could spend all day at work.

We spent the time before and after school at the home of a neighbor. Then, when Momma got home, we'd come running. "Just give me five minutes," she'd often beg. Then after five minutes it was time to cook dinner and go through evening chores. Momma didn't like to cut corners, but sometimes she'd hem our pants with masking tape, and when the hem would start to come loose, and the tape would show through, "I'd be so embarrassed," she says. "But what could I do, there wasn't time to sew."

Momma was a gentle soul with perfect, middle-class, colored-girl manners and sensibilities, except when she drank hard or cussed and grew bitter about my daddy. All the books and movies said life would turn out different if you looked like my momma. That her kind of beauty so thoroughly insulated a woman from bad endings that she just had to steer her course with the right dress and colors for her hair and nails to sail into a beautiful, financially secure horizon. Turns out that's not even a fantasy that works well for white women. And for years, it served my momma ill. In some ways it caused her to underdevelop her natural creativity, brilliance, and self-reliance. To stay with Daddy past the point where staying was good.

After twenty-two years of marriage, much of it hard time, Momma divorced my daddy and remarried. A few years later, on

Father's Day in 1985, my father, who had been an alcoholic and a paranoid schizophrenic, killed himself. I was eighteen years old.

My momma is a different woman now than the one I remember growing up with. Or perhaps her real self was always overshadowed by drama and work, familial responsibilities and hurt. Perhaps we loved the promise of a mother we sensed in her, as much as we loved our lovely, overwhelmed, often sad mom herself. She still likes her high heels and tries not to go out of the house without carefully considering how her nails will match her jewels will match her purse. But she's a stronger woman than anyone thought she was. Stronger, certainly, than she thought she was.

She and her second husband divorced rapidly, and she set about buying her own house and building her own financial resources. Sometimes she's made peace with her choices; in other cases she's learned to live with her regrets as she's watched a lot of other folks die with theirs.

A couple of years ago, when my momma retired after thirty-two years with the Chicago public schools, she told my sister and me the story of what happened to that old abandoned house that used to sit next door. The one she called the city on time after time, worried because the house was a beacon for winos and children.

That house burned down, didn't it, my sister Lisa asked, and Momma got a funny look on her face. "I burned that house down," Momma said. "Me and Mrs. Tate."

In her essay, *In Search of Our Mothers' Gardens,* Alice Walker writes, "And so our mothers and grandmothers have, more often than not anonymously, handed on the creative spark, the seed of the flower they themselves never hoped to see; or like a sealed letter they could not plainly read." Walker's words make me remember the women who've come before me. I do not fool myself into thinking I have all the best qualities of my mother and grandmothers. I, most accurately, have their best and their worst qualities, but I have better choices and perhaps the luxury of a greater tendency toward self-reflection.

Sometimes at night I feel the women in my family close to me, cheering me on or fussing me out. Sometimes I think I see them in my own daughters. Savannah is the fastest child in her class and Sydney can sit at the computer making up stories for hours.

Jessie Mae, Susie, and Mabel made their own way. They made mistakes and carried their regrets, like scars or secrets, to the grave, willing that some parts of life would be different for their children. I am still learning new things about Betty Lou, who just bought a retirement house, her first brand-new home, near my sister Lisa in North Carolina. Her anger and sadness when I was a child have made me refuse to surrender to anger and sadness as an adult. And her courage lets me know that sometimes, to keep your kids safe, you may have to burn the house down and just add that to your pile of secrets.

Around my house, I like to plant flowers to honor and remember. Rosebushes for my children, lilacs for Grandma Mabel, a vegetable garden to work in every spring and summer and make me think of Momma.

I don't have a plant for my hard-cussing Momma Susie yet. That one requires an extra measure of thought. Something resolute and thorny, but beautiful in its best season, to a certain kind of eye. Something with long branches that break off into seedlings or trees. A plant that refuses to perish without water and won't wither with the dying of the light. A black woman's plant that curses the irritations that flow, like water from the ground, only to become among its most enduring parts.

Would that I could find her a sturdy little Motherfucker.

4

Mom in the Mirror

Ah wanted to preach a great sermon
about colored women sittin' on high, but
they wasn't no pulpit for me.

ZORA NEALE HURSTON,
*Their Eyes Were
Watching God*

I USED TO BE AFRAID of having children.

Black women weren't supposed to be scared of kids, I knew. "A black women is the mother to the world. Look at our history," wrote author Martha Southgate in "An Unnatural Woman," an essay about her own ambivalence about having children. "All the babies we've raised. Our own and other people's. By necessity and by choice."

I kept it mostly to myself, but I worried I wasn't grown enough to be somebody's mother. I obsessed about being too stretched out in body and in mind to still fit into my narrow skirts and tightly focused career plans. I whimpered because my wedding day had been lovely, but a baby meant I was married for real, for real. I was twenty-six and had been married one month when I found out I was pregnant. And I was dumbstruck.

In hindsight, however, there may have been clues that it was coming.

I had been experiencing strong bouts of baby lust, whipping my head around to see infants in strollers and pressing my face to an office window when a *Washington Post* reporter brought her newborn daughter to the newsroom. The day after we got married, I'd told my husband Ralph that it was either buy me a kitten or I'd be pregnant inside of six months. Also, I hadn't really been using birth control, so I realize the argument could be made that I was actually longing for a child. And perhaps deep down, or even just below the surface, it was true. But on the surface, I was reeling. Babies changed things—passions and proportions and sometimes possibilities. I wasn't yet a reporter for the *Washington Post*—that was still my dream. I hadn't even written for a daily newspaper. While working as a news aide for the *Post*'s Metro section, taking news tips, delivering mail, and sending faxes, I had been looking for opportunities to network and write in the hopes that it might happen for me one day. But a child could take me seriously off course.

Socially, I had made other young friends and was just starting to go out. My jeans were cute and my hair finally flipped into a perfect imitation of the young careerist Marlo Thomas in *That Girl*. I was feeling myself and didn't want to give any of that up. I needed the reassurance of a fantasy girl, the kind Hollywood is supposed to serve up in abundance. But the only glamorous young mother I remembered clearly from television was Elizabeth Montgomery in *Bewitched*, and I couldn't be Samantha because my own powers were not yet strong.

Maybe it is because I've always had a writer's love for characters and stories, an active imagination, or the penchant for drama that can come with growing up in a volatile house, but I've always looked to television and movies to help find pieces of myself.

Because sometimes, I've seen me most clearly in reflection—or discovered myself hiding in metaphor.

I remember fighting once with my college boyfriend. He was often snarling or shoving or punching holes through the drywall next to my head. But this time was worse than any of that, and I could feel a creeping ugliness pulling on my life, changing my predictions and all the good things the seers always said about me. As I lay curled in a ball crying on my apartment floor, one of my best girlfriends rubbed my back.

"Lonnae, do you remember Sister from *Sparkle*?" she asked urgently. "Do you remember how pretty she was and how ugly she died? That's going to be you if you don't get away," she told me, and an instant, iconic movie image flashed between us—the actress Lonette McKee as Sister, popular and lively, turned out and destroyed by the hard-living Satin and her own inability to break free. A ghost of things to come, my friend suggested in movie shorthand, and her words felt prescient and real. And later, but not too late, I left.

At thirty-seven, I am too young to remember some of the earliest popular portrayals of black women in film. I never saw Lena Horne or Dorothy Dandridge. Growing up, I mostly caught big-screen images of black women rebroadcast on television, and only a few of them stayed with me.

Even as a young child, I was hurt and humiliated by Rhett Butler's anger at Scarlett for trying to flee the ravages of Sherman's march through Georgia with, among others, Prissy (the black actress Butterfly McQueen), whom he called "a simple-minded darky," in the 1939 movie *Gone with the Wind*. And while I didn't relate to Mammy's lush black physicality played as asexual foil to the delicate, manipulative Scarlett, I have always been struck by the authority of actress Hattie McDaniel, who famously responded that she'd rather play a maid than be a maid when criticized about her string of servile roles. In the movie, she and Rhett actually *flirt* about the petticoat he bought her and she lifts her skirt to show it off. At the time, I quite remember feeling grateful that she was even being acknowledged as a women, such was my internalized feeling of erasure at her portrayal, and I knew there must be more to her story. (Nostalgic mammy lore notwithstanding, I later learned the economics of slavery demanded that no black woman's sexuality went unexploited. This was as true for the young, the old, the pregnant, and the nursing as it was for the mammies. Mayhap it was even true on Tara.) There has always been more to the story of black women than Hollywood has ever been interested in telling.

There have been volumes written about the dearth of substantial movie roles for people of color. Their titles largely tell the tales. There's *Toms, Coons, Mulattoes, Mammies & Bucks: An Interpretive History of Blacks in American Films,* by Donald Bogle. There's "Sapphires, Spitfires, Sluts and Superbitches," the chapter written by Elizabeth Hadley Freydberg in the book *Black Women in America.* In a 2003 *USA Today* article, writer Kelly Carter maintained that despite Halle Berry's Oscar the year before, the first ever by a black actress, "black actresses still face piles of scripts filled with prostitutes, drug addicts and jive-talkin' characters." So it is no surprise that while growing up, it was television rather than the largely one-note roles of black women in movies that most keenly shaped my perceptions of race and femininity. Or, more often, forced me to come up with my own.

The early years of television brought *The Hazel Scott Show.* The elegant, sophisticated star was an accomplished pianist and entertainer and was married to the dynamic Harlem congressman Adam Clayton Powell Jr. Though her show was well received and seemed to portend a time of enhanced opportunities for a diversity of images for black women, she was caught up in the McCarthy-era blacklisting of entertainers, and her show was canceled after a few months. What followed was television that appeased the conservative, pre–civil rights sensibilities of the times.

"Did somebody bawl for Beulah?" McDaniel said in the post–World War II opening of the radio show *Beulah*. The program, which told the story of another kindly black maid, initially starred successive white men affecting thick black dialect, before starring McDaniel. By the time the show moved to television, the role was played by the deep blues woman Ethel Waters, who is credited with adding dimension to the title character. Author Donald Bogle describes the character as:

> a warm and winning hefty, full-figured, and good-hearted "colored gal" with a deep hearty laugh. Employed by a middle-class white couple named the Hendersons, who had a cute little son named Donnie, Beulah was ever ready to solve the family's problems. She didn't seem able to exist without them.

Of course by the early 1950s, the ideal of the faithful mammy had long been established. In the decades following the Civil War, Southern county seats erected mammy statues in their town squares to honor the nurturing "loyal servants" of the Old South. (There were plans to erect one in Washington, D.C., until the National Association of Colored Women said I don't think so.) And ads for Aunt Jemima declared how that out-of-control mammy delighted in keeping her pancake recipe secret so only her master and his friends could savor their good taste. *Mmmm-hmmmm.*

At the other end of the continuum of images for black women was the character of Sapphire Stevens, a television archetype from the early 1950s CBS comedy *The Amos 'n Andy Show*; a program widely seen as insultingly reliant on exaggerated caricatures of black culture. Like the characters of Aunt Chloe in *Uncle Tom's Cabin* and, of course, Mammy in the novel *Gone with the Wind* (who was a mammy to white folks but had only harsh words for her man), Sapphire was television's version of the shrewish, ball-breaking, emasculating black woman. Count on Sapphire, with eyes rolling and tongue lashing, to keep her husband, Kingfish, in check.

Although hugely popular, *The Amos 'n Andy Show*, the first with an all-black cast, was canceled in 1953 after protests from groups like the NAACP and possibly out of appeasement to advertisers who feared their products could be tainted by close association with blacks. At the time, one advertising agency executive, referring to blacks on television, noted in *Variety*, "the word has gone out, 'No Negro performers allowed,' " and it would be nearly another twenty years before another all-black cast was in prime time.

My own earliest memories of black women on television begin with a fleeting image of Julia Baker and her son, Corey, in the NBC drama *Julia*. Diahann Carroll played the title character, a nurse and single mother trying to raise her six-year-old son after her husband was killed in Vietnam. It debuted to controversy in 1968, when detractors accused it of being soulless and safe in an era when urban discontent was playing out in burn-baby-burn refrains.

I only recall a single scene from the series, which ended in 1971. It was just an image really. Carroll was hugging her TV son and I remember having the keen sense, even as a very young child, of how special that felt. A pretty black woman was loving a black child, and I was validated by a picture that I recognized and that recognized me back. My earliest years of television watching were like that, sprinkled with occasional black people. Nearly as sketchy is my one memory of high school counselor Liz McIntyre—Denise

Nichols—in the early 1970s ABC drama *Room 222*. Still, those brief images were just more reinforcement of my overall certainty that black women worked. Even in outer space, Uhura, the lovely Nichelle Nichols, could always be counted on to get somebody on the phone for *Star Trek*'s Captain Kirk.

And if the picture wasn't exactly right, if the sisters on television didn't seem subject to everyday stresses, didn't get tired or laugh or cry—didn't drink beer, didn't talk about politics or white people, eat pigs' feet or press hair—I was able to forgive them their shortcomings. If anything, I learned the valuable lesson about how none of that is supposed to show on the everyday face you give the world.

A number of television movies also accompanied my growing up in the 1970s. There was *Get Christie Love!* (which became a series) with actress Teresa Graves as the beautiful policewoman title character. "You're under arrest, sugah," she said, packing heat and taking bad guys down. There were serious dramas of poverty and courage, like *Sounder* and *The Autobiography of Miss Jane Pittman,* both starring the majestic Cicely Tyson, who many viewers remembered from the short-lived 1963 CBS series *East Side/West Side*.

And of course there was the groundbreaking ABC miniseries *Roots,* based on the Alex Haley book about his family's triumphs and tragedies during slavery. *Roots* first aired when I was in fourth grade, immediately expanding notions of race and history in popular culture. But even though every kid in school and on my block got to watch it, even though my teachers talked about it each day and movie-of-the-week music rang in my head, *Roots* carried a "parental guidance suggested" warning that was the kiss of death for viewership among children in the O'Neal house. When *Roots* came on, we had to get in bed and I was in high school before it aired again. By then, my school was majority white, *Roots* was a rerun, and none of my teachers seemed inclined to talk about it at all.

Made-for-television movies and rebroadcasts of theatrical releases notwithstanding, my most vivid memories of black women on the tube came with the Norman Lear sitcoms of the mid-1970s. Florida Evans, a housekeeper character on the show *Maude,* was spun off into the CBS sitcom *Good Times,* which aired from 1974 to 1979 and centered around the lives of the Evans family in a Chicago housing project. Florida, as played by Esther Rolle, sounded a singular, asexual note, nurturing her family and supporting her strong-willed but perpetually laid-off husband, James. Her daughter Thelma was beautiful and jiggly and winsome, but she mostly just fought with her brother, the clownish J.J., who emerged as the show's star. The single neighbor Wilona, who late in the series adopted young Penny, played by Janet Jackson, was interesting and fun, but the series ended shortly after she began getting serious time on screen.

The decade also brought black-centered sitcoms such as *The Jeffersons, Sanford and Son*, and *The Flip Wilson Show* to television every week, with characters like Florence the maid and George Jefferson's long-suffering wife Weasy. There was the scowling Aunt Esther ("you ole fish-eyed fool," she'd call Fred Sanford) and Geraldine, who was feisty and sexy but was, after all, Flip Wilson in drag.

There were now black characters in my life, but none who spoke to me like the thoughtful children on *Little House on the Prairie* or *The Waltons.* None who were beautiful with kick-butt jobs like the sleuths on *Charlie's Angels* or, later, the coolly elegant Stephanie Zimbalist from *Remington Steele.* None who married exciting and well, like Susan St. James on *McMillan and Wife*, or had the perfect combination of vulnerability and strength, like Lindsay Wagner in the *Bionic Woman.* None who helped a lonely, creative child dream of herself.

In her book *Bone Black*, cultural critic bell hooks remarks that little is contemplated about the interior world of black girls in the culture. Not even an acknowledgment that that contemplation has been missing. She quotes Toni Morrison, who explained that she wrote her Pulitzer Prize–winning novel *The Bluest Eye* to give voice to "the people who in all literature were always peripheral—little black girls who were props, background; those people were never center stage and those people were me." She didn't just give us black girls, hooks says. She gave us "girls who were struggling to confront and cope with pain. And most of all she gave us black girls who were critical thinkers, theorizing their lives, telling the story, and by so doing making themselves subjects of history."

But I didn't read Toni Morrison when I was young. I read Harlequin romances and I watched television. I took lessons from all the characters I saw, weaving their parts into my black middle-class template to make me a girl suit. And I added the significant, value-affirming messages from the thin white women who belted out songs in glamorous commercials for dime-store perfumes.

> Kinda young, kinda now
> Charlie
> Kinda free, kinda wow!
> Charlie

Or:

> I've been sweet
> And I've been good
> I've had a whole full day of
> Motherhood
> But I'm going to have an Ambiance night

Or, most especially:

> I can bring home the bacon
> Fry it up in the pan
> And never, ever let you forget you're a man
> 'Cause I'm a woman
> Of Enjoli

Those women were compelling and beautiful. There was power and authority in their voices, and presumably they smelled good. When I was young, the women who had my face didn't have the kind of life I fantasized about living. And the ones who had my fantasy life didn't have my face and didn't know anybody who did.

Perhaps that's why I was positively giddy when I was in college and NBC's *The Cosby Show* debuted in 1984. Watching the show in prime time, I finally saw myself in Lisa Bonet, the quirky young actress who played Denise Huxtable. She was pretty and funny and smart. Her family was accomplished and ethnic without making the two seem mutually exclusive. Bonet was my very own "It" girl until she left the show, and even then, I continued to pine for her. I eagerly followed her movie career when she made the 1987 *Angel Heart* with Mickey Rourke (although I could only imagine the things my Momma Susie would have to say about a white man kissing on your breasts).

Later, I became a die-hard fan of the character Whitley, played by actress Jasmine Guy on *A Different World*. Her world wasn't so different. She was young, educated, lovely—all the things I longed to be—and every time she was on screen I was riveted. I would call up good girlfriends during commercials, and we would dissect characters and plot lines and, especially, dish about what Whitley was wearing. I still remember the episode when Whitley married her college sweetheart Dewayne Wayne. It featured Diahann Carroll and Ron O'Neal, Cree Summers, and newcomer Gary Dourdan, now of *CSI* fame. The people were stunning, the flowers elegant, and *Ave Maria* filled my mind with the promise of endless love. I taped that episode, and before my own wedding in 1993, I watched it over and over and over again.

But when I became pregnant, I had no modern television images of young black mothers to inspire me and help guide me to a self. Nobody who came from what Jacqueline Jones calls a "pioneer generation," someone who interacts significantly with the mainstream culture without ever having experienced legalized racism. Nobody with my history and my mandate who still wanted hip-hop and high-heeled boots. Nobody who wanted to write and mother and rock her thing (because although the sitcom character Murphy Brown was a journalist and later became a mother and a phenom, she was older, her world was lily-white, and she didn't seem to rock anything I wanted at all). Once again, I was forced to reach into my bag of tricks—into history and literature and popular culture. I plumbed the folkways of black folks to help assemble what motherhood would look like on Lonnae.

Most viscerally, I drew from Alice Walker. Do you remember Oprah Winfrey as Sofia in the 1984 movie *The Color Purple*? In one memorable scene Sofia was in a juke joint arguing with her ex-husband, Harpo, while her new boyfriend looked on.

"Whatchoo doin' here?" Harpo asked, ". . . just as scandalous, a woman wit' chillen in a juke joint at night."

"A woman need to have a little fun, Harpo," Sofia said.

"A woman need to be at home," he fired back, glaring at them both.

The boyfriend hugged Sofia tight to his lap. "Hey, I don't fight my woman's battles," he said. "My job is to love her and to take her where she wants to go," and the two laughed conspiratorially.

That scene lingered in my mind because Sofia had a rack of kids. She was no lingerie model, but she was strong and confident and possessed eminent domain over her body, her choices, and the brother who was waiting to take her *there*. There was beauty and power in the customization of her womanhood. And glorious possibility. Children come, thighs thicken, and still we dance.

On the surface, actress Pamela Anderson and Victoria's Secret model Stephanie Seymour seem to have little in common with Oprah Winfrey's Sofia. But both were also women I emulated when trying to invent myself as a mother. The television sitcom mothers I grew up watching in reruns—June Cleaver, Margaret Anderson, Carol Brady, nice ladies with orderly houses and sage advice for their kids—had largely been desexualized. But Anderson and Seymour built a self *based on* sex. They were my age, and Seymour already had one child when she was palling around on video with rocker Axl Rose. These women, along with Vanessa L. Williams and Demi Moore, chose motherhood and then chose to bend popular culture renderings of motherhood along the way, and I wanted to follow in that tradition (without the implants, boozer husbands, or tattoos).

Fortunately, I had help: two of my best girlfriends from childhood were also pregnant around the same time. In high school, my dear friend Terina was like "The Girl from Ipanema," and if I ever lost her in a crowd, I simply followed all the heads that had turned to stare and smile as she walked by. My girlfriend Shonda, the homecoming queen, was a doll-face with the kind of figure that the Commodores surely had in mind when they sang about a woman built like a brick shithouse. (They shortened the 1977 Motown hit, to "Brick House," but of course black folks, with strong memories of houses that lacked indoor plumbing, always heard between the lines.)

The three of us were young and nervous, wondering what kind of mothers we were going to be. We had college degrees and husbands, post–civil rights emancipations and subscriptions to *Glamour*, and we were all determined to have something just a little different from the mothers who preceded us. We bonded over our pregnancies and swore solemn vows. That marriage and children wouldn't mean we would just let our essential selves go. We promised we would hold on to our spark, our personal space, our workout schedules—whatever it took not to wholly give ourselves over to maternal, overwhelmed, soft-focus imitations of our younger, more ambitious selves.

While my friends and I considered ourselves striking out into new-mom territory, looking back, it seems like we were just part of the wave of young women who must have grown up watching those same Enjoli commercials and taking up the challenge.

In 1978, Barbara Eden's way-sexy mom in *Harper Valley PTA* was comical farce. Now, on any given day, newsstands are likely to feature articles on married or pregnant celebrities as "haute mommas." In 1997, actress Hunter Tylo successfully sued Aaron Spelling for firing her from the steamy nighttime soap *Melrose Place* after she became pregnant. The actress and mother of three, who was eight months pregnant at the trial, convinced a jury she was still hot enough for the role of prime-time siren.

There's Sarah Jessica Parker, star of *Sex in the City* and mother of a young son on the cover of *People* magazine, or model Rachel Hunter as the bikini-clad fantasy-girl mom on a rock video. A few years ago, model Cindy Crawford reprised her Super Bowl Pepsi-Cola commercials, retaining the sultriness but adding two toddlers in the back seat of her minivan. In a lot of ways, it is a time of heightened expectations and, unfortunately, stresses, because anytime Hollywood gloms onto an image for women, it can get tyrannical quick. This "new momism," beautiful, patient, and enchanted, is part of what authors Susan J. Douglas and Meredith W. Michaels railed against in their book *The Mommy Myth*.

Still, despite the rigid, overly saccharine, unforgivingly Hollywood turn that the mom image has taken, ten years ago my friends and I simply longed for healthy preservation. Every bit as important as prenatal vitamins, we said. And while we didn't have money for personal trainers or makeup artists to airbrush on that rested, radiant glow, we had obsession. Like sisters swearing a blood oath, we vowed we'd always rock it and call each other out if we didn't. Of course, we did learn to make allowances for story time at the library and trips to the Wal-Mart. (It's like my Aunt Jackie, an agoraphobic who entertained in silk lounging outfits and sued people for a living, always said: You've got to know your limitations.)

Now when I watch *The Cosby Show* with my own kids on Nick at Nite, I no longer see myself in Denise Huxtable (although I still wish Lisa Bonet acted more). I'm checking for Clair, the lovely lawyer, wife, and mother of five who makes Dr. Huxtable grin. In her groundbreaking book *Having It All? Black Women and Success*, journalist and author Veronica Chambers (who compliments friends for looking "very Audrey" over lunches in Manhattan) profiles black women who have drawn upon all parts of the culture to make recombinant selves. She dedicates the book in part to "The Clair Huxtables Everywhere," such is the resonance of this character.

Clair still seems to exude an authority and self-possession that I have only ever pretended, but she does give me something to shoot for. A Varnette Honeywood, just like hers, hangs on my wall (of course, I'm thinking hers was an original), and I even watch those old episodes carefully to see how Clair yells at her kids and then try to yell at my own kids the exact same way. Although her little daughters had thick, kinky hair like my little girls, and I've never seen Clair Huxtable dig into a jar for the last dregs of Ultra Sheen, I appreciate her presence in my family room. And it's deeply comforting to know that my own children, who fancy themselves Olivia or Rudy or Vanessa, will never have to watch television and wonder if anyone else sees them—at least as children.

I still don't quite see myself in prime time—and, in many hard-fought ways, don't need to as urgently. But the television landscape has also changed markedly in the nearly thirteen years since *The Cosby Show* left the airwaves. Rudy, Olivia, and Vanessa notwithstanding, my own children face different, and in some ways more worrisome, problems in terms of seeing their reflection in popular culture.

A while back, I walked into the family room and found my daughters watching an episode of the UPN series *The Parkers* with my eighteen-year-old niece Brittany, who recently moved in with us from St. Louis to attend a nearby college. I reacted as if they had been exposed to pornography. During the school year, my girls are allowed to watch two hours of television a week, Fridays and Saturdays usually. During summer vacation, they get an hour a day, but I haven't kept that as a hard-and-fast rule. We sign up for a few camps and outdoor activities, but we try not to overschedule the kids, and that leaves a whole lot of free hours in the day, time when friends aren't outside and the backyard has lost its allure. Time when four big, bored, brown eyes are looking to Momma for fun! and Momma is having her own fun! on deadline. It is those times when our one-hour rule can stretch into a Nickelodeon marathon—but only on approved shows, and *The Parkers*, about a black mother-daughter college duo, was not on the list.

I hadn't seen the show although I was somewhat familiar with the face of its attractive, ubiquitous star, Mo'nique, and I counseled myself to keep an open mind. I'd heard the jokes about how UPN stood for "U People's Network" for its heavy lineup of bad black shows, but since *The Parkers* was one of the most popular among black viewers, perhaps there was something there, I thought. I wish I had thought twice.

All it took was for daughter Countess Vaughn, the "hip, young, albeit not-too-bright daughter Kim," according to the show's web-site, to show up with a half-done gold weave and I was through. I recoiled and immediately ordered the girls upstairs. In that moment, something in me snapped, and I simply could not stand gag after gag of cartoonishly black television an instant longer. It's a sentiment shared by a lot of folks I know.

"It's all the weaves that are killing me," concurs Dawn Fong, a friend of a friend, an executive assistant at BET and single mom to twelve-year-old Dalia. Dalia watches a lot of old sitcoms, *The Cosby Show* and *Good Times* on Nick at Nite because "I've seen most of the episodes. They are not introducing anything new. Whether good or bad, I've already gone through it," Fong says. She doesn't do *The Parkers* or any of the black shows on UPN (or suggestive videos on BET, for that matter). "They are just too silly for me and I can't relate," she says. "It's not a reflection of my family, my immediate friends, or my immediate community." With respect to *The Parkers,* Fong says, "I don't want to be that type of single mother, so that show doesn't appeal to me. She's a good comedienne, but not for my child."

My friend Mae Israel, an editor at the *Washington Post,* laments that kids' programs "are just horrible!" Mae also doesn't allow her nine-year-old daughter, Maya, to watch any of the black shows on UPN. "I think there is too much buffoonery," she says. "Quite frankly, I view the TV as an enemy combatant that can suck the creativity, imagination, and interest in reading and writing out of our children. One hour at a time."

I go back and forth about which shows I let my girls see. We watch a number of old black sitcoms, *Good Times* and *Sanford and Son*. But even the modern shows I think are fine in general—the Disney Channel's *Sister, Sister* and *That's So Raven*—often are too exaggerated, move too fast, and are interspersed with too many Buy me! Try me! You're nothing without me! commercials. And, as Dawn points out, "Lord, do all the little black girls on television have to have long hair? I try to teach my daughter that she can be beautiful without a weave or without long hair," she says. "You come into our communities and we don't all have long hair. It varies."

Everywhere except modern shows for black people on television.

Our new O'Neal Parker house rules? The girls can watch an hour of cartoons, they can watch additional shows on a case-by-case basis, but they can watch all the TV Land shows they can stand— *The Andy Griffith Show, Bonanza, The Addams Family*—family programs I watched growing up. Last year, in an Associated Press article by Lynn Elber, actor Robert Townsend, CEO of the cable network the Black Family Channel, pledged to offer well-rounded, fully nuanced stories of black life and talked about how television helped his mom raise four kids on her own. "I was watching *The Andy Griffith Show* and Opie's lessons were my lessons. I think he taught me well," Townsend said. "He reinforced what Mom was teaching me and the church was teaching me." Although those old programs are almost totally devoid of black faces, I reason that by not seeing themselves at all, black kids can at least fantasize about where they would want to stand, as opposed to seeing a "not too bright" young black woman in an off-track gold weave and thinking perhaps that could, or should, be them as well. And it stuns me that even in this new millennium, these are my options—and have been for years.

Writing for the *LA Weekly* in 1999, around the time NAACP president Kwesi Mfume was threatening suit over the lack of diversity in television, columnist Erin Aubry Kaplan reached some of the same conclusions:

> I would like to cast an unpopular vote: I don't want to see any more new black people on TV. With all due respect to Mr. Mfume, enough is enough. With few exceptions, the black television presence has come to mean fetishized ghettoism or insipid vamping on the middle class, buffoonery across the board, nonexistent character development—to the point where the only black programs I watch with any regularity are TV Land reruns of *Sanford and Son* and *The Flip Wilson Show.* They at least represent the high point of what's always been a nadir. In the black-consciousness '70s, the characters of *Sanford and Son* and even *Good Times* were engineered with some dimensions beyond skin-color pathology, which is why they endure as family in America's collective TV memory, occupying as definitive a space as the Cleavers and the Bunkers. A generation ago, black characters in even the cheesiest shows earnestly aspired to some kind of progressivism—Linc in *The Mod Squad,* the inner-city hoopsters in *The White Shadow*—but in the age of crack cocaine and Def Comedy Jam, blacks are mined almost exclusively for hood sensibilities or comic relief, frequently both.

These days, as I try to help my kids navigate the television minefield, or more often just boycott it all together, I do continue to look, just a bit and without much hope, for modern images of black motherhood. Maybe to try to pick up helpful hints, time-saving tips, or rhythm and blues clues from other mothers who are walking my way. Maybe just to see myself and get a high five. Perhaps because I don't have it all figured out, I still value creative input, making me eager for the *Reader's Digest* with a pregnant Soledad O'Brien, CNN anchor and already the mother of two, on the cover. I'll scan *Jet* magazine with the glamorous Holly Robinson Peete talking about how she "holds it down" as an actress, mother of three, and NFL wife, and another *Jet* featuring "TV's Hottest Moms." I hadn't seen most of the shows it highlights, so I sat down to watch *All of Us, Half and Half, Girlfriends,* and *My Wife & Kids* starring Tisha Campbell-Martin. (I grew up along with Campbell-Martin in *Rags to Riches, Schooldaze,* and *Martin,* and her prodigious talent has always outshone her material.) I also rented the first season of *The Bernie Mac Show,* the smartest, funniest thing I'd seen in a very long time.

Although much of the comedy was slapstick, which isn't my cup of tea, the actresses were amusing and attractive. There were more black women faces than I had imagined, albeit of a similar look, making me, ironically, still hungry for color and texture and diversity. There were more black mothers. But I still found myself waiting for Denise and Whitley, Clair and Cicely. I still found myself waiting for that breakout role and that breakout black woman who resonated, who talked some good stuff, who *spoke to me* instead of just making me laugh.

Part of the problem can be blamed on the limitations of sitcoms, says Valerie Boyd, journalist, professor, and author of a forthcoming book on black women in Hollywood. It is difficult to do a fully realized character in thirty minutes. There's a foil, a setup, and a resolution, and with one exception, all the black shows that have survived more than one season have been comedies. (That exception was the Showtime drama *Soul Food,* which ran from 2000 to 2004 and centered around three sisters. Boyd calls those characters nuanced and richly revealed, and I make a mental note to add the series to my DVD rental list since I only saw the first two episodes, which were promising, but problematic.)

Boyd cities Eleanor, actress Ella Joyce, from the Fox television series *Roc* (one of my favorites from BC—before children), which ran in the early 1990s, as one of the best black female character roles. Eleanor, who didn't have kids, worked as a nurse and she and husband Roc (Charles S. Dutton), clashed about running the house. Boyd calls her a "down home, regular sister. Working and feminist in her way—politically aware, and outspoken while still being supportive and attractive in a very accessible way."

Boyd also speaks highly of Lilly Harper from the early 1990s NBC drama *I'll Fly Away.* Lilly (Regina Taylor) was a writer, she put everything in her journals, and stories were told from her perspective as a single mother and budding civil rights activist. (The story was set in 1958–1960, and she played a domestic.) But, of course, that show was canceled too soon as well.

Sometimes when I'm scanning the television horizon, I pause on *According to Jim,* starring Courtney Thorne-Smith, or *Still Standing,* with Jamie Gertz. I remember both stars from earlier, more vivid turns on camera: Gertz in *Less Than Zero, Lost Boys,* and *Gilda Radner: It's Always Something;* Thorne-Smith in *Melrose Place* and *Ally McBeal.* I can't help but feel vaguely disappointed at the departure their new roles seem to represent; dismayed that they're paired on screen with slobs. It feels, inexplicably, like they've sold me out, like we grew up together but now they've stopped striving (though Jamie does seem like she's reclaiming some of her attitude and

Jamie-ness). Like they aren't interested in working, however imperfectly, toward more egalitarian marriages, greater self-fulfillment, more flattering outfits, or some small piece of modern motherhood. Of course, perhaps their roles are just a simple reflection of the fact that some white women have different imperatives, and certainly more television options to choose from, and that simply makes my own lack of options more glaring.

If prime time leaves me largely unmoved, advertisements do offer me a few women I can embrace. "Moms have changed, shouldn't the minivan," a commercial for the Nissan Quest intones, and I'm all a-twitter. The ads feature women of different races loading violins or kayaks or huge yoga balls into their hatchback. Women sporting interests and confidences and full engagement with the world, not to mention kids. I also break for Motrin commercials, again featuring women of different races, with the secret of self-possession—"moms who don't fool around with pain." And while I'm not fifty, I say right on to all those postmenopausal women suffering bone loss, smiling, painting, and walking the beach talking about how "this is an amazing age, the age of Fosamax."

Finally, I confess, every Monday through Thursday in the lunchroom at work, I'm the only reporter glued to the soap opera *The Young and the Restless*. It's got glamorous people, engaging plot lines, and the Winters, a black family I adore. Kristoff St. John (who I wrote when I was a kid and he was a *Bad News Bear*) plays Neil Winters, and Victoria Rowell (who also starred in *Diagnosis Murder*) plays Drucilla Barber Winters. He's the CEO of a billion-dollar company, she's a former ballerina and company spokesmodel. They're raising a teenage daughter, and this year they've added a compelling storyline about foster parenting. Rowell herself was raised in foster care, and in one exchange, she argues passionately with her husband telling him they had much to offer and it was time for them to step up. It is a powerful scene, and I love that Rowell brings her life and voice to daytime television.

In another scene, the Winters are making out on the couch and he's telling her, "I love it when you get mad excited about something. You look so sexy, Momma, I love you so much." As a viewer, I love a good love jones. And I appreciate seeing these two beautiful black people represent without being corny or clichéd—even if Drucilla did sleep with her brother-in-law, her sister slept with her husband, and it's hard to tell which of the brothers is the Winters' daughter's daddy. (Got it?)

"The best art shows us the world," writes Martha Southgate in "An Unnatural Woman." And that's why I find bits of truth, small pieces of insight and inspiration, in creative offerings from others; in books and music and, yes, often, in television series and reruns and movies of the week. Though the demands of kids and the solitude of writing are often incompatible, children can help ripen you to life, Southgate adds. "My children force me, not as often as I should, sometimes resentfully or with exasperation, to look at the world," she says.

Or to see it differently.

I used to be afraid of having children, because I wanted something more from life and from motherhood than what I had already seen. I longed for an image to shoot for, like I had done so many times before when childhood hurt, when fantasies were all I had to sustain me and imagination took me to a dreamy place that helped quiet my most churning fears. I was afraid, but when I was seven months pregnant with my first child, a contaminated water scare warning pregnant women to be on guard, a high-profile child murder, and rising violence in the streets replaced my large, amorphous fears with deeper, more concrete terrors. And the fierce protectiveness I felt for my unborn child allowed me to know that my heart and courage were growing in proportion to my belly. I wrote about my new fears and great expectations in an "open letter to Baby-X Parker," a baby I now loved, and in 1993, *Washington Post* columnist Donna Britt turned that letter into a column. Her editor, Jo-Ann Armao, the deputy assistant managing editor for the Metro section of the *Post,* published it, and my reporting career began with an internship a year and a half later. Since then, some very good editors have given me skills, but it was the babies I was afraid to have who made my need to write bigger than my fear of failing at it; who made me pregnant with resolve. It is my kids who have given me deeper connections, keener insights, or at least a whole lot more raw material to draw from.

And it's just too bad that Hollywood doesn't see those dimensions in grown-up black women—and doesn't want to hear our stories. But I'm no longer a child and that lack of validation no longer disproves I exist. My children have good books and good pictures of brown girls and me to help them navigate the television dial. And, at least for now, I have my Motrin commercials, *for moms who don't fool around with the pain of not having a prime-time dramatic show on network television.*

Besides, there's always the fierce and funny Clair Huxtable, reminding us of ourselves on Cosby reruns on Nick at Nite, or even Samantha from *Bewitched,* because now my powers are strong.

5

Action Verbs and the Meaning of Sacrifice

Black women sitting at home reading
bedtime stories to their children are just
not going to make it.

Frances Beal,
Double Jeopardy:
To Be Black and Female

I THINK I MAY BE getting carpal tunnel syndrome, I told a
friend recently. As a reporter, I pound the keyboard for a living,
sometimes typing out thousands of words at a clip, but I do not believe it's just my job that's causing me the repetitive stress injury. I
think it's years of combing my children's hair.

Sydney and Savannah are very kinky girls.

I typically don't do a lot of elaborate styling with their hair, although if they had their druthers, I'd be much more talented, and
they'd look like Alicia Keys every day. I'm from the simple, old
school of straight parts and Original Formula Ultra Sheen, but even
relatively easy ponytails of twists and braids add anywhere from fifteen minutes to an hour or more of labor to my morning.

That's every morning, just the same as it did for my momma before me.

Whether I'm running late for an early interview, or was up the night before sick with what felt like Ebola, we fill a spray bottle with water and select colored hairballs with barrettes to match. I take a rat-tail comb and use their noses to guide my part straight back. I twist, I braid, I detangle, I sweat.

Unless you have a child whose hair goes out instead of down, it can be difficult to quantify the pressures, time and otherwise, that a kink coefficient can add to your day. Hard to describe the necessity of gripping a hairbrush until your knuckles whiten and your fingers begin to spasm. Or to convey the ritual constant—sometimes affirming, sometimes tearful—stretching back over all the generations we remember, of planting a daughter between your knees and trying to bring a diasporic sensibility to the Africa growing from her head.

We're the only people on the planet with hair like this, a coworker with locks once told me. It was an affirmation of the glory of natural black hair, and I believe in that glory. We read *Happy to Be Nappy* in my house (although Savannah, especially, questions that logic: "Mom, do you know what 'nappy' means?" "It means hard to comb." "I don't know if I should be happy if my hair is hard to comb, but, well, okay") and the girls often wear their hair in cottony Afro puffs secured with a hairball. I don't chemically straighten my children's hair, although we do get it hot-combed on occasion, and I encourage black girls with all kinds of hair that what they've got growing is lovely.

Still, *Happy to Be Nappy* notwithstanding, black-girl hair is complicated; especially tangled. Sometimes I don't let my kids mess theirs up by swimming or squirming too much in their seats. Sometimes I don't allow them to play in the sandbox or scratch their head when it itches bad. Sometimes even my husband sees me as the bad guy, unduly restrictive and unnecessarily stern. But then, it's a black woman thing, and I'm not sure if other folks understand. In a September 1997 *Allure* magazine article, "Not so Black-and-White," author Debra Dickerson compared black women's obsession about their hair to white women's neuroses about their weight. When my daughters come to me with the vague sense that, as girls, they are not quite American enough for the American Girl catalogs, I'm the one who has to find the words to prop up their egos. I'm the one who takes the time and does the work every morning to tell them they're beautiful and to make sure they have a good face, which always, always means a neat head of hair, for the world—and the one who feels bad if they don't.

It is black women who have always known that when little black girls go out of the house, the non-nappy world doesn't open its arms to say we cherish you, we accept you, we love you just the way your are. And if your hair is all over your head, because after all, left to its own devices, all it wants to do naturally is stand and salute Amen-Ra, well, that's just fine by us. The world doesn't say that, and neither, in large measure, do other black people. It's like my friend Stephanie, a journalist and online producer for AOL, who hails from Washington, D.C., points out: Growing up, if kids came out of the house ashy, or with their hair nappy or their noses running, folks always whispered that their mommas didn't care. . . .

In her book, *It's All Good Hair,* author Michelle N-K Collison talked about how her typically less than successful struggles to keep her daughter's hair neat became fodder for public comment and running jokes. After a while, she wrote, her day-care provider took over the job. "Finally, she just said, 'Bring me a brush and comb so I can do Maya's hair here.' "

I've sent my girls to friends and neighbors to do something

special to their heads, and last year, a little neighbor girl called to ask if I would do her hair and I was up parting and twisting for hours. Whenever I'm traveling without my daughters, making arrangements for somebody to comb and brush the girls out is one of the most crucial logistics I figure. When I took Sydney to Guatemala, women would carefully inspect her and murmur approvingly about all the work I put into her hair. Each of my own day-care providers has also styled the girls on occasion (and if they didn't initially know how, because neither Cousin Kim nor the nanny we call "the Señora" really have kinks to speak of, they learned quickly).

My former neighbor, Cathie, a finance director for a national association, is the most meticulous woman I've ever known. Her only child, Khadijah, whose skin is so dark and luminous it ought to have its own crayon, is the most well-appointed child. I used to tease Cathie about the lace socks she'd buy to go with Khadijah's school uniforms and the deep iron creases that were even starched into her gym class sweats. I teased her with a mixture of wonder and envy because in the ten years that her child has been on earth, I've never once seen a hair out of place. That's just what we learned to do, Cathie explains nonchalantly, and if she has gotten up at four o'clock in the morning, every morning for ten years to make that happen, to make sure that she doesn't have to rush and that she and her daughter are both pulled together with their best face for the world before work and school, well, such is the way of things.

Cathie and her husband, Leo, an associate director at an international human rights organization, hail from Louisiana and remember segregated schools. They remember when segregation ended and all but the poorest whites went to private schools. Cathie remembers when folks thought is was a scandal for little dark girls to wear light bright colors. You kept your hair neat and your clothes

neat and your house neat because everybody, even teachers, expected it, she says.

Maybe that's because neatness was one of the primary ways for
blacks to express dignity and self-definition—a first line of defense,
and not just to the outside world. In his book *The Fire Next Time,*
James Baldwin tells his nephew that his daddy, Baldwin's brother,
was a lost man, ruined because, deep down, he believed all the dirty
things white folks said about him. It's why in the book *Living In,
Living Out,* elaborate ritual was made out of dressing and grooming
young black women from the South in preparation for the trip up
North to work as domestics and why, during the civil rights movement, activists put on their Sunday best, even when they knew their
clothes might get splattered with blood.

In my house, hair doesn't have to be fancy. It doesn't have to be
wavy or cascade down my children's backs. "Cascadade," said the
"Little Girl with Blonde Hair" from Whoopi Goldberg's 1984 one-
woman show, when she played a black child who ties a sweater
around her hair to pretend it was long. It's the same thing my
friends and I did when we played "Charlie's Angels." The same
thing I saw Sydney and Savannah do a couple of years ago.

In her essay "Anger in Isolation," author Michele Wallace writes:
"On rainy days my sister and I used to tie the short end of a scarf
around our scrawny braids and let the rest of its silken mass trail to
our waists. We'd pretend it was hair and that we were some lovely
heroine we'd seen in the movies. There was a time when I would
have called that wanting to be white, yet the real point of the game
was being feminine. Being feminine meant being white to us."

In my house, it doesn't have to cascade, but it has to be
groomed, mostly groomed, or at least tied up with a scarf. This
daily ritual can be a wonderful piece of creativity and bonding—
and it can numb my fingers until I can no longer twist open a jar

of Blue Magic. But like so many of the things of motherhood, it is work that is largely unheralded, and in my house, it is always my perceived shortcomings that my children like to make center stage.

Choose your verb! said the public service announcement, one of my favorites, designed to combat childhood obesity and get kids moving. It was a delightful piece of instruction, so right there in my family room, we took up the challenge.

What's your verb? I asked six-year-old Savannah, and she said her verb was to run or to play on the computer or to hug her little brother.

What's your verb? I asked Sydney, ten, and she said her verb was to draw, or to act, or to ride her bike.

Okay, what's *Mommy's* verb? I asked the girls expectantly, and Sydney thought hard for a moment.

"Mommy, your verb is to sleep," she finally said, grinning widely. My own smile faded.

"To *sleep?* Are you sure that's it?" I asked, disbelieving. This was sooo not the verb of my self-concept. "You don't think Mommy's verb is to write, or to cook dinner, or even to dance?" I asked. (For crying out loud we were taking African dance classes every week!) Later, with the kids off somewhere playing, I was still smarting, feeling waves of existential angst and mentally ticking off the long list of what I thought my verb actually should have been.

How about to wash clothes or to iron or to volunteer in everybody's class? How about to pay cash money for wrapping paper I don't need? I thought crossly. How about to write on deadline? Or hell, to have sex when I don't feel like it?

How could my daughter think my verb was to sleep when one or another of my children always wakes or wanders or wants things in the night and I stumble over shadows to put them back to bed. When most mornings, I'm up by six-thirty and I haven't slept past eight-thirty in the morning in over ten years. When somebody is forever pulling on me, when everybody wants something from me, when I am the indispensable person in my house, and when it's me they want, it mostly means that nobody else will possibly do.

For Mother's Day a few years ago, I wrote a piece for the *Washington Post* magazine about taking a year off from work to travel with my kids and freelance and live a Donna Reed fantasy of gleaming hardwood floors. And about my subsequent decision to return to my reporting career, committed to a four-day-week schedule, better rested. I began the essay about being sleep-deprived. About driving home late from some event I had to cover as a *Post* Style writer with the windows down and the music blaring, pinching myself to try to stay awake. As a reporter and mother of two young girls, with a husband who commuted to Philadelphia all week, I was always pushing myself, and I wrote that this time, fatigue pushed back—hard.

I wrote about how my husband found me that night, with the car still running, asleep in the driveway.

It seemed unfair and maybe a bit cruel that of all the things I was trying to do and all the people I was trying to be, of all my action words, Sydney thought my verb was to sleep. (My friend Stephanie's eleven-year-old daughter Jordyn said her verb was to yell.) Then one of those old black voices chimed in to remind me that fair had nothing to do with anything at all.

In Toni Morrison's 1988 Pulitzer Prize–winning novel *Beloved*, an escaped slave woman tries to kill her children and does succeed in murdering her (crawling-already?) baby daughter, when the slave catcher threatens to return them to bondage.

The novel was inspired by the 1856 story of Margaret Garner, a fugitive slave from Kentucky, who fled with her husband and four children across the frozen Ohio River. A short time later, they were discovered and surrounded.

> The husband of Margaret fired several shots, and wounded one of the officers, but was soon overpowered and dragged out of the house. At this moment, Margaret Garner, seeing that their hopes of freedom were in vain, seized a butcher knife that lay on the table, and with one stroke cut the throat of her little daughter, whom she probably loved the best. She then attempted to take the life of the other children and to kill herself, but she was overpowered and hampered before she could complete her desperate work. The whole party was then arrested and lodged in jail.
>
> The trial lasted two weeks, drawing crowds to the courtroom every day. . . .
>
> But in spite of touching appeals, of eloquent pleadings, the Commissioner remanded the fugitives back to slavery. He said that it was not a question of feeling to be decided by the chance current of his sympathies; the law of Kentucky and the United States made it a question of property.

"Mamma, did you ever love us?" Hannah asks her mother, Eva Peace, in Morrison's 1973 novel *Sula*. When Hannah and her brother and sister were small, Eva's husband left her with $1.65 in her pocket, three beets to her name, and a winter to be endured. One day, Peace deposited the children with a neighbor, promised to return the next day, and instead returned eighteen months later with two crutches, a new pocketbook, and one leg—and whispers that she threw herself under a train to collect the insurance money. "Did you ever, you know, play with us?" Hannah asks.

"Wasn't nobody playin' in 1895," Peace tells her daughter. "Niggers was dying like flies." Since coming back for her kids, Peace always wore skirts, and stockings, and beautifully heeled shoes to show off the shapeliness and tone of her remaining leg. "What would I look like leapin' 'round that little old room, playin' with youngins with three beets to my name?"

"I know 'bout them beets, Mamma. You told us that a million times," says Hannah.

"Yeah? Well? Don't that count? Ain't that love?"

Sula is a brilliant piece of fiction, of bone memory, no doubt, and maybe memories of broken bones as well.

In 1955, fourteen-year-old Emmett Till of Chicago begged his mother to send him to Mississippi to spend the summer with his cousins. She sent him with strict instructions about how to navigate the Jim Crow South. At a drugstore in Money, Mississippi, he is alleged to have whistled at a white woman. His momma, Mamie Till-Mobley, said she taught Till to whistle because he stuttered and whistling helped him talk. Either way, the white woman took offense and three days later Emmett Till was kidnapped from his great-uncle's home. When they found his body in the Tallahatchie River, one of his eyes was missing. His head was bashed in. He had been shot at close range, and a 125-pound cotton gin fan had been tied around his neck.

The casket with Till's remains was welded shut, then sent to his mother in Chicago. Mamie Till-Mobley insisted on opening it. Then she insisted on leaving it open for the funeral so a nation on the brink of change could see what racism did to its children, and its men.

In the summer of 1999 at a housing project in Washington, D.C., Helen Foster-El was enjoying the evening air, talking to a neighbor, and watching her grandchildren and other children play when gunfire erupted nearby. Foster-El quickly rounded up all the children in sight, ushering them to safety, shielding their bodies with her own. Before she could make it inside, she was shot in the back and in the leg. She died before the ambulance pulled away from the curb.

Angela Davis writes that there is something concrete and non-mystical about black mothers in their myriad acts of resistance and heroism. It is the experience of motherhood under duress. In her critique of the abolitionist novel, *Uncle Tom's Cabin*, in the book *Women, Race and Class*, she writes that author Harriet Beecher Stowe failed to capture this essence in the gentle, Christian part-white character of Eliza who is drawn in the Victorian mores of the time. Eliza, a sheltered house servant, fearful of her husband's passionate hatred of slavery, is driven to the superhuman feat of spiriting her child over a frozen river to elude slave catchers. In reality, argues Davis, it is not just motherhood, but the very specific condition of motherhood under oppression, that has left black women with a tradition of endurance and sacrifice.

History has not required that I display what one essayist calls "the monstrous potential of love." It has not compelled me to slit my baby's throat to spare her from an unspeakable fate. I have not needed fidelity enough to walk twelve miles one way to visit my children on another plantation (like the mother of Frederick Douglass). I haven't had to swallow my own horror and heartbreak to show a nation the tortured body of my only child, and I've never dodged bullets. As a mother, I have not been required to make those kinds of sacrifices—only to be mindful that other mothers have.

In 1998 my husband, who worked as a sales rep for a large pharmaceutical company, was offered a promotion. He had finished his M.B.A. the year before and he was eager for the additional responsibilities his promotion to the company's corporate headquarters outside Philadelphia would entail. I was pregnant with Savannah that year and looking forward to taking time off and then getting back to my still new job as a Style reporter for the *Washington Post*. I hadn't had a traditional career path. The *Post* was my first (and only) daily newspaper job, and although people thought my writing showed promise, I still had a great deal to learn. We arrived at an impasse, my husband and I. He wanted to move and I wanted to be still. He wanted to grow in his career and I wanted to grow in mine and we wanted to be together, but our jobs were far apart.

I knew a lot of women would have followed their husbands. Would have altered their ambitions or put their aspirations on hold, believing it was for the good of their family. I understand and respect that decision as a viable choice for some women to make. But my husband and I had just weathered a difficult time, had just dealt with some unfinished emotional business that got put off when our first baby showed up so soon after we were married, and neither of us wanted to add another resentment. Gifted with options, suffused with entitlement, and tasked because I was a writer who needed to write, I chose something else. I did not believe it would be a good thing for my family if their indispensable person was a bitter woman, or for me to feel compelled to make choices I knew I could not live with. I decided to stay and continue to work for the *Post*. And for two years, beginning when my oldest daughter was four and my second daughter was a month old, my husband drove back and forth to Philadelphia, living away the better part of every week.

I brought in a young cousin from Illinois to live with us to help. Cousin Kim lacked direction and focus and was looking forward to a change of scenery. And, as a half-black girl who'd always passed for white, she was looking forward to getting in touch with her black side. I've often joked that she may have gotten a little more than she bargained for.

After a six-month maternity leave, I returned to the *Post* and left Savannah in Cousin Kim's care. She watched her for a time, but later worked and went to school herself. I dropped off Sydney at preschool and Savannah at day care, and Cousin Kim picked them up. I figured out dates and logistics for dance and gymnastics. She cooked or ironed uniforms and learned how to braid little black girl hair. I breastfed for a year and worked late, and she sometimes stood in for nightly games of Concentration.

By the second year, the strain of being momma and mostly daddy began to show. There were times when I was so tired I felt drugged. I fell asleep in my clothes. I woke up in my shoes. One early morning, Sydney stood by the side of my bed, told me she was hungry, and asked if I could fix her breakfast. I thought about ordering her back to sleep. I thought about telling her to grab a Pop-Tart from the pantry. I thought for a while about how I wanted to cry. Then I got up and fixed her something to eat. Because I don't remember exactly how the women I grew up with held it all together, but I don't ever remember them sleeping through breakfast.

"You got big dreams? You want fame? Well, fame costs and right here's where you start paying." So said dance instructor Lydia Grant in the 1980s television series *Fame*.

With help from neighbors, who pitched in to occasionally take the kids, fix dinner, or offer words of support, we zoomed or, often, stumbled through our days, Kim and I. At work, I raised my voice and sometimes wrote stories that made me go deep. An old, old black man called me after I wrote a story about Kim who, although biracial, had always called herself white. It was intimate and controversial and prompted a flood of letters and calls and invitations for my cousin and me to talk about the story on television. That old man left a message saying he was calling on behalf of himself and his wife to say that they were proud of me. My mind can scarcely hold the thought of that black man with the years falling from his voice—what it may have meant for him to be proud of a young black reporter or the grace that allowed me to hear him say it. I just know that if I don't do anything else, that message will have made all my writing worthwhile.

I don't pretend that my struggles make me any different from other mothers who feel the burden of history and the burn of personal ambition and the weight of children planted on their hips. My fervent prayer is that they make me kind of the same. That the universe will record that I tried to represent.

Of course, the universe will undoubtedly recognize that having money and options makes the representing just a little easier.

My sister Lisa had less money and fewer options when her own kids were young, and she has always been a steady presence in my life, has always stood a fixed distance ahead to offer lessons or parables or cautionary tales for me to ponder.

At twenty years old, Lisa dropped out of college to marry her high school sweetheart. She was pregnant with my nephew Brandon and had just finished college a few years later when her daughter, Ryan, came along. A while after that, her high school sweetheart, whose arms I used to jump into when I was a little girl, changed into someone we didn't know, someone who didn't quite want to work or stay home at night with kids. He changed into a man who wanted the streets more than he wanted the young wife who loved him.

When she was twenty-three and her husband was not around, my sister went grocery shopping. She came home with bags of groceries, a baby carrier, and her two-year-old son trailing behind her. She couldn't pull right up to the front of her townhouse, so she had to carry the groceries up the three steps to her back door. "I meant to throw a couple of plastic bags of groceries up on the steps and then go back to the car to get some more," Lisa says. Instead she threw the baby carrier with her six-month-old inside. The baby was fine. She didn't even cry. But my sister did.

A few hard years later, with help from my mother's sterling credit, Lisa bought a house and continued raising her kids alone. She divorced her husband and, in her early thirties, remarried, moving from the south suburbs of Chicago to Johnston County, North Carolina. She and her husband, Darryl (who is from Centralia and was sweet on Lisa when they were kids and we were visiting for summer vacations) have a young son, Darryl Alexander, who is eleven days older than my Savannah. She earned a master's degree in 2000 from North Carolina State University, and she's an assistant principal of a magnet middle school fifteen minutes from her house.

In many important ways, my sister, now forty, has prospered and moved past the trauma of her young life. Except our struggles always seem to leave tracks in the snow. Not footprints exactly but grooves or indentations or even ridges, worn like the bodies of black women, where the ground has been rubbed into monuments by all the times we've laid across it doubled over, rocking back and forth.

And they leave tracks in the souls of the children who follow close behind us. When my nephew Brandon was about to graduate from high school and Ryan had been accepted to an elite private boarding school, Lisa wrote her kids a letter, just to clear some things up.

I know I push you guys sometimes and I may seem too rigid, however, please know that I only want the best of all things life has to offer for you. You can't slip and slide by in anything. Anything of importance in having (education, marriage, career, even a clean house) takes work. If you don't put in the time and effort, things will fall apart very quickly.

You may have noticed I like things in order, and if it seems I go overboard sometimes in these pursuits, I apologize. For a lot of my life, things were in chaos, so now structure for me is a wonderful thing. . . . Also, you may have noticed that I'm a somewhat serious person, not exactly your lighthearted gay type of person. If we have not had enough laughter and fun, perhaps I can start over with your kids and be the fun grandma. I'll try, I promise. . . .

Brandon, when you were nine months old, my father committed suicide. . . . I think I hung in there because of you. You were an infant and you needed me so. . . .

I've already told you that I got pregnant in college; however, that was my mistake, Brandon, you never were thought of as a mistake. . . . I have never regretted having you. Please know that I've done the best I could, given sometimes negative circumstances. Part of the reason I divorced your father was so you wouldn't have all your childhood filled with drama . . . that can lead to an unhappy adulthood. Don't be bitter, make a vow to improve your children's lives and your own.

Ryan, a wife is supposed to be loved and respected, never called out of her name or yelled at like a dog. Always remember you can be unhappy by yourself. Always do what's best for Ryan and her children. . . .

Always know you will always have my love . . . whatever you choose and wherever you go.

I listened to my sister's letter, to the power of her words, and I remembered that after all, she was the one who was supposed to major in journalism. I listened to her letter and I heard Eva Peace explaining to her daughter that it's hard to play when you need to figure out dinner and the roof over everybody's head. I heard echoes of author Russell Banks in his book *The Sweet Hereafter*, about a small-town bus accident that killed fourteen kids and ruined the parents, who sometimes hold it together only because they've got somebody else who needs them to make it.

I remembered when Lisa worked full-time as a teacher but couldn't afford health insurance, so she prayed even harder than most that her kids wouldn't get sick or injured. And she got our cousin, Lana, the granddaughter Momma Susie sent through medical school, to diagnose Brandon's scarlet fever over the phone and call in a generic prescription.

And Lisa was middle-class.

I once read that the older sister clears a trail for the ones who come behind her. That she's on point, out front, putting her body in the way of cold realities that stick and accumulate and bury you if you don't figure out how to keep going. From a good ways off, she turns around to say Go back! Don't come here! Take a different path! My sister sacrificed for her children, who are intelligent and compassionate and sometimes keep their rooms fairly straight. And she condemned a bad road for her only sister, who might otherwise have married and had a baby in college as well. She pointed out a way where the ground was more forgiving and wound through more beautiful, well-compensated places. It's another sacrifice worth noting and one I try to be mindful of for all the little sisters coming behind me (and for my niece, Brittany, and Cousin Kim, who've lived with me and think that I have a least a few of the answers).

Of course sometimes, even when you see a path that does not beckon, you can still be the kind of woman who reads other women's signs.

Not long ago, I was sitting in the home of Joby Dupree, a neighbor who happens to be the great-great niece of Zora Neale Hurston. Joby was an accountant for ten years before she quit, forfeiting roughly half of her family income and scaling back housing and lifestyle choices to begin what she calls her second career: home-schooling her three academically gifted children for eight years. She's now earning her teaching certification so she can take what she's learned into a broader classroom.

For a long time, living in Florida and Tennessee, Joby says she felt like she was the only black stay-at-home mother and the only one home-schooling her kids. "I still think society as a whole and even the black community is not cognizant that there are African American stay-at-home mothers. In [media portrayals], they're heroin addicts or welfare moms. They're not seen as making the sacrifice to be at home with their children."

Then she moved to her current home in Prince George's County, Maryland, and started meeting other black at-home moms. In 1997, Joby helped found the national organization Mocha Moms—a support group that has, according to its website, "adamantly refused to compete in the alleged competition between 'stay-at-home' mothers and 'working' mothers commonly referred to as the 'Mommy Wars.'"

The website goes on to say:

While many of our members have eliminated employment altogether, others work part-time, flex-time, night shifts, have home-based businesses, consult or freelance from home or have chosen alternative, less demanding career paths so that they are more available to their families. Our goal is to support the decisions made by our members. We will never pass judgment on mothers who choose to make or are forced to make different decisions for their families.

That means, "I don't try to tell people what they should or shouldn't do, I can only tell you what has worked for me," Joby says. "So many people come out and say this is what you should do or shouldn't do. You don't know me, you don't know my family, and you don't know my children. Tell me what worked for you and maybe I can try it."

In October 2003, the *New York Times* magazine ran "The Opt-Out Revolution," a controversial, widely read piece profiling educated, successful women who have chosen to cut back or quit high-powered jobs. While a 1998 essay in the *Washington Post* magazine detailed the same phenomena and included the perspective of another Mocha Moms founder, Cheli Figaro, a Columbia Law School grad who quit the Commerce Department after the birth of her son, the *New York Times* piece made no reference at all to women of color (or, by the way, the men who now supported these women).

A June 2004 essay about opting out in the libertarian *Reason* magazine says, "It's amusing to see the 'opting out' trend treated as news, considering that the story has been around for the last 25 years or so—that is, for as long as women have been on the career track in significant numbers." But that *Reason* article also neglected to mention contemporary black women (like those in Mocha Moms) or any history of those who tried to opt out of field work after Emancipation. Who, in the late nineteenth and early twentieth centuries, opted out of living in as Southern domestics or took in laundry (my grandmother in the 1930s and 1940s) and boarders when they moved to the cities nearly a hundred years ago to try to come up with a better work-family balance of their own. And I assume that for the middle-class black club women of the early 1900s, with children, college degrees, careers, and crusades, trying to work from home doesn't count at all. It is precisely this inability of some women to see beyond themselves, to appreciate other struggles or glean insight from other histories, that helps make much of the current work-family debate seem so shrill and intractable—why, for women like me, it so sorely lacks resonance and rigor and, most assuredly, soul.

Joby talks about being one of two black children in private school when she was young and how alienated she felt, especially when a teacher told her class that blacks were genetically inferior. She talks about how when her own children were preschoolers (her daughter is fifteen, her twin boys are fourteen), they hid their black Fisher-Price Little People and only played with the white ones and the Asian ones and the ones that had straight hair. "My kids were two years old, what had I ever done to make them dislike or not want to play with black dolls?" The answer was nothing, she says. It's just in the air.

Which is why Joby says she "has to do more," and in her passion, I hear echoes of club woman Mary Church Terrell. For mothers who raise their kids in the main culture it's less of a problem (although surely mothers of fat kids who want to be thinner, gay kids who contemplate suicide, the little girls with dark hair who talk incessantly about wanting to be blonde can at least partially relate), but black mothers have to be more deliberate about their choices. They have to buffer the images of black people children can get from teachers or television or pull from the ether.

For parents who want an academically rigorous environment for their kids, that can often mean sending them to all-white places. For eight years, Joby chose to give her children that academic rigor at home but says, "When I send my kids out in the world, I have to shore them up in their blackness. I have to do that at home because they won't be getting that in school."

I am moved when I listen to my neighbor talk. She has shared her insights in conferences and classrooms and in small spots on radio and television. She tutors (one of her students is my daughter Sydney), and she's in school now so she can give back more by consulting or running her own classroom. Her wisdom is bracing and gathered over long years spent in singular focus.

It is a focus I have not had.

Doesn't it feel like we're always going to wonder what treasures we left undiscovered on the path we didn't walk, even if we've worked out what's best for us or are at least engaged in an ongoing calibration.

I've got a running joke with my editor. Often on deadline I'll send her messages lamenting how I gave up a promising career in the french fry arts at McDonald's. Sure, there were those nasty basket burns to contend with, but sometimes the lure of a job that doesn't ask much of me is seductive. Sometimes I pass those folks who work construction, especially the ones whose job it is to change the sign from STOP to SLOW, and wish I only had to move in two speeds. That my labor was uncomplicated and my thoughts were my own. It's my fantasy of a simpler life.

Just like sometimes I fantasize that I could be the kind of woman who remains at home or even home-schools her kids. But I took my Aunt Jackie's advice a while ago and I know my limitations. So does my neighbor Joby, and presumably so does every other woman who makes choices in her life—choices that all involve sacrifice—and that, of course, recognizes the deep historical privilege of black people even having choices at all.

"I wouldn't change a thing. I don't regret what I did," Joby says.

Still, sometimes she looks at women her age who have been working in their fields for decades. "They are lecturing, they've got their Ph.D.s, they're doing consulting," she says wistfully. That could have been her. But "you can only do so many things with your life."

Always there is more time than life, I can hear my Spanish teacher in Guatemala saying.

It feels like a grown-up thing to understand that women get to customize their lives—that they have to pay the bills or play to their personal strengths and then, if they're smart, they can borrow, sample, remix each other's best ideas.

Joby still loves to read aloud to her kids—she's read them the whole Harry Potter series—so when I was having a problem getting my oldest daughter to read more, she suggested I find a book about a little black girl in elementary school. I went out that day, focused on finding Sydney just the right book, and she read it in two sittings. I find much to admire in what mothers who work at home accomplish, and perhaps if I am humble enough, I can learn from them without feeling diminished by their choices.

And they can maybe be glad that I can write it all down.

Still, all my work and pondering aside, I really do think I'm getting a bum rap in my house. Not long ago we were on our way to Baskin-Robbins, and my husband, Ralph, and Sydney were talking. "Sydney, now, you know if Mommy only has money for three scoops of ice cream, that doesn't mean you'll get one and a half scoops and she'll get one and a half scoops. That means Mommy will get three scoops of ice cream and you'll get none," Ralph said laughing. "And then she might give you a little bit of hers."

Sydney looked at me and nodded her head. "I have noticed that's true, Mommy," Sydney said.

I met my husband's and my daughter's gaze square on.

Whatever.

My children hurt me when I breastfed, but my son Satchel was the worst. From the beginning he was greedier and clamped down on me harder than the girls. Early on, an infection made nursing agonizing. Later, he bit me so hard I thought he had taken my nipple off. He hadn't, but the blood that soaked through my shirt was only partially diluted by my tears. I continued to breastfeed for nearly two months after that.

I didn't breastfeed because I was trying to be superwoman, because it did such amazing things for my bustline, or, after a while, even because everyone says it's best for children over the long haul, although that was my initial motivation and I believe it to be true. I breastfed because it was the sweetest thing I've ever known. And when I close my eyes, I can still feel warm, panting baby breath rooting around the hollows of my neck. Because in a still and quiet time, if I sat in my glider and rocked my babies in my arms, doesn't my Lord know, that was the rock of ages.

My children are my joy and my primal passions, but I have others as well, and that's something they need to understand. If need be, I would lay down my life for my kids. But what I won't do is stop living. Eva Peace gave up a leg, but nobody could have asked her to give up the skirts that showed off the curve of the one leg she had left.

In her essay "Elementary Lessons," Rita Coburn Whack writes, "If we run ourselves ragged taking care of everyone else's needs, leaving no time for ourselves, we teach daughters that other people are worth more than they. And sons learn that women are only for the beck and call of men." I push back against all the things that leave me empty or burn me up too quick. I stand up to all the people who try to take me from myself when I'm working so hard to have enough of me left to give them. If my children think I sleep a lot or that Momma is going to make sure she gets all three of her scoops, then so be it. Let them remember it well when they become mothers and have to struggle to fortify themselves because there's always more to do.

My kids may not know that the seams in my mothering used to be chasms that almost swallowed me whole. Nor do they need to. I didn't understand my mother's sacrifices when I was a child, but I understand better now, and I put my faith in the fullness of time when all things are revealed. When my children are grown, I hope they will also remember that I volunteered in their classes, went on their field trips, and combed their hair lovely until my hands began to tremble. I hope they remember that Momma showed up. That I made sacrifices.

And I hope they love me for it.

6

White Girl?
Cousin Kim Is Passing.
But Cousin Lonnae Doesn't
Want to Let Her Go

Cousin Kim had been living in my home a little over a year when I felt compelled to write out all the unspoken things that were passing between us about culture and ethnicity.

This article was a deeply personal exploration of race in my home and my family and, by extension, other families who have straddled the color line. While it landed Kim and me in the middle of a nationally televised conversation about race, it also started a more personal dialogue in my living room that continues with Kim, and sometimes other family members, still. It was first published August 8, 1999, and is reprinted here with the permission of the *Washington Post*.

I don't know if I would say the same things if I were to write this article now. But perhaps that is only because I said exactly what I was feeling then.

I HAVE A TWENTY-YEAR-OLD white girl living in my basement. She happens to be my first cousin. I happen to be black.

Genetics is a funny thing. So are the politics of racial declaration.

My five-year-old daughter, Sydney, calls her Cousin Kim. Kim's daddy calls my mother his baby sister. Kim's father is black. Her mother is white. And Kim calls herself white. At least that's what she checks off on all those forms with neat little boxes for such things.

She grew up in southern Illinois. Sandoval, population about 1,500. There were thirty-three people in her high school graduating class. Counting Cousin Kim, there was half a black. I used to think Kim lived in a trailer park. But one day she corrected me. We live in a trailer home, she said—"my mother owns the land."

The black side of Kim's family is professional. Lawyers, doctors, Fortune 500 company execs. We have an uncle who got a Ph.D. in math at twenty-one. The white side of Kim's family is blue-collar. Less formally educated. Some recipients of government entitlement programs. Not to draw too fine a distinction, but color is not the only thing that separates us.

I brought Kim to Maryland to live with me after my second child, Savannah, was born. She is something of an au pair, if au pairs can hail from Sandoval.

Back home, Kim had run into some trouble. Bad grades, good beer. She came to D.C. to sort it all out. To find a way to get her life back on track. And she came to get in touch with the black side of her family—and possibly herself.

She may have gotten more than she bargained for.

This is a story about how a close family can split right down a color line without ever saying a word about it. The details belong to Cousin Kim and me, but the outline is familiar to anyone for whom race is a secret or a passion or an issue or a decision. The story is scary in places. Because to tell it, both Kim and I have to go there. Race Place, U.S.A. It is a primal stretch of land. It shares a psychic border with the place where we compete for the last video, parking space at the mall, or kindergarten slot in that elite magnet school. Where we fight over soccer calls and elbow each other to secure Tickle Me Elmos for our kids. It is the place where we grew up hearing black people smell like copper and white people smell like wet chickens. Where everybody knows that whites are pedophiles and gun nuts. And blacks smoke crack. Where interracial couples still bother us.

You've gotta pass through Race Place in order to make it to Can We All Get Along?, but most everybody is looking for a shortcut.

For Kim and me, there are no shortcuts. We meet in the middle, from opposite sides of a racial divide. It is the DMZ and our shields are down. We may lose friends, black and white, for telling this truth so plainly. Still, alone together, we begin.

THE FIRST TIME

Do you remember the first time somebody called you "nigger"?

I do. I was on vacation in Centralia, Illinois, where both of my parents were born and raised. Five minutes from where Cousin Kim grew up. It was the early 1970s, and I was maybe five years old.

Two white girls walked up to me in a park. They were big. Impossibly big. Eleven at least. They smiled at me.

"Are you a nigger?" one of the girls asked.

On the segregated South Side of Chicago where I lived, it was possible for a black child to go a very long time and never hear the word "nigger" directed at her. But I wasn't on the South Side, and after five years, my time was up.

I stood very still. And my stomach grew icy. My spider senses were tingling. Where had I heard that word before? "I, I don't know," I told her, shrugging my shoulders high to my ears.

The first girl sighed, exasperated. Then the other repeated, more forcefully this time, "Are you a nigger? You know, a black person?" she asked.

I wanted to answer her. To say something. But fear made me confused. I had no words. I just stood there. And tried not to wet my panties.

Then I ran. I turned quickly to look over my shoulder just in time to hear a rock whiz past my ear and plop into a nearby creek.

"You better git, you little Ne-gro!" somebody else, a white boy, yelled at me from a few feet away. I kept running, and this time, I didn't look back.

For the rest of the day, I harbored a secret. I harbored the shame for longer. I knew I was black. I had found out the year before. I remember because I had confronted my father, demanding to know when my blond hair and blue eyes would kick in. Like the Miss Breck shampoo girl on television. Like the superheroes on *Super-friends*.

Only white people have blond hair and blue eyes, my dad said. "And we're black."

The wicked witch, the headless horseman, the evil stepmother, and all the bad guys on *The New Adventures of Scooby Doo* wore black. Black eye, black heart, Black Death. Black ass. Mine was a negative, visceral reaction to the word.

Five years old was old enough to know I was black. It was old enough for somebody to call me a nigger.

And it was certainly old enough to feel like one.

That would be the first time.

ONE BLACK DROP

It is early June, and Cousin Kim and I are about to watch *Roots,* the landmark 1970s television miniseries about a slave family. Kim says she's heard of the movie but has never seen it. So I go to queue the video in the cassette player, but first I make a cup of tea. And straighten the pillows on my couch. Then I check my voice mail.

I am puttering. Procrastinating. Loath to begin. Because I don't know if our blood ties are strong enough to withstand slavery. And I am scared to watch *Roots* with a white girl. Scared of my anger. Scared of my pain. Scared that she won't get it. Scared of how much I want her to. Scared of the way race can make strangers out of family.

It has been nearly a year since Kim first came to live with me. She was a cousin I barely knew. She had visited my husband and me in the summer of 1994, when our daughter Sydney was a baby. The first time she had ever seen so many black people in her life, she would later say.

Before that, there were brief visits with my mom and quick kisses at my college graduation. Over the years, I heard much more than I ever saw of Cousin Kim. Kim's father had a black family. His kids were adults when Kim was born. Later, his wife died. And though they are now a public couple, my uncle and Kim's mom never married.

My girls adore Kim. And when she goes to get Sydney from school, the little black prekindergartners rush her at the door, greeting her with wide smiles and hugs and shouts of "Hi, Cousin Kim!"

This past year, we've laughed over sitcoms and shared private jokes. We've talked about old boyfriends, gone shopping, and giggled over family gossip. Still, up to now, we've never been down that black-and-white brick road.

I was shocked to hear that Cousin Kim considered herself white. I found out only because she had to fill out some forms to get into community college. Because I asked her if they had a box for race. Then I asked her what she checked. I was ready to tease her pointedly for checking off "other." In between. Not quite either.

I was prepared to lobby—to drop science about the "one-drop rule." In slave days, that meant that if you had a drop of black blood, you were singing spirituals and working for somebody for free. Trying not to get beaten, and trying to keep your babies from being sold—even if the massa was their daddy. Color gradations were a legacy of the plantation system. And although light was favored, one drop gave us a common destiny. Shackled all of us darkies together.

Later, one drop meant that blacks were able to form a common cultural identity. To agitate for the common good. Because light mulattoes lynched as easily as dark Africans. But one drop also meant there have always been those who could pass. Who required writ, or testimony, or a declaration of intent to make them black. For whom race has always been a choice.

Cousin Kim would be one of these. Her eyes are bright blue-gray and her skin has only a suggestion of color. Generations of careful breeding have worked out all her kinks. To white folks, she looks white. And mostly, that is how they treat her. Like one of their own.

Still, I was ready to cast her lot with the sisters. You know half-black is black, I was ready to say. I was ready for "other." I wasn't ready for "white." Or that familiar sting of rejection.

PASSING AWAY

I have The Sight. Like my mother before me. Like most black people I know. It is a gift. A special kind of extrasensory perception. We may not be clairvoyant enough to determine the location of the rebel base. Or have the telekinesis it takes to shatter a glass ceiling.

But we can spot some Negro on you from three generations away.

It reveals itself in a flash of expression. A momentary disposition of features in repose. The curl of a top lip that seems to say "Nobody knows the trouble I've seen."

We have The Sight because we are used to looking at black people. Used to loving them. We know the range of colors black comes in. Because there's always somebody at our family reunions who could go either way. And because we are a worldly people, and we know how these things go.

The Sight is a nod to solidarity. It is a reaction against dilution and division. It is the recognition that when people face overwhelming odds, you need to know who can be compelled to ante up and kick in.

We use it to put a black face on public triumphs that look lily-white. And to "out" folks who might act against our interests without sharing in the consequences.

No matter how many times she thanked "the black community" for embracing her music, we knew Mariah Carey was part black. And long before he opened his mouth, we saw something in Rock Newman's eyes, even though they are blue.

When people wanted to call actresses Jennifer Beals or Troy Beyer beautiful, we were eager to point out their black roots. Eager to claim New York Yankee Derek Jeter and Channel 4 newscaster Barbara Harrison. Old folks swear Yul Brynner was black and that was why he kept his head shaved. And speculation persists, despite the fact that Georgia representative Bob Barr has affirmed his whiteness.

Understand. It's not that we don't respect Tiger Woods' right to call himself a Cablinasian. We just don't think it will help him get a cab in D.C.

My cousin calls herself white and I see a side of me just passing away. Swallowed up by the larger, more powerful fish in the main-stream. And I wonder if that will be the future for my family, some who look like Kim—others who look like me but have married white, or no doubt will. And I wonder, ultimately, if that will be the future for black people. Passing themselves right out of existence. Swearing it was an accident. Each generation trading up a shade and a grade until there is nothing left but old folks in fold-up lawn chairs on backyard decks who gather family members close around to tell nostalgic tales that begin "Once upon a time when we were colored . . ."

And I think to myself, I wish there were some things that we just wouldn't do for straight hair. And I think of the struggle and the history and the creativity lost. And I trust that the universe will reg-ister my lament.

When my cousin calls herself white, I see red. And I hear echoes. "Well, I don't really consider myself black . . ."

Or maybe it is laughter.

THE REAL WORLD

Cousin Kim is having a hard time with *Roots*. Not her own, the movie. I'm not having an easy time myself.

She isn't ready for the stuff they left out of her history books. I am unable to restrain my commentary. Or my imagination. Sometimes my tears.

Ever heard of Calvert County, I ask Kim bitterly when a teenage African girl is sold at an Annapolis auction as a bed wench to Robert Calvert. Kim didn't know that Maryland had ever been a slave state.

There is a scene where kidnapped African Kunte Kinte won't settle down in his chains. "Want me to give him a stripe or two, boss?" the old slave, Fiddler, asks his Master Reynolds.

"Do as I say, Fiddler," Reynolds answers. "That's all I expect from any of my niggers."

"Oh, I love you, Massa Reynolds," Fiddler tells him. And instantly, my mind draws political parallels. Ward Connerly, I think to myself. Armstrong Williams. Shelby Steele. Hyperbole, some might say. I say dead-on.

"Clarence Thomas," I say to Cousin Kim. And she just stares at me. She may be a little tender yet for racial metaphors. I see them everywhere.

Kim is twenty in the way of small-town twenty-year-olds all over the country. Her best-best friends are Jenny and Nikki and Theresa. They send letters, e-mail one another, and run up my phone bill. She takes classes, takes care of my children, and passes time painting her nails and watching *The Real World* on MTV. I tease her about being Wal-Mart–obsessed.

Cousin Kim walked out of the movie *Glory* when she was in eleventh grade. When Denzel Washington got lashed with a whip and cried silently. Couldn't handle it, she said. "I just didn't want to see it. I couldn't stand the idea of seeing someone literally beat." Avoidance and denial are twins in my family. In others as well.

When Kim was growing up in Sandoval, they didn't celebrate

Black History Month, she says. "Not even Black History Week. We just had Martin Luther King Day."

The town was not integrated. Her father was the only black person she saw regularly. "And I don't consider him black," Kim says. My uncle is not one to disabuse her of that notion.

Kim's dad ran his own sanitation business. He was a hard-working, astute, sometimes charming businessman. A moneymaker. And my mother says people used to say if he had been white, he would have been mayor of Centralia. Of course, Kim has never heard this. In fact, "we've never had a conversation about race in my house," Kim says casually. And for a moment, I am staggered. But I am not surprised.

MAKING THE GRADE

My mama's people have always been color-struck. Daddy's, too, for that matter. Black folks know the term. It is part of an informal caste system that has always existed in the black community.

It is a form of mental colonialism. A shackle for the mind. A value system that assigns worth and power to those traits that most closely resemble the massa.

If you're light, you're all right. If you're brown, stick around. If you're black, get back, people used to say.

I am light; my husband is dark. When my daughter Sydney was born, everybody wanted to know who she looked like. They weren't asking about her eyes. They wanted to know what black folks always want to know when a baby who can go either way on the light-dark thing is born. Whose color is she? What kind of hair does she have?

The hair can be a tricky thing. Nothing for that but to wait a few months until the "grade" comes in good. But for color, we've got it down. We're a race of mad scientists, fervently checking the nail beds and ear tips of newborns to precisely determine where they'll fall over the rainbow.

My paternal grandmother was a very light woman with straight hair and black features. She had an inspection ritual she performed on all new babies in the family. A careful once-over to check for color and clarity before she pronounced judgment. I didn't know this until I introduced her to Sydney when she was about six months old.

She sat my baby on her lap. After a few minutes, she announced her findings. "Well, her color is good. And her hair ain't half bad considering how black that nigger is you married."

Hmmmm.

You know these days we try to stay away from divisive pronouncements on color, I wanted to tell her. We don't want to handicap our daughter with crippling hair issues.

But please. My grandmother might have hit me if I had tried to spout some nonsense like that. More to the point, particularly among the elders, there is a certain unassailable quality to the color caste logic. A tie-in with life chances. And my grandmother was nearly eighty. So I took the only option available under the circumstances. I smiled sweetly and said thank you. Because, after all, this was high praise.

"Watch out for your children!" had been a favorite admonition passed down from my maternal grandmother. The one I shared with Cousin Kim. She wasn't talking about bad influences or oncoming traffic. She was talking about a kind of Breeders' Cup standard for black love. At least the kind that ended in marriage. Light skin, good-hair (a compound word), light eyes. That was the Triple Crown.

Early on, I learned there is a premium placed on my particular brand of mongrel.

I am Red, as in Red Bone. Or Yellow, for High Yellow. Or light, bright, and damn near white.

I used to be able to break into a full genealogy incantation in an instant, with attention paid to the whites and Native Americans in my family tree. Because that white girl was still running around my head asking me if I was black. Because black and ugly always came in the same breath.

But I credit white folks with my slow evolution toward racial consciousness.

We moved to a suburb of Chicago when I was nine. And we arrived squarely in a middle-class dream.

I had always been shy. A good student. With long hair. Teachers loved me. And always, a few black girls hated me. "White dog," they called me—no, wait, that's what they called my sister. I was a "half-white bitch." Theirs was a reaction. A rage. A demonstration of the only power they had, the only power perhaps they thought they would ever have. The power to bully. But back then, I didn't know that. I had "A Foot in Each World" but couldn't get my head into either.

I don't remember my moment of political and aesthetic epiphany. It was more of a slow dawn, I think. An incremental understanding of the forces that were working around me. Certainly, watching white folks pack up and leave the neighborhood in herds made an imprint. And when a white boy spat on me at a park, I took that very personally. But it was the trickle of small slights that accumulated over the years that combined to make one point very clear.

High Yellow was just a lighter shade of black.

To be in Chicago in 1983 when Harold Washington, a big,

dark, deep-black intellectual, was elected mayor was to see the face of racism. To watch the way that hate contorts the features and purples the skin. White folks were rabid. Foaming at the mouth. A few white newscasters could barely read their copy. A flyer circulated through my high school featuring a big-lipped black caricature chowing down on watermelon. The city would have to be renamed Chicongo, it said. And I understood.

Ultimately, race is political. And I am a partisan.

Sometimes I still hear that white girl ask me if I am black. And now I have an answer.

Pitch.

Cold.

Blacker than three midnights.

As black as the ace of spades.

I'm so black that when I get into my car, the oil light comes on.

I've decided that it is unhealthy for us to surrender to white sensibilities, including the ones that mock us from inside our own heads.

We have all been guilty of dumbing down our expectations of white humanity—like white folks can't process nappy hair—and it's time to help them raise the bar.

PLAYING THE RACE CARD

Kim has a friend whose daddy was in the Ku Klux Klan. A poster-sized picture of a finger-pointing Klansman adorned her living room wall. "I felt like Clarice Starling in *The Silence of the Lambs* whenever I went over there," Kim says. "Like the first time she went to the jail and saw Hannibal Lecter."

The father didn't ask if Kim was part black. Kim didn't tell. She just sat on the edge of the couch with her hands and legs folded. "I kept praying, oh God, he's going to see something on me and know that I am mixed." So she stared straight ahead. And she sucked her lips in a reverse pucker the whole time she was there. Trying not to make herself too obvious, she says. Trying not to look black.

When she was in fifth grade, Kim's dad took her to a basketball game. And the bleachers went silent. Then they got whispery. Some folks already knew her dad was black. After that, everybody did.

"They used to tease me," Kim says with a shrug. She is reluctant to talk. So I press her. "Let's see, it went something like this, "Nigger-lips, nigger-lips, nigger-lips." Kim won't look at me.

The grandparents of one of Kim's friends didn't like black people. They didn't know about Kim's daddy. When the girls visited these folks, they weren't allowed to watch *The Cosby Show* because the grandfather didn't want a black man in his living room.

"I hate the N word," Kim says. It is late. We've finished another installment of *Roots,* and Kim is unsettled. Ready to talk. Tripping over her pent-up thoughts. "Whenever somebody said 'nigger' in class, everyone would turn around and look at me. I hate that word. I hate that the first thing they associate with that word is me."

When she was a freshman at Sandoval High, Kim wore a T-shirt with Martin Luther King Jr. on the front and Malcolm X on the back. "They all looked at me as if to say 'Oh, my God, she really isn't white.' " She grins when she says this.

Around 1993, Kim says she started getting into the "movement." Started watching *Yo! MTV Raps* and *The Cosby Show.* Started being hungry for black culture.

She gave a civil rights speech to her sophomore English class. Her teacher thought it was a little angry. That summer, when my daughter Sydney was a baby, Kim came to D.C. We toured the White House and saw the first lady. But it was the Father's Day tribute at a friend's house where a group of us read proclamations and praised all the things we loved best about black men that got her. That let her know there was a different world than where she came from.

Her mother said she seemed different when she returned. Kim says she's always been different. In a town where everybody knows everybody and the social hierarchy is simple and uncolored, Kim is an anomaly.

"I've never technically fit in Sandoval," Kim says. "I've never had the small-town mentality. Then, after I moved out here, I thought maybe I do. Maybe I'm just a little bit country.

"I'm really trying to figure out who I am."

Some of that goes with twenty-year-old territory. It's a no-woman's-land. Biologically grown, legally not quite, emotionally uneven. But Cousin Kim's twenty is more complex than most. She's never tried to deny the fact that her dad was black. But she has never had the resources or the tools to embrace that side of herself. She is provincial. Unexposed. Underdressed as a black girl. Searching.

On the phone or when she goes home to visit, Kim is still white. But in my house, she is a real root sister. Neither are affectations. It's just the way her cards fall. Kim is, I suppose, the ultimate insider. Privy to our private jokes. The ways we laugh at white people. And at each other. A black spy in her world. A white fly on the wall in mine. A study in duality.

We have also had some growing pains in my house. And I am quick to assign blame. Quick to play the race card.

Cousin Kim smokes. I am hard-pressed to name anybody else

who smokes. Especially anybody young and black. I want her to stop, and I make the questionable leap. "You need to leave that nasty white girl [expletive] alone," I tell her. Initially when I said it, Kim just looked at me meekly. Now, she gives me the finger.

Ours is a jocularity. Aided by silent code. Reinforced by a power imbalance.

Reverse racism, I suppose some would call it. I don't think so. I believe white folks would know if blacks were ever to really reverse racism. We call them countermeasures. Cousin Kim, I ask her, if you hate me because I am black and I hate you because you killed my babies, is that the same?

It is a rhetorical question. Because in my house, we do not hate. We merely understand that there are those who do. So we strive for balance. We try not to resort to negative campaigning. Sometimes we succeed. Occasionally we fail. But we always make the effort. Because fear leads to anger, anger leads to hate, and hate leads to suffering. We do not need Yoda to tell us this. It is something people on the dark side have always known.

KILLING ME SOFTLY

A couple of months ago, Katie Couric made me mad. I had to vent with Cousin Kim. For a week, the *Today* show devoted a segment to tracing family histories. And Couric's roots go back to Alabama. When cotton was king and the Courics were part of the ruling family.

You could buy fertile land cheap, the segment said. And the Courics did. The family prospered and included a Civil War governor and a member of Congress.

Couric toured the family cemetery and recounted the stories behind the headstones. Then she said, "Slaves lie in unmarked but well-tended graves nearby."

That was it. No acknowledgment that these "slaves" were people her family bought and sold. That some of them might be her kin. That no matter how smart or talented or hardworking she is, her privilege was codified, her head start generations long. That it came at the expense of somebody else's freedom. No mention of any attempt to trace those other lives to see how they fared. Maybe that would have been too much to hope for. But how about an expression of regret. A mea culpa. An "I'm sorry—wish you were here."

Genealogy is about "our simple stories, not forgotten," Couric said. Interesting choice of words. Black families have stories, too. Ones we don't forget. That get passed down to our kids.

My great-grandmother shot a white man who tried to rape her in Mississippi, and the family had to scatter. My grandmother's family, who hadn't been able to get in on that fertile-land-for-cheap deal, was dirt poor, and although she was the only one of her people to finish high school, there was no money for college. At seventeen, my mother sat outside a Birmingham train station crying because they told her she was too colored for the white side and too white for the colored side. On a family vacation, we were turned away from an empty motel lot because the manager said there were no vacancies. In college, when I told a white journalism professor I wanted to work at the *Washington Post,* he said, "Doing what? Sweeping floors?"

Cousin Kim, I say. Which is better? The kindly massa or the sadistic overseer? And Kim doesn't answer. Neither, I tell her. They are the same. Two parts of a whole. Today, folks won't just walk up to you and call you "nigger-lips." Well, they might, but mostly it is the benign racists who are killing me softly. They don't recognize themselves in the mirror. They didn't mean anything by it. They harbor no ill will. They just don't care enough to step outside their comfort zone.

I understand that proclivity. Often I share it. Most of us are too self-involved to dig up the psychic pain of others. But when your family has owned slaves, indifference is a self-indulgence you forfeit.

Over two hundred years of chattel slavery. Another hundred years of terrorism and de jure Jim Crow. Thirty-four years—one generation—of full legal enfranchisement. I don't know, seems a little corrupt for white folks to cry color-blind now. We go to the Race Place because these days, I find privileged indifference as culpable as malice aforethought. When you step on my toes, I may not retaliate in kind, but you must know that I will say ouch. Loudly. Such that it disturbs your peace. Then you say, "I'm sorry." Then help me heal. After that, we can all get along nicely.

Cousin Kim nods her head yes. I believe she really gets it this time. But perhaps that's just wishful thinking.

BLACK FOR ME

Cousin Kim and I have watched all six parts of Alex Haley's *Roots*. And three parts of *Queen*. Then we did an hour of WHMM's *Black Women on the Light Dark Thing*. We have talked and we have shared. And still she is white. And I am as black as ever.

"We're lucky," the biracial woman Alice said in *Queen*. "We can choose. Who'd choose to be black? Black is hard. White is so much easier."

Still.

I want my cousin to be black for me. For the little girl who ran from a rock thrown at her head. For all the niggers I have been. I want her to be black because I'm still afraid of casual monsters in white-girl clothes. Not because they might hurt me, but they might hurt my children. Not because they hate. But because they teach five-year-old black girls to hate themselves. And black people of all ages to suck in their lips.

Cousin Kim still chooses white not only because she looks white, she says, but "because I was raised white," and because most white folks don't know the difference. Probably it is easier. Maybe to some people she is selling out—but I also know that is an option a lot of black folks would like to have.

If I'm honest with myself, maybe I'm one of them. At least sometimes, if I think about my husband or brother getting stopped by the police for speeding. Or maybe at Tysons Corner, when tears burn my eyes as I watch a salesclerk wait on everybody but me. My anger is hot and righteous. But I'd give it up for a simple "May I help you?" any day.

Every day the world lets me know I'm black. And I wonder what it would feel like not to carry that, just for a while. Probably guilty. Probably relieved. Probably a lot like Cousin Kim.

There are no easy choices, but I think I understand my cousin's. Maybe I did all along. I just had to tell our story to realize it. But understanding and acceptance are not the same. Cousin Kim is white but conflicted, and I still sting with rejection. So alone together, we linger.

THE MAGIC KINGDOM

Race. The final frontier.

The Race Place isn't crossed in a day. You can't pass through it in the time it takes to watch a miniseries. We traverse the Race Place in fits and starts, inch by inch, over the course of a lifetime. Or maybe two. Sometimes our progress is steady. And sometimes we are dragged for miles back to the beginning, chained behind a pickup truck, and have to start all over.

The overarching reality is that realities overarch. And jockey for head space.

The extremes are easy to condemn, but the vast middle is where most of us live. Where we raise our families. And where we hope that life's lessons land a little softer on the behinds of our children than they did on our own.

A few days ago, Cousin Kim said she got into an argument with her ex-boyfriend over *The Wonderful World of Disney.* The characters in the old cartoons are racists, Kim said. Look at the crows in *Dumbo.* "I won the argument," she says. "He told me 'Kim, you think too much.' "

Cousin Kim smiled. And I smiled. Because this is what I want for her. To think. To challenge. To recognize. To get it. If she does that, then maybe she doesn't have to be black.

Still, I can't help giving her a silent "right on, little sister." You just take your time. We're family. And I'll be here to hip you up if you ever change your mind.

Bring Home the Bacon

Why should well-salaried women marry?

ALICE DUNBAR-NELSON,
"THE WOMAN"

MY MOMMA HAILS from the "God bless the child who has his own" school when it comes to a woman having her own money—although she didn't get through her hardest classes until she was middle-aged. She worked as a schoolteacher for decades but divorced two husbands before she began taking control of her money—spending what she wanted and saving for her retirement—before she stopped asking a man's permission for the things she wanted to buy.

Momma tells stories of my father one day announcing he'd bought her a Mother's Day gift, then coming in the house with a new mop bucket and wringer. He drove a convertible Cadillac (gangster whitewalls, TV antenna in the back) and she talks about how he once offered to buy her a fur coat. Wanting to be practical, she suggested a new prefab garage instead and ended up with neither. (My sister and I have subsequently persuaded her against fur.) She talks about faithfully turning over her paycheck every two weeks for decades, trusting she'd always have a husband and that he'd always take care of everything. She was in her mid-forties before she realized she'd have to take care of herself. And she's always hoped her daughters would start their financial self-care earlier, husband or no husband, just on GP.

A couple of years ago, after nearly ten years of marriage, I finally decided it was time for me to have my own bank account—something my husband knew nothing about. He's a good man, but I'd heard too many stories of the way the lights get shut off, and the mortgage goes unpaid if a man decides to flip on you. I watched my sister struggle to pay bills when her marriage dissolved and agonized with my good friend Terina (the girl from Ipanema) who got divorced one day and got evicted from her home not long thereafter.

An imminent flip didn't appear to be on our marital horizon, but my need for my own account felt sophisticated and empowering. It felt like I had learned from the bitter lessons of the women in my family and that I was in keeping with a valued black tradition—one that's always recognized that a black family might go under without a woman's contribution, so she made sure she had one. It's a tradition that stretched into the time my momma was a girl and black woman earned twenty-three cents on the dollar and continues today, with black women earning 68 percent of the weekly pay of white men.

"Set something aside to buy the baby milk." I could almost feel my grandmothers, secret-keepers all, nodding their assent.

"Always keep some pin money tucked away," (Grandma Mabel).

"You got your own money, you don't hafta ask nobody for shit," (Momma Susie).

"Never, ever, ever, leave home without your feisty [Jamaican for 'rude'] money—enough change for a phone call, and if not taxi fare then at least two tokens," says Joan Morgan's mother in *When Chickenheads Come Home to Roost.*

I make a good salary, but my husband makes more. Joint accounts have meant he's always had more to say than I've cared to hear about what I've wanted to buy. I've been very fortunate to be able to take extended leaves of absence to have babies and to write, and even for the indulgence of reenergizing myself because I can't write when I'm too tired to think. But extended leaves have meant extended periods of being subsidized. Times when I've pieced together a living from occasional speaking engagements or freelance assignments. Times when I've had to beg or borrow or barter (*hello?*) with my husband for items I've deemed essential.

In many ways, these kinds of trade-offs go against my basic programming. I've worked since I was sixteen years old, taking orders and mopping floors at McDonald's for minimum wage. I worked on my college campus from the time I was a sophomore, even though I came into a bit of money after my father died and could have just focused on my studies. I took time off before I got the job at the *Washington Post,* and friends would joke about me sitting on my apartment porch reading when they got home from work, but that was only possible because there was money in my account.

In an essay for the *Post,* I once wrote, "I can be obsessive, compulsive, a little freaky when it comes to control. Sometimes I think I can bend spoons with my mind." I once heard Ashley Judd tell an interviewer, "I want what I want when I want it." I don't quite have it like Ashley Judd, but insofar as I can, I simply want to be able to chart my own path, to shore up my inner accounts, to be well stocked in my things, even when my thing is as simple as a supply of eight-dollar patchouli incense sticks that make me feel groovy.

During my extended absences from the paper, my husband

would tease me about always having a scheme about money. I simply called it working my plan. Like most of the women I know, whether they work in the house or get out and hit it every day, I'm always thinking of ways to increase my bottom line and give me the added satisfaction of having a little something on the side. I was on unpaid leave when I wanted to take Sydney to Guatemala. Although there wasn't nearly the money in our budget for this, I promised the *Post* and *Essence* magazine articles about the trip and was able to secure some up-front travel money to make it happen.

It was after returning to work from one of these extended absences that I decided to open the account. My husband's money was our money, I reasoned, but at least some of my money had to be my own. He doesn't have the same love of books and antiques and knee-high boots that get the covetous glances in the Starbucks. He is, at times, skeptical about my insistence that eyebrows arched and nails done can be the key factors in aiding my productivity. You just don't want me to be cute, I sometimes accuse him, and in my mind, that makes him a dishonest broker, trying to keep me from the full glory of a salon-perfect roller set. It's just the kind of thing that puts me on the phone with my momma. Because even when I've disagreed with her, seems like I've always harbored the deep-seated belief that my momma knows best.

When I was little and feeling bluesy, sometimes Momma would step in with a "feel-better." Some M&M's for my silent tears after a blood test at a ghetto clinic where the technician talked on the phone and stuck the needle in my seven-year-old arm over and over and over again because, she said, during lulls in her conversation, my vein kept "rolling." There were grapes, after I fell and scraped my knee and eventually one-pound bags of soft-bake cookies when I was in high school and substituting chocolate chips for sex (a fact that didn't become apparent to me until after I started having sex).

My candy feel-betters turned into the occasional suit from BCBG, but the essential premise remained the same. A pick-me-up for rough days or a little something to take care of yourself after you've already taken care of home.

A couple of years into dating, Ralph and I decided to move in together and Momma was shocked, offended, *scandalized* by the notion that I was actually considering contributing money for something so base as rent. "If he wants you to be a kept woman, then let him keep you," Momma said dramatically. Though I dismissed her outdated relationship model and paid an equivalent amount in other bills and groceries, technically I never did fork over a dime toward the rent.

Momma has always had a pretty woman's notion that there's only a finite amount of time that you can use what you've got to get what you need. But the concept is ageless. Joan Morgan also points out, "I got my start as a writer because I captured the sexual attention of a man who could make me one. It was not the first time my externals would bestow me with such favors. It certainly would not be the last." Momma is not one to be drawn into a discussion of sexual attentions, but if one of her daughters needs a flat front skirt to even out her proportions and give a nice little lift to her bottom, well, in her mind, that's a legitimate investment that might pay dividends in unforeseen ways—might be just the thing to help you out with that whole room of one's own. She recognizes it just requires an initial cash outlay.

After nearly a decade of marriage, with a good job, I reasoned it was time I had a separate account for my own kids' feel-betters and trips to the teacher's store to outfit their walls with maps and because—*yes, lord*, mayhap I got to have a new pair of shoes. (It's those white women in those commercials again, what do they say, beautiful and I'm worth it?)

I was proud of my little account, the one I put jointly in my mother's name and kept secret. Maybe that's why I accidentally left the passbook out one day and my husband found it. He was more bemused than hurt at the discovery. *You went to a bit of trouble with that one, didn't you?* I'd like to think his winning attitude would still hold true even if he one day discovers how much of his paycheck he regularly contributed to my Dignity and Independence fund.

A women's heart is a deep ocean of secrets. . . .

A friend and colleague, *Washington Post* financial columnist Michelle Singletary, who writes "The Color of Money," says this is a no-no. She maintains that separate accounts are not a good way for a couple to max out their financial potential. She does, however, understand the many deep places our money urges can come from.

In her book *7 Money Mantras for a Richer Life,* she cites a mutual fund company's survey that finds African Americans making more than $50,000 a year are more than twice as likely as whites to lend financial support to friends and family beyond those living in their homes. It's a finding that resonates with me because of the cousin who lived with me for two years searching for new direction, the good friend who stayed with us for a year and a half to get hold of her finances, the troubled brother for whom I've bought clothes and wired money, and his daughter, my niece, who attends community college and lives with us now.

I am reminded of girlfriends who've taken guardianship of younger half-siblings, allowed adult siblings to move in, or regularly send money to support other households and folks who haven't quite made it to the middle class. That sense of obligation to family and friends, that sending of remittances, seems an old tradition for all the people in this country who feel a deeply internalized commitment to the folks they left behind in another country or another economic strata—and for all the black folks trying to get somewhere themselves even as they wearily try to bring everybody else along.

Michelle talks about being raised, along with her four siblings, by her grandparents. Raised on her grandmother's $13,000-a-year paycheck because her "papa, rest his soul, was a drunk." He often drank up his paychecks, necessitating frequent search-and-rescue operations to get his money before he got to the bar on Friday. Or sometimes crawling along her grandparents' floor, at the urging of her grandmother, to take cash from her father's pocket after he passed out.

"So you see, I understand why, if you grew up not having enough, you want so much now—even if it means going into debt. I understand the urge to give your children what you feel you were deprived of as a child. I know how it feels to want to buy stuff to fill up the sadness and emptiness you feel because of your childhood traumas," Michelle writes. And she is correct, I do have childhood traumas that fill me with wants and make me want something different for my kids. But while they surely take money, my different somethings still manage to feel like something very basic.

Not long ago, Ralph and I were out for our weekly Saturday "date night," cruising the parking lot of a local restaurant and noticing the fancy foreign cars, the drop tops, the Pirelli tires and Spreewell rims, and I was suddenly led to an inescapable conclusion. "We do not have a phat ride," I told my husband. We still drive the medium green, four-cylinder, rear-wheel-drive Isuzu Rodeo he bought me ten years ago. It's not surprising. I just got my first laptop to replace the six-year-old computer I had been using, and friends constantly tease me about the "1998 technology" on my cell phone or about how the hang-up button is gone and I have to grip it with two hands to get decent reception. While I'm always in fantasy mode about that new navy blue Nissan Quest or covetous of the reliable, up-to-the-minute technology of friends, what I hunger for most intensely are options.

The option to travel, to take dance classes; the cash to pay someone to clean up my house or do the wash if that's what my soul needs; the ability not to have to stay in a job, or a home or even in a marriage if it's not a good place to be. I hunger, in the midst of all my running around, to be still for a bit. To take time off, to sit with myself so that when folks come grabbing at me, I have the reserves to be a more patient mother, a more caring wife, a more giving friend, a more thorough reporter. I hunger for the resources that give me options, including the option to be a better woman than I would otherwise be.

Even beyond my real love of nice things, it is that deep pool of wants that most appropriately connects me to a wide sea of other women. Most especially to black women who a hundred years ago realized that bringing something besides greens to the table was one of the best ways to make sure they'd always have a place there and something to say about the decisions that were made around it.

Alice Moore Dunbar-Nelson, born in 1875 to middle-class black parents, was a writer and a second-wave feminist before the first wave of feminism had even gotten the vote. She graduated from Dillard University, studied at the University of Pennsylvania and Cornell, and wrote poetry that caught the attention of the eminently renowned poet Paul Laurence Dunbar. They married, and she became a nationally prominent poet in her own right before later ending their stormy five-year marriage. She continued writing and teaching and having numerous relationships before marrying a second time to Robert John Nelson and helping edit his weekly newspaper. In her essay "The Woman," Dunbar-Nelson intimately ties a woman's independence and finances to her overall well-being. For the single, "well-salaried woman," she writes:

Take the average working-woman of to-day. She works from five to ten hours a day, doing extra night work, sometimes, of course. . . .

Her earnings are her own, indisputably, unreservedly, undividedly. She knows to a certainty just how much she can spend, how well she can dress, how far her earnings will go. . . . To an independent spirit there is a certain sense of humiliation and wounded pride in asking for money, be it five cents or five hundred dollars. The working-woman knows no such pang. . . .

It is not marriage that I decry, for I don't think any really sane person would do this, but it is . . . this rushing into an unknown plane of life to avoid work. Avoid work! What housewife dares call a moment her own?

Numerous, powerful examples of black women abound, anchored in that same tradition. Before she became Madame C. J. Walker, the legendary entrepreneur and philanthropist who died in 1919 as one of the wealthiest self-made businesswomen in the country, and whose cosmetics empire endured until the mid-1980s, Sarah Breedlove was the first free child born to her parents in Delta, Louisiana, in 1867. Orphaned by age seven and raised in a climate of white terrorism and score-settling after Emancipation, Breedlove married at fourteen to escape the home of a cruel brother-in-law, but she became a mother and widow by age seventeen.

"Rather than be destroyed, Sarah learned to turn her vulnerability into resolve and resilience," writes her biographer and great-great-granddaughter, A'Lela Bundles. Client by client, she built a cosmetics empire, employing thousands. She funded scholarships, helped the NAACP establish homes for the aged in St. Louis and Indianapolis, and made the largest single donation to the National

Association of Colored Women to purchase the Frederick Douglass home in Washington and turn it into a museum.

Oseola McCarty of Hattiesburg, Mississippi, spent her entire working life washing and ironing other people's clothes. In 1995, at eighty-seven years old, she told of being frightened when she was a young child and her mother had to leave her alone to work as a cook and selling candy at a local schoolhouse. It was during those times Miss McCarty resolved that she would save up her own money. She started ironing clothes and putting the money away young. In sixth grade, she left school to care for an invalid aunt and never returned. Later she also cared for her mother and grand-mother before they died. She continued washing and ironing for generations of Hattiesburg's "best" families. She lived frugally, never owning a car, and put her money into certificates of deposit and conservative mutual funds.

When it was time to decide where she wanted her money to go, Miss McCarty was clear. She left some to cousins and to her church, but the bulk of it, $150,000, was to be used to endow a scholarship at the University of Southern Mississippi, a school she had never seen. "They used to not let colored people go out there, but now they do, and I think they should have it," Miss McCarty told re-porter Sharon Watz.

"She seems wonderfully at peace with where she is and who she is," said a vice president at Miss McCarty's bank. And perhaps she was. But perhaps it was just too complicated to go deeper and imag-ine that old black woman in three full dimensions—too complex to struggle with the notion that she might have had her own dreams once upon a time, dreams that were circumscribed by race and sex. Perhaps it requires too much figuring to calculate exactly how much Mississipi soap powder it took to wash those dreams away.

It is that self-reliant train of thought, often coupled with bitter visuals, that helps inform the tradition of nearly every black woman I know. My Grandma Mabel sold eggs, took in white women's wash, and wrote stories for lurid romance magazines; her sister, Ella, owned a family dry-goods store and bought real estate; Momma Susie loan-sharked; her daughter, my Aunt Jackie, sued people and lived off a shrewd real estate investment. By hook or by crook, the women in my family kept their own pool of money, their own counsel, and, perhaps, if nothing else, the enduring sanctuary of their own interior worlds.

It is a self-reliant strain that spans class and geographic lines. My friend Marcia Davis, a *Washington Post* editor and fellow member of my Sojourners book club, hails from a family of working-class women—a grandmother who sharecropped and came north to St. Louis in the late 1950s and a great aunt, a domestic nurse's aide, who was helping to raise Marcia into her eighties. In her early thirties, Marcia bought the home of Sterling Brown, the distinguished historian, folklorist, and first poet laureate of Washington, D.C., and is now helping to raise her nine-year-old cousin Dave.

"The messages were spoken and unspoken," Marcia says. Men were mercurial, engaged in their own struggles with oppression and patriarchy, or maybe off wrestling demons, but women were there day after day, working hard at low-wage jobs, holding everything together. A male relative said she needed to make sure she always had her own money. " 'As women, you'll need that kind of independence,' he told me." And when her stepfather's marriage to her mother broke up and she watched her mother struggle to secure "not just her own money but her own life—to be her own person," that was the evidence that helped prove those words to her.

Kim Greenfield Alfonso, a family friend and my husband's former boss, and now a vice president for a medical supply company outside Washington, has a different family story, but the salient points remain familiar. She and her siblings were raised upper-middle-class in Washington. Her mother was a nurse and her father began one of the first African American HMOs in the country. "There was no question we were going to have not just an education, but double degrees," Kim says. "That's your way to earn an income, to be free, to have power over your own life," she heard repeatedly growing up.

"The second message I got loud and clear was I was not going to be dependent on a man," Kim says. Her mother, especially, would stress, "You're going to marry for love because you're not going to need the money. And why? Because you're going to have your own. What you're going to want from a man is love and companionship, but if anything happens, you're not going to get caught like a lot of women get caught."

Her commitment to career and constant savings and investment is something that's continued through her eleven-year marriage to a prominent Washington businessman. "When I dated my husband, he used to laugh because I always wanted to make a point to him that I was somebody who was bringing something to the table and he would have to come correct." The couple, who have a five-year-old daughter, have almost never had money issues, Kim says. "Neither one of us is frivolous, but if I go out and spend $300 here, $400 there, I don't think about it. I don't have to say anything to him." He buys artwork, and when she had to buy her first car after more than a decade of company cars, she bought the luxury model she wanted, in cash. They have a joint account and separate accounts, and their daughter has an account for college.

For the most part, she says, they live below their means. "We could have a bigger house, yes, but we realize we want to save money, and we have a daughter with visual issues [congenital eye problems that have required surgeries and a rigorous course of treatment] and want to make sure we have a legacy we leave her."

Strategies for financial stewardship and independence are among the advice she has shared with black girls, including the homeless girl she mentored for five years and invited to her wedding. And it is advice she has shared in her various capacities with local outreach and social organizations, including the D.C. Coalition for 100 Black Women and Jack and Jill. The bottom line: "I like nice things, I'm too old and I make too much money to have somebody question my new pair of shoes," she says.

I feel exactly the same! Except sometimes my well-developed sense of entitlement doesn't square exactly perfect with the cash on hand in my checking account. That's why, occasionally, I'm forced to borrow from other black traditions to make it all work.

Not surprisingly, it's my sister Lisa who has most directly advised me on romance and finance and the intricate play between the two. Whenever I'm in a quandary about a sum of money, it's my sister who breaks down columns and adds the figures up. Who is mostly practical, with just a touch of larceny in her heart. She double-coupons and does deep discounts. She works in June for what she wants to buy in December. She says "I'll gladly pay you Tuesday for a hamburger today."

Sometimes it gets annoying, like when she "accidentally" hangs up on you and waits for you to call her back, swearing you got disconnected, so she can save on the long distance. But it was Lisa who first taught me to sneak a dress past my husband. Who taught me to say I had had it forever and he'd just overlooked it, or told him that she bought it for me herself.

When her first marriage was going bad, and who knows where their money was going, Lisa started a small savings account in her own name, a college fund for her kids, even if she could only put away $25 a month. After they divorced, Lisa says, "I used to bring dinner home for the kids from the [school] cafeteria at work," where black women cooked greens and ham, turkey and dressing. Lisa first turned me on to designer labels, and she still had her Gucci purse from college, but she was shopping for food at the cheapest grocery store around.

She recalls standing in the line one day with too many groceries and not enough money. "I was so embarrassed, having to tell the cashier to put this back and put this back. This black woman behind me offered to buy my groceries. She said, 'Honey, you don't have to be too proud to take it,' but I was too proud to take it. When the kids went without Halloween costumes I wouldn't let Mom or [my mother-in-law] buy any, so we just put some kind of makeup on their faces and went on." Even during those tough times, she says, she had the deep satisfaction of being able to provide for herself and her kids "without a man. And I can still do that," she says. Even though her husband makes good money and loves her deeply.

My sister still puts some of her money away against a rainy day. Against hard times and human nature. And she puts money away so she can occasionally browse through Ann Taylor. Because difficult financial times and austere financial measures have left her serious, and always older than her years. But they haven't completely taken her soul. "You have to get some enjoyment out of life," my sister says, and as always, I hear echoes.

After a late start, my momma also became very shrewd with money. She bought a brand-new house this year, one year after retiring from the Chicago public school system. She put 10 percent down and she didn't have to sell her old house to do it, or to make her payments. She started out modestly after her second divorce.

"Every two weeks, every time I got paid, I'd put $35 into one little IRA and maybe I don't know the exact amount, maybe $100 every pay period, maybe about $200 a month into a tax-sheltered annuity." I didn't live flamboyantly, she says. Then she admits that red convertible Firebird she bought new and ran up and down the street might have been a tad flamboyant. But even in her mid-forties, with heartache and tragedy behind her, she was, after all, still beautiful Betty Lou underneath all those years of being elegant Elizabeth. Little by little, Momma put away her money or reveled in new purchases and adjusted to the unexpected turn her life had taken. She made independent decisions and a lasting impression on her daughters.

When my niece, Brittany, moved in with us, Momma sent her the money to buy a car. And, since college, whenever I've needed anything, help with a down payment on our first new house or, later, a new suit my husband says wouldn't be practical, Momma has always been there.

I was reminded of her example watching the 2004 Summer Olympics trampoline competition. Watching a gymnast jump very high and seeing his coach come from nowhere to slide a cushion out of bounds before he could land badly. That's what Momma does, I said to myself, reflecting on the importance of having enough resources not only to stand on your own but also to keep someone you care about from falling. I thought deeply about the profound historical import of black women with cushions to soften missteps and mistakes, to keep the people closest to them from crashing through the floor. Then I thought about the historical shame that so many black women, making pennies on the dollar, and vulnerable to bad life choices, didn't have cushions to offer. And it all makes me think about the myriad ways I want to be there for my own children, so they can jump as high as they're able.

I think a person is blessed who is able to give emotionally and financially, my momma says.

I no longer have my own separate account, although I reserve the right to establish another one, if not keep it a secret. Perhaps I just wanted to prove I could do it, even to myself. Perhaps my life is too crowded with old souls to ever be caught without a Plan B. Perhaps it's just that my mother's story—part example, part cautionary tale—is too powerful a parable for me to ignore.

These days, my husband and I pool our money and we work for the good of the house. I respect when he feels he needs to spend money on something—a new generator so we won't be the only house on the block without power in a storm, karate lessons, or even that annual trip to Miami with "the bros" for the black film festival, although he's not even remotely connected to the motion picture arts and sciences. Within reason, he gets to have his stuff.

And so do I.

In her book *Successful Women, Angry Men,* author Bebe Moore Campbell details all the ways couples striving to have egalitarian marriages can find themselves at less than equal. While black women have developed certain strengths from a long history of pulling double duty in the workforce and at home, she writes, they are still not exempt from the powerful pull of traditional gender roles and how they can introduce tension into the best-intentioned relationships.

My husband grew up watching his father make nearly all the decisions about their family finances. But I make more money than my husband's blue-collar father or my own decidedly white-collar father ever did. So I consult, I compromise, sometimes I even cajole, but I've learned to have my say. Besides, if things don't go my way, I can always call my momma.

I think about my job and my marriage and the beauty of wanting to stay in both because it's where I want to be, and not because I could never afford to leave. I don't have a phat ride, but my head is fairly clear and my life is sprinkled with options that have helped me out when the terrain has gotten rough.

God bless the child, says Momma. And generations say, Amen.

Fry It Up in the Pan

Do you want it on your rice and gravy?
Do you want it on your biscuits, baby?

JILL SCOTT

I WAS ON THE PHONE with my girlfriend Lafayetta one day,
when she started talking about a pot of chicken she was making.
This was a familiar subject for Lafayetta. She was always cooking
food and talking about food and talking about the food she was going to cook. Nearly a decade ago, I wrote an essay about how I considered myself a "philosophical vegetarian." About how I was
considering making a dietary change but the evocative cooking traditions in the black community, and the connectedness I felt to
them, held too much sway. In the essay, I cited Lafayetta as "the
soul food high priestess of my under thirty set."

A woman who warned, "Okay, you go ahead and feed that big
ole black man salad if you want to."

Lafayetta's nickname was Pepper when she was growing up in
the Jackson Five hometown of Gary, Indiana (where my daddy was
a schoolteacher and administrator for twenty-three years). She was
nominated as best dancer at Horace Mann High School and had

been a proud member of the Stoney Jackson Fan Club. She's a suburban, middle-class nurse now, but her way-ethnic bona fides are unassailable.

On the phone that day, her chicken conversation got involved, and, as usual, I got caught up in a comfort-food trance. See, Lafayetta has a way of making recipes sound like folklore and a long list of ingredients hit the ear like syncopated rhythm.

"I had a whole chicken, so I cut it down the middle to flatten it out so it would cook easier and season easier. I just flattened it out in the pan and seasoned it with seasoning salt and garlic powder on both sides. I usually cook for the week, so when I have baked chicken, I'll do a chicken soup or have baked chicken and a chicken chili. The soup is my Grandmother Lula Hart's old recipe. I just get the egg noodles and get like five pieces of chicken. I use two, three cups of water. I just add regular salt, pepper, garlic powder—all of this while the chicken is boiling. Then I take it out of the pot and debone it and pull the fat out of it. I put the meat back, then put in the margarine and noodles. That's all I do."

As in many cultures—Italian and Mexican spring readily to mind—cooking traditions hold a special place in the black collective psyche. It's why Democratic strategist Donna Brazile, who in 2000 became the first black women to head a major presidential campaign, chose the foods she learned to make as the child of a working-poor family in Kenner, Louisiana, as recurring metaphors for her memoir, *Cooking with Grease: Stirring the Pots in American Politics:*

Grits in Louisiana are stirred with butter, and sometimes cheese, but rarely plain. When I got to Washington, D.C., however, I tasted some on Capitol Hill made with onions and garlic, and they were delicious, too. I discovered that maybe I'd stir the pots in D.C. after all.

And like all the traditions that have imprinted us most deeply, these have long roots. "It is true that domestic life took on an exaggerated importance in the social lives of slaves, for it did indeed provide them with the only space where they could truly experience themselves as human beings," writes Angela Davis in *Women, Race and Class.*

In *Labor of Love, Labor of Sorrow,* Jacqueline Jones maintains the domestic work of black women on behalf of their own has been inherently political, from the slave cooks who fed runaways to the grandmothers who kept the steady stream of civil rights marchers fed.

It was blacks who were the architects of most of what passes for Southern cuisine, says Joyce White, author of *Soul Food: Recipes and Reflections from African American Churches.* Its origins stretch back to slave raids that were sometimes conducted in specific West African regions where planters were known to grow rice. She points out, for example, that while gumbo is considered a Creole dish, it was, in all likelihood, invented by South Carolina slaves who took it with them to Louisiana, and the name actually comes from *kingumbo,* the Bantu word for okra. It was blacks who cooked for the Southern planters' grandest occasions, and after Emancipation, black homesteaders often became hog farmers, accounting for our long-running love affair with chitlins and pork chops and all things pig.

Allegedly, according to White, a slave once made a delicious lemon pie and when the master loved it and wanted to know what kind of wonderful thing he'd created, the brother replied, "It's jes pie," and that's how chess pie, which can be made with chocolate, pineapple, or lemon, became a popular Southern confection. White, who comes from the South, says black women have a long history of cooking because those were the only jobs available to them and because black patrons weren't allowed in white restaurants. "We went to church, we went to each other's homes," she says. "That's where . . . our lives took place. That's where we did a lot of our eating."

In the mid-1960s, White became an editorial assistant at the *Ladies' Home Journal,* one of the first black women to work in that capacity. Black faces were absent in places where domesticity was celebrated. Still, black folks had long ago learned to celebrate their own. White saw how her mother and aunts marked their week by cornbread or flapjacks and put on great feasts for the most meaningful times of their lives, and watched the joy that came back their way. It was "anointed" work, says White, of black women cooks.

My friend Lafayetta just says, "That's where I get my applause."

In his standup routine in the 1986 comedy *Raw,* Eddie Murphy talks about the big lumpy "welfare burgers" his mother used to cook: a counter to his deep longing for McDonald's—"I got something better than McDonald's," she would tell him. A burger bursting with green peppers and dripping with juice enough to turn the bread gooey and tear it into holes. Murphy talks about getting into a fight as a young man once and calling his mother crying, needing her words, hungry for the warming comfort one of those welfare burgers could provide.

So I know the ritual and lore and the deep caretaking that cooking represents for black people, but it was much more than psychic memory that moved me to call my friend Lafayetta that day. She is a wife and mother of a preschool daughter. She brought her teenaged brother to Maryland to live with her in 2002 after his parents became unable to care for him. She's a cardiac nurse and sometimes works a twelve-hour shift, and when she says, "I cook for the week," I hear a blueprint, a guide, a helpful hint about organization and making it all work. I hear a very specific way of taking care of home that calls out to me every time.

I feel loved when I walk into Lafayetta's house and she asks if I've eaten. "Look in the fridge," she says. "I've got some roast in there, I made some potato salad the other day. Should be some macaroni and green beans near the back. Just let me know because I've still got that pound cake from this weekend. I just made a fresh pot of iced tea." I love my friends just as much, but when you walk in my house, could be I'll offer you a sandwich and a glass of water. And this time, listening to my friend, I was (once more) inspired to change all that.

I got off the phone with Lafayetta that day and ran straight to the grocery store. I bought a whole chicken and a jar of chicken bouillon. I bought celery and onions and came right back to my kitchen. I put on Grandma Mabel's old apron, the one I like to think smells like her even though she died years before I was born so any thought of her smell is just a comforting bit of fiction.

I started to work on the chicken, but very quickly the work got hard. Turns out, I had never in my life cut up a whole chicken. What the hell, the store has all the chicken parts you want, already cut up. They got more legs and breasts in a package than even a chicken on the heaviest steroids can grow. Besides, it's nasty work. So while my mother used to wring chicken necks and pluck off their feathers when she was a girl, I never even bothered to learn to cut one up. Maybe it's because I had a small knife (do they call those paring knives?), but my chicken bones just weren't breaking right. My chicken didn't lay flat in the pot. My hands were slimy and my good feeling was slipping away.

I managed to come up with something for dinner that night. But it wasn't anything like what Lafayetta had described. *Got to know your limitations,* Aunt Jackie's words echoed through my head. Note to self: *You are not Lafayetta, and you have no business pretending to be.* Bumping up against my limitations is part of the reason why, more than three years ago, when I was pregnant with my son, I hired the Señora, Dona Patti, to help out with the house and kids. She arrived every morning to do light housekeeping and laundry and, initially, to watch Savannah, my second child, then Satchel, my third. Over time, our relationship grew and so did her responsibilities. Routinely, they now also include cooking because, as luck would have it, I hired a Mexican woman not unlike many of the black women I've known my whole life. A designated cook in her family. A woman who loves you with food, who started making Satchy hand-rolled tortillas and fried eggs for breakfast as soon as he got four teeth in his head.

Early in the relationship, the Señora made no comment about leftovers, or the lack of leftovers, available in the fridge. But after a while she started to engage me. She asked about certain ingredients or asked for help understanding a certain English cooking instruction. But I wasn't particularly passionate, so this happened infrequently. Later our familiarity grew and Dona Patti began meeting my friends. I would often host get-togethers—baby showers or book readings—and she quickly caught on that it was always my best girlfriends who did the cooking for these occasions. She would ask pointedly who would be cooking for my various "fiestas," wanting to know if Lafayetta was coming over to help.

My good friend Dana, who used to do catering on the side, lived with us for a while. She'd often cook big dinners, roast beef and fresh green beans on Sundays, and Monday mornings, the Señora would say, "I see Dana cooked." Or "Tell Dana dinner was good." After a while Dona Patti started cooking dinner for me as well, and I developed favorites like her lentil soup or tacos and tortillas with homemade salsa. She'd make frijoles and rice on Mondays, and we'd eat off of it for part of the week. Whenever possible with my husband, but most especially with the kids, I passed a number of her dishes off as my own. And since the Señora speaks only a few words of English, I had no fear she'd contradict me.

Recently she brought her newborn granddaughter, Litzy, to the house for a visit. I was baking cookies for my girls, but I became so engaged with the baby that I overcooked three successive batches. I blamed it on the baby, but the Señora just smirked. She picked up Litzy and cooed to her in Spanish, murmuring all sorts of falsehoods about how Señora Lonnae couldn't cook. First off, I set the record straight. "*Yo puedo cocinar*, I can cook, you better recognize," I told the baby emphatically ("*tal vez no muy, muy bien*").

Secondly, *whatever*. Somehow I find a way to work it all out.

Still, I always remember somebody being in the kitchen when I was growing up. My grandparents owned a restaurant, Momma cooked every night, and every Sunday, my daddy would pull out the electric griddle and make an elaborate production out of breakfast, moving about the kitchen, calling himself the "chef extraordinaire." I liked the hum and bustle and busyness of these times and wanted to join in. In fact, one of my earliest memories is of trying to make an egg. I got as far as cracking it on the counter and letting it drop to the floor before somebody grown shooed me away.

I grew up in a kitchen with great imposing pots and cast-iron skillets—frying pans without adornment or pretensions of anything other than black folks' work, in a time when "nonstick" meant you rubbed steel wool over the pork chop leftovers, scouring the pan until hunks of meat came nonstuck. A time of dumplings and gravies and jars of bacon drippings left in a can on the stove to be recycled into unsuspecting green vegetables, altering their character and rendering them virtually inorganic. A time of soul food and the constant gathering around to eat it. But by the time I reached an age to learn to cook, books and television had captured my imagination. My home life was often troubled and dramatic and I lost myself in my head, in an entire world of fantasy and escape. And you have to be present to cook if you don't want to burn yourself or set something on fire. Momma made dinner every night, but she was, admittedly, just an average cook—hampered by the pressure that any misstep could bring mean-spirited teasing and taunts from Daddy and his mother, Momma Susie. And likely hampered by the fact that some of her dishes, like salmon and rice, or the tuna noodle casserole she says she got from Aunt Carolyn, tasted to my young mind like a particularly evil punishment.

But Momma always looked good at the stove. She stayed in her heels and her skirts from work so when Daddy came home, she was outfitted and lovely. It was that image and television images of glamour and sophistication that stayed with me most and caused me to turn from a notion of myself that could be validated by a well-seasoned plate of greens. Myrna Loy wasn't slaving over a hot stove for her husband in *Shadow of a Thin Man.* Besides, I told myself, I wouldn't ever have to worry about cooking because somebody was gonna take me out to dinner every night.

Surprisingly enough life hasn't quite worked out like that for me. So for a long time now, I've been trying, off and on, to play catch-up, to stir up a part of myself. I was in college the first time I tried to fry chicken. It was the summer after my freshman year and I was living in the apartment of an older sorority sister. I dipped the chicken in egg, because seems like I had heard other folks say that made it more savory, but I didn't know I was also supposed to dip it in flour. My grease was too hot and I ended up burning the chicken in a stank, scorched mess, angering my roommate and causing her to marvel that I was so profoundly unschooled in even the cooking basics.

A year later, I was with my boyfriend at the apartment of one of his boys. The fellas were in the living room and that left it up to the women to cook. I was in the kitchen with a girl named Ellen, whom everyone called Dodie, a pretty girl with hard edges, as I recall. This time I was eager to prove myself. To fit in and not make such oddball mistakes. I knew you were supposed to dip the chicken in flour so that's what I did. Then I seasoned it with salt and pepper all over. Dodie came and stood next to me. She looked at the chicken, then looked at me, and I got what had become that familiar sinking feeling telling me I had done something wrong. Something that meant my program was off and perhaps just a little less than authentically black, because after all, black girls could cook, no? She studied me for a moment. Then, without a word, she rinsed off all my chicken and reseasoned it first, before redipping it in the flour, and that's how I learned to fry chicken.

I went to school at Southern Illinois University, about an hour south of my grandparent's home in Centralia, and one day my boyfriend and I decided to visit. In Centralia, where he ran the Confectionary for about fifty years, my grandfather, Papa Lonnie, was known to most as Chef. He was a simple, hardworking country man with a beaming, Louie Armstrong smile, and a love of food and all kinds of food lore. He still called all his favorites by their Southern nicknames. As a kid, I sat with him one day while he was eating a biscuit, except he called it a "cat head."

Why in the world, I asked, slightly alarmed, did he call it a cat head.

My grandfather just grinned. "Lookadat thang. Don't dat look like a cat head to you?" he asked, holding it up, turning it in the light. I couldn't see it myself, and I was not really in a place to be able to appreciate the etymology of the old Southern food traditions, to understand that biscuits were cat heads and watermelons were letters from home. One day, my grandfather sat on a tree stump in front of his house eating a "letter from home" and laughing as white folks drove past, some swerving or nearly ramming their cars to turn and gawk at him, a dark black man on a tree stump chowing down on watermelon, a real live postcard from Jim Crow.

When my boyfriend and I arrived at the house, my grandfather, naturally, asked if we wanted something to eat. When the boyfriend said sure, Papa Lonnie turned to me impatiently, "Baby, go 'head and fix your young man a plate," he said.

"Um, Papa Lonnie, I'm in college. I don't really get down like that," I started to tell him. Then I remembered I was trying to be a good black woman (a *good* black woman), so I headed for the kitchen and got my young man a helping of beef with a couple of cat heads and a side of mashed potatoes.

In school, I regularly dined on noodles and tuna and yogurt. I sometimes put on domestic airs offering visitors freshly brewed coffee, though most of the folks who came to see me preferred a fresh-brewed *beer,* or at least a glass of Kool-Aid. I had an apartment and I was playing house, so food rituals were starting to mean something to me. But I was young and searching, trying on different parts of myself and walking them out into the real world to see how they looked. And slaving over a hot stove still looked nothing like me at all.

My boyfriend didn't seem to mind that I couldn't cook anything more than burgers, but clearly, in a lot of other eyes, having a man changed things. It altered folks' expectations, adding a variety of culinary feats to my list of things to do. It let me know the gaps in my résumé were problematic, and even though I thought I was cute, that wasn't going to be nearly enough for me to be taken seriously.

My sister, Lisa, was already a young wife and mother by this time and on her way to becoming a very good cook. If she ever had any illusions about how often she'd go out to dinner, she had already gotten her comeuppance. When she was a kid, Lisa had been less of a dreamer, more careful to watch my Aunt Nellie working in the kitchen, a great big woman for all those big pots, and paying attention as Momma Susie baked. She even learned to make my father's favorite cream puffs before he died.

Her first husband liked to cook as well, and she watched him and asked her own mother-in-law for her husband's favorite recipes. She began a tradition of making gumbo every January 1 and inviting friends over to celebrate the New Year. It's a tradition she left alone when she and her first husband split up. Later, when she was dating again, she made some fried chicken and commissioned her ex-mother-in-law to make sides of fried cabbage and macaroni and cheese. When the new guy came over, Lisa served him a delicious dinner, including the side dishes she quite naturally passed off as her own.

Food and sex, the kitchen and house politics have always been intertwined. "Baby, are you hungry? Can I fix you something to eat?" or "Get up and get it your damn self" have alternately presided in the places I've lived and the stories other folks tell as well.

Limited as they have been in other avenues of power and expression, women, and most creatively, black women, learned to play and fight in the few arenas that were open to them, which is why, in 1974, hot grits that stuck and burned became the weapon of choice in the hands of a lover spurned by soul singer Al Green. Why a close friend recalls an urban legend told to him by his mother about a black man who "beat his wife's ass" and then went to sleep. How he woke up to the smell of bacon frying and told himself, "Damn, that's a good woman," before drifting back off. How he woke up again when she was pouring bacon grease in his ear.

In the 1959 Lorraine Hansberry play *A Raisin in the Sun*, the young wife, Ruth Younger, is annoyed at her husband, Walter Lee—annoyed because they're poor, because they live in an overcrowded apartment with one bathroom between two families, because she's overworked and overtired and might be pregnant with their second child. It's too much annoyance for a workday morning, so Ruth just asks Walter what kind of eggs he wants and when he says, "Not scrambled," she proceeds to scramble them anyway.

And, of course, slave history is rife with tales of poisons and masters who were always afraid a black cook might try to exact a bit of revenge on the family.

Food is often used as code for when something's gone wrong. But also for when things are going deliciously right. When they were feeling a particular kind of good, bluesy black women like Bessie Smith bragged, "Nobody in town can bake a jelly roll like mine." Etta James wanted no misunderstanding when she sang, "All I want to do is bake your bread / Just to make sure you're well fed."

A few years ago, I was watching the HBO movie *Boycott*, and laughed at the confidence and playful sexuality of the church cook who handed Jeffrey Wright, playing Martin Luther King, a hot plate of food. "I hope Mrs. King don't get jealous," she said.

In 2000, on her sumptuous track, "It's Love," Philly songbird Jill Scott continued that tradition—saw where we was hungry and raised her voice.

> Love, love, love, love, love, love
> Do you want it on your collard greens?

Do you want it on your candy sweets?
Do you want it on your pickled beets?
Give it to me, give it to me, give it

Soul food, I believe they were talking about; about how it's a powerful thing when a woman, can, you know, cook, burn, keep people satisfied. "Food is sexy," writes Vertamae Smart-Grosvenor in *Vibration Cooking*, and you "can tell a lot about people and where they're at by their food habits. People who eat food with pleasure and get pleasure from the different stirring of the senses that a well-prepared food experience can bring are my kind of people."

My husband is routinely complimentary about my cooking. And the times when he's not—when he's pointed out a singed pastry or an extra-chewy tenderloin, when he's thought it okay to say one of my meals isn't quite up to snuff—I've taken those times personally. I've reminded him how easily he could be sleeping alone. Then the teasing stops.

Still, sometimes I get wistful imagining I could be that kind of women who commands authority and respect in the kitchen, too. I hunger to know what it would be like to add another layer to my chocolate cake, to the list of things I like to say I do well. But I'm a cook with only about five really tasty dishes to her name. And evidence to suggest that stories about how I threw down in the kitchen will not be part of my legacy is rapidly piling up against me. For example, when Cousin Kim moved in with me, she lost thirty pounds in three months. I didn't think too much of it. I have a busy house and Kim had been feeling a bit pudgy anyway. Then last summer, my niece, Brittany, moved in and lost thirteen pounds in a month and a half.

What can I say? We do a lot of salads and I don't often bother with gravy since mine tends to be lumpy, prompting comments from my kids that make me mad. I don't eat pork chops or ham, and although I now fry chicken well, I don't like how the smell of deep-fried Crisco lingers. I am hampered in my cooking glory by a lack of time or attention or, at some level, a depth of knowledge and skill—and by the fact that I'm not a big eater, except when my low blood sugar has made me voracious. But I never have been a woman to let a material reality get in the way of my vision of how things oughta be.

Because I sample and I'm quick on my feet, because I hear the call of history and put a premium on folk traditions, I decided not to let the fact that I'm just an average cook keep my family from having our own soul food memories. In fact after the success of the 1997 movie *Soul Food*, about an extended family in Chicago who worked out their kinks over weekly meals, I borrowed an idea from a colleague who started giving his own Sunday dinners for friends and family. I used to invite the people closest to me into my home for food and fellowship. I stuck to my best dishes and had better cooks bring along theirs as well (though, as designed, I got most of the credit for pulling everything together). The food was hearty, especially appreciated by my bachelor buddies who were lean in the limbs from having to fend for themselves. My friends are artsy and accomplished, thoughtful and funny, and as we broke bread, we talked politics and popular culture, history and hip-hop. We turned on the stereo and DJ'd our own after parties, dancing with our kids. We made the joyful noises of folks who knew what it was to be comfortable in their own skin.

My Sunday dinners reminded me of home, only different. And nobody was falling out drunk. Sometimes you can never get the things you never had, but sometimes you can. You can surround yourself with friends who love you and accept your shortcomings in the pot roast department. You can give of your gifts and they can give of theirs, and that can be enough not to remind you not exactly of the home you had but the one you always wanted and so you deliberately made it so.

My friends have given me baby showers for each of my three children. They've always put their foot in whatever they've cooked up, but the last one, for my son Satchel, was something different altogether. They made jerk chicken and collard greens. Peas and rice and gumbo. They had fresh flowers in unexpected places and arranged the table professionally, heating the food with chafing dishes. "Wow, you have friends who come in to cook like this for you," one of my colleagues remarked. My hostesses Lafayetta and Dana and Stephanie accepted rave reviews the whole afternoon, although Stephanie cooks more like me, so she was just asked to be on beverage and paper product duty. ("Girl, I can't mess with them," Stephanie said. "Lafayetta made some pizza on a damn stone. I was just, like, Wine anyone? I was a hell of a pourer.")

I haven't given up the idea that one day, I, too, am going to break out and get all brand new in the kitchen. But I have come to believe I may be under something of a curse when it comes to getting my just deserts. Routinely, if Dana or Lafayetta or my good friend Liana, a mother of five who knows what it is to nourish, is coming to visit, if it's another cook I really want to impress, something goes inexplicably wrong with my meal. It's undercooked or it's overcooked or my noodles stick together. It has happened so often, I am convinced the universe is trying to keep me humble; to let me know I can't have more than my fair share of gifts. A few months ago I thought I had beaten this jinx. Dana called last minute to say she was stopping by and my dinner, chicken and rice and mushroom sauce, was already done. I took it out of the oven piping hot and congratulated myself that this time nothing would get in the way of my full cooking recognition. I left the casserole dish covered on top of the stove and ran to the 7-Eleven to get something to drink. Back at home, I was setting the table when suddenly, out of the blue, my casserole dish exploded, sending bits of chicken and glass flying. Apparently, I had left the eye to my electric stove on, or at least that's what I was supposed to think. Whatever. Dana arrived a short while later, to my customary apologies, and assured me dinner was very good and that I had done a very good job picking glass shards out of the rice.

Although my passion for cooking comes and goes, I do routinely bake brownies from scratch as appreciation gifts for the teachers and bus drivers at my kids' school. (Although last year, I used the wrong-sized glass dish and they were a little scorched on the edges and doughy in the middle. I simply decided it was the thought that counted. And, like Kate Reddy, the heroine in Alison Pearson's novel *I Don't Know How She Does It,* I like folks to think I bake from scratch.)

I still hedge my bets and sometimes make Sydney and Savannah's favorites, mashed potatoes or potato salad or spaghetti, in the hopes that they might remember a few of my dishes fondly. And in due time, I will send them over to apprentice in the kitchen of friends and family, something I've considered doing myself if I ever reach that magic place where life holds more time. I also frequently ask for help from my mother-in-law, Ma Evelyn, who lives ten minutes away and is always generous with her time and cooking advice.

"History resides in many places. It is in our memories of family and the stories passed down to us. It is in our hometowns and home countries, even in customs we have maintained," says the introduction to *The Historical Cookbook of the American Negro.* Maybe that's why last summer, when my cousin Ronald came to visit before he was sworn in to the Supreme Court bar, he baked us a chocolate pie and we swapped stories of Momma Susie.

Soul Food author Joyce White laments that cooking may be something of a dwindling art for modern black women who are squeezed for time and worried about breaking their nails. I take her point, but while there are more doors opened to us, creating more opportunities to channel our energies and talents, I believe a core of skill and knowledge and barbeque lore will always be around. "We are a people," Alice Walker points out in her foreword to the Robert E. Hemenway biography of Zora Neale Hurston. "A people do not throw their geniuses away."

Five or six years ago, I picked up my sister's tradition of making gumbo for the New Year. Of inviting friends and family over to celebrate and sending a big bowl out back to Miss Cathie, next door to Wardell and Jennifer, or home with our friend J.R., whose wife, LaFonda, always sends him over with a Tupperware bowl. I never had a recipe although by this time I should know it cold. But I don't. Instead, every New Year's Day I spend hours on the phone with my sister, calling her after every step, after I boil the chicken and cut the onions. After I fry my smoked sausage and again when I add my crab legs.

I don't bother to memorize it because I prefer that time with my sister, visiting over the miles, and talking about our hopes for the New Year all through the day.

My gumbo is good, and maybe someday, my cooking for the rest of the year will catch up as well. But even if it doesn't, it's not like I'm going to let that keep me from gathering everyone to the table.

Never Let Him Forget

I was so pretty that mens brought me
breakfast in bed. Wouldn't let me hardly
do no work at all.

> SONIA SANCHEZ,
> "JUST DON'T NEVER GIVE
> UP ON LOVE"

THERE IS A SCENE from the epic 1956 Cecil B. DeMille production of *The Ten Commandments* that stayed in my mind when I
was a child. As a girl, I loved Charlton Heston. I grew up with a recurring rescue fantasy and he always fit the hero bill—a strong and
courageous man, a man of biblical proportions, I thought. But in
The Ten Commandments, I couldn't help but notice it was Nefertiti,
talking about all that myrrh perfuming up her hair, who wielded
her own special kind of power. It was more earthly than ethereal,
with a feel of depth and mystery, but it was a force nonetheless, a
power to compel.

Nefertiti had thrown herself at Moses' feet when he faced judgment in the court of Pharaoh and sobbed as she was promised to
Ramses as the future queen of Egypt. But when Moses came back

around, no longer a fallen prince but a messenger of the Almighty sent to free his people from slavery, Nefertiti, who had also come into her own, was quick to hem him up. Quick to let him know she could be a powerful ally or a fierce opponent. "Who do you think can harden Pharaoh's heart?" she asks Moses. "Or soften it?"

In that moment, I knew she was talking about using what she had to get what she wanted. That she was talking about laying it down and whipping it on him. And even if I wasn't exactly sure what "it" was or how "it" worked, I knew instinctively "it" could tip the scales and bend things in favor of the queen. Now I'm grown, with three kids, and I must admit, I've been an "it" girl for a long time. And while I don't know if what I'm serving up would be enough to free the Hebrews from Egypt, I have it on good authority it'll take you to the Promised Land. Which sounds right because I do pride myself on being a woman of many talents. Like Nefertiti, they are skills I like to use to bend things toward a favor all my own.

If I want to go out alone with friends on a Friday, I start being real nice to my husband the Sunday before. I cook a good dinner a couple of nights in a row and keep the house orderly and straight; but since I know how to play to my strengths, I keep my trump card tucked away 'til later. I like to use it when I want to go out, but it works just as well when money's tight and I still want a pricey pair of new shoes, or I need my husband to loan us his generator to power the neighborhood block party. I start dropping hints about whatever it is I want. I start talking about how happy it's going to make me, and I remind him how a happy wife does such happy things for her man. And that usually closes the deal and makes for one big happy family.

There's a certain sensual fluidity I like to bring to my suburban pantheons. A quick tap on my husband's backside during the school sale at Target to say *Baby, I dig how you gangstered that opening in aisle five*. Perhaps a lick to my lips at family bowling when our eyes meet as the song overhead begs "Love me 'til my tension's gone." Do you remember Will Smith in *Men in Black*? When he put on his suit and dark glasses, turned to Tommy Lee Jones, and said, "I make this look good." Well, that is *exactly* how I'm going to rock a Dodge Caravan. I reject the notion that minivans desexualize. After all, sex is the reason I need one in the first place. That's why on a recent car-shopping trip, while my husband sat in a minivan driver's seat, I sat behind him cooing, "Baby, you look so good, that's all you," and rubbing his head while the car dealer looked on, befuddled. He must not know the sexiest thing on earth is a black man in a ride that keeps everybody safe and allows enough room between the seats so that Cheetos thrown from the back don't land upside your head.

My *Washington Post* computer screensaver used to read "I Got Me a Man Named Dr. Feelgood" until I worried the other reporters might try to scoop my good thing. Once, I was supposed to meet up with girlfriends for drinks at a popular all-male review, but when plans fell through and my friends couldn't make it, I stayed for the show anyway, then came home and told my husband all about it. And last Halloween, with a bucket of candy at the door and *Pop Halloween Hits* looped on the CD, friends and I sat around the kitchen table wearing cat ears and drinking wine, missing untold numbers of trick-or-treaters because we were making off-color jokes about all the love we like to save for special occasions.

It seems such a natural, easy thing now for me to play with the authority I've assumed over my sexuality and the power I've learned to appreciate and most definitely to wield. To use hyperbole and swagger in the cultural tradition of making my own myth (except, don't misunderstand, I'm the real deal). But it hasn't always been so. And the fact that it is, now, for women like me, is significant, and worthy of comment. Although it's an area that's inherently personal, since a hundred years before their white counterparts found the words to speak it, black women have known that the personal is political. It's the bodies of black women that have been among the most politicized terrains on the planet, and used to be there was little more public than black women's sexuality. Sometimes that's still the case.

From 1619 to 1865, black women did not own their babies or their bodies. They were inspected and poked and sold on the auction blocks. They were raped and sexually subjugated by white men and mated with other slaves so their children could be added to the master's bottom line. Internationally, whites titillated themselves lining up in France to gawk at Sara Baartman, the young South African tribeswoman, dubbed the Hottentot Venus, who became an icon of black female sexuality and racial inferiority In 1810, when she was twenty years old Saartjie "Sara" Baartman, was taken to Europe and exhibited naked, in a cage, in European capitals. Her large derriere and distended labia were seen as "somatic evidence of the lasciviousness of blacks, a racial characteristic." In *Bulletproof Diva*, essayist Lisa Jones raises the intriguing possibility that Baartman's notoriety was partially responsible for the rise in popularity of the corset in Europe that gave white women higher busts, rounder hips, and exaggerated proportions of their own. In death, Baartman's sexual organs were preserved and displayed in a Paris museum as recently as 1985. In 2002, the French government returned her remains to South Africa, with apologies.

Stereotypes of sexually rapacious blacks had origins that stretched back to Europeans' first contact with Africans. In *Stolen Women: Reclaiming Our Sexuality, Taking Back Our Lives,* Gail Elizabeth Wyatt, a psychiatry and biobehavioral science professor at UCLA, details those early encounters. She writes that African women didn't cover their breasts (breasts were viewed as symbols of life, not sexuality), that women nursed their children openly, and sex occurred outside of religious control, although not outside of tribal norms and rituals. Europeans used these initial observations as the basis for stereotypes, and the contention that blacks were hardly more than animals in their sexual appetites was part of the justification for slavery. And slavery forced black women to make desperate decisions about resistance against or capitulation to the sexual demands of whites, and to suffer the consequences. Acquiescence could mean estrangement from other slaves and being sold from loved ones by oppressed, vindictive white women who often found their high, chaste, pedestals a desperately lonely perch. Resistance could bring severe physical punishment. It's a point vividly made by folklorist and author Zora Neale Hurston in the novel *Their Eyes Were Watching God*:

> "It was de cool of de evenin' when Mistis come walkin' in mah door. She throwed de door wide open and stood dere lookin' at me outa her eyes and her face. . . .
>
> " 'Nigger, whut's yo' baby doin' wid gray eyes and yaller hair?' She begin tuh slap mah jaws ever which a'way. Ah never felt the fust ones 'cause Ah wuz too busy gittin' de kivver back over mah chile. But dem last lick burnt me lak fire. . . . But then she kept on astin me how come mah baby look white. She asted me dat maybe twenty-five or thirty times, lak she got tuh sayin' dat and couldn't help herself. So Ah told her, 'Ah don't know nothin' but what Ah'm told tuh do, 'cause Ah ain't nothin' but uh nigger and uh slave. . . .'"
>
> "She went to de foot of de bed and wiped her hands on her handksher. 'Ah wouldn't dirty mah hands on yuh. But first thing in de mornin' de overseer will take you to de whippin' post and tie you down on yo' knees and cut de hide offa yo' yaller back. One hundred lashes wid a raw-hide on yo'

bare back. Ah'll have you whipped till de blood run down to yo' heels! Ah mean to count de licks mahself. And if it kills you Ah'll stand de loss. Anyhow, as soon as dat brat is a month old Ah'm going to sell it offa dis place.' "

And in real life the consequences could be even worse. In her book *Black Women in America, A Historical Encyclopedia,* Darlene Hine tells the story of a young Missouri slave girl:

Celia was fourteen years old in 1850 when she was bought by Robert Newsome, a seventy-year-old farmer. On the way home from the slave auction, he raped her. He raped her repeatedly after that until the night of June 23, 1855, when she resisted him with force. At that time, Celia, nineteen years old, was pregnant for the third time and had been ill for at least four months. According the court testimony, Celia had told Newsome that she would hurt him if he raped her while she was still sick. Despite her warning, he came to her cabin that night to force sexual intercourse upon her. Celia, who armed herself with a stick, struck him twice. He died immediately thereafter, and Celia was charged with first-degree murder.

She was later hanged.

Wyatt writes about James Roberts, a freed slave who, in his "Narrative of James Roberts," tells of how fifty or sixty black women were bred on his plantation. How they were impregnated solely by whites in the hopes that their children would bring top dollar. "From these women, 20 to 25 children were born and sold away when they were ready for market," Roberts said. In slave times, women were often given thin or ill-fitting clothes, and modesty was additionally often subservient to the hard realities of bending over and squatting in fields to perform their labor. This was offered as further proof of black sexual aberrance. After Emancipation, sexual relations became one of the primary areas in which former slaves could act upon their freedom. With the end of Reconstruction, blacks were once again forced into political and economic subservience, so the ability to travel, and, most especially, to choose who they wanted to love became among the clearest lines of demarcation separating slave days from free ones.

Still the stereotype of the insatiable black woman, who gave rise to the oversexed black man, who was a constant danger to the virtue of white women, continued and grew as a justification for the lynching that became widespread. "Black men were thought capable of these sexual crimes because of the lascivious character of the women of the race in a time when women were considered the foundation of a group's morality," writes Paula Giddings in her essay "The Last Taboo." This notion became a deeply entrenched flip of historical reality. Journalist Ida B. Wells found that in only a fraction of the hundreds of lynchings she investigated were blacks even accused (never mind found guilty) of rape and that black women, vulnerable from working as domestics in white homes, faced constant threat at the hands of white men. This is supported by one study, which found that in the period following Emancipation when interracial marriage was banned, the number of biracial children in the United States actually increased.

It was Wells' findings and her international antilynching crusade that prompted James W. Jacks, president of the Missouri Press Association, to write that all black women were "prostitutes, thieves, and liars." Black women's outrage at this slander sparked the black women's club movement. This is why that early-twentieth-century movement of middle-class black women devoted so much energy to ladyhood and propriety—because they were obsessed with defining themselves and debunking the stereotypes that were used to murder their sons and husbands. For women like educator and feminist Anna Julia Cooper, who was widowed young and never remarried, it also prompted extreme denial and a near sexless persona in favor of total sacrifice to the cause of uplift. Maxine Clair, author and George Washington University English professor, recalls growing up in Kansas City when black teachers were compelled to resign once they got married or became pregnant, so as not to despoil their image of chastity. Clair says although laws mandating resignation for white teachers were rescinded in the 1940s, the custom continued for black teachers, especially in small, Midwest school districts, well into the 1950s.

My Grandma Mabel came out of that clubwoman tradition, and maybe that's why she had to completely split off a part of herself to secretly write stories for pulp magazines. It is why she drilled decorum and respectability into my momma's head. Perhaps that is why my mother never said a word to her daughters about sex, never helped me fashion a healthy self-concept or set of rules as I grew out of my girlhood, never taught me the facts of life.

Maybe that accounts for why Momma turned so cruel and judgmental when my sister became pregnant in college. And all of that is certainly why I have had to come up with an approach to sexuality all my own, one that is influenced, in many ways, by my mother's conservativism inflected with that clubwoman tradition. But one that, you know, samples elsewhere to customize my rhythms. Because there are other, earthier traditions I like to claim as well.

These sexual traditions are most especially exemplified by the blues music that sprang from the complex realities faced by the black working class, like my father's people, in the first half of the twentieth century. They are expressive traditions reflective of grappling and coping and coming to terms. And of trying, whenever possible, to nudge those terms in more favorable ways. They are traditions that borrow empathy and passion from exultations of the sacred—"Make a joyful noise unto the Lord, all ye, all ye lands"—to try to score a bit of heaven in secular places:

> Send me a Zulu, a voodoo, any old man,
> I'm not particular, boys, I'll take what I can."
> (Ma Rainey,
> "Lawd, Send me a Man Blues")

It is music derived from a black aesthetic, but a commercial offering as well, exaggerated for purposes of art and performance, and, of course, for commodification, because, as Ethel Waters pointed out, this was "clean" work. Unlike scrubbing toilets and dirty laundry. (A sentiment analogous to Hattie McDaniel's famous I'd rather play a maid than be a maid. A sentiment that can be carried forward through the bare-chested banana dances of Josephine Baker and even, to the get-paid exhortations of rappers Foxy Brown and Lil' Kim.)

In her book *Blues Legacies and Black Feminism*. Angela Davis points out that women were the first professional purveyors of blues music, the first to be recorded on wax. The blues created a discourse and women were able to bring their issues of poverty and abuse and love and heartbreak to that discourse, "making women's lives equal to that of men." The search for agency and the meanings of freedom informed blues music. And for black people who, after hundreds of years, could finally lay claim to partial ownership of their bodies, that freedom was most immediately sexual. "In women's blues, which became a crucial element of the rising black entertainment industry, there was an even more pronounced emphasis on love and sexuality," says Davis. "The representations of love and sexuality in women's blues often blatantly contradicted mainstream ideological assumptions regarding women and being in love."

I wanna be somebody's baby doll to ease my mind
  He can be ugly, he can be black, so long as he can eagle
    rock and ball the jack.

(Bessie Smith,
"Baby Doll")

They were songs that, although exaggerated for effect, gave voice to black women's aspirations for greater economic, political, and sexual equality. They refused to surrender to the stereotype of the black women as "debased Jezebels," and, as important, they refused to consign themselves to a sexless counterstereotype requiring surrender of their newfound sexual autonomy. Seeking their own space, they were sometimes "wild women blues" that recognized middle-class conventions, which were supported by greater access to resources and buffers to racism, had little to do with the working-class black women who were most directly vulnerable to violence, privation, and economic and sexual exploitation.

You never get nothing by being an angel child
  You better change your ways, and get real wild

(Ida Cox,
"Wild Women Don't Have the Blues")

They were songs with themes surely cosigned by large parts of my extended family.

The women on my daddy's side were pragmatists, working-class black women who seemed, if not wholly to own their sexuality, to at least be comfortable with bringing it up in casual conversation. These women were studied professors of sexual politics, and my own instruction started young. At fourteen, I was visiting Momma Susie's sister, my favorite, Aunt Ellen, when a cousin stopped by to say she was moving to Washington, D.C., to live with her boyfriend, the father of her baby. My aunt was livid. "You move in with a man, you ain't nothing but an unpaid 'ho," Aunt Ellen told her. "Hell, the only time you a paid 'ho is when you get married."

This stayed with me. Not the least of which because it was the same summer I had been glued to the television, transfixed by the wedding of Prince Charles and Princess Diana. I keenly sensed a dichotomy, a disparity, a bit of psychic dissonance in the messages I was getting. But like even young black folks, my double-think, double-consciousness skills have always been sharp, so I simply registered both messages and kept stepping. From an early age, I began to understand (abstractly) that sex was currency. Legal tender. Negotiable for all debts public and private. My family featured extended marital relations and extramarital relations, passions and children of passion, and a certain internal logic structure that, although difficult to deconstruct, effectively kept folks from getting shot. I obviously took note of all this. Still, it didn't become personal until later.

I was a nerdy child growing up. I didn't get my cool until I got much older. And I was very nearly Victorian when it came to thoughts of romance. I turned away from the television screen when Catwoman, Julie Newmar, would flirt with Batman, Adam West. (Of course when black actress Eartha Kitt replaced Newmar for the final season the sexuality was ratcheted back and that became less of a problem.) And in one episode when Batman came perilously close to kissing some woman and finally intoned "man cannot live by crime fighting alone," I THOUGHT I WAS GOING TO FAINT.

Not only was I lost in my television world of fantasy and escape as a preteen, I was also a bookworm. I learned the facts of life (*Eew!! Gross!!!*) from a pregnancy book I covertly checked out from the adult section of the library. But from the time I was about twelve until I left for college, what I loved to read more than anything in the world were Harlequin Romances. I chain-smoked them, sometimes ditching school to read two a day. I had favorite authors like Janet Dailey and Carol Mortimer, and I had the formula for love down pat. They always featured about 188 or 189 pages of smart virginal heroines, and rich older men. The more interested I became in boys, the more obsessed I was with my fantasy of how my love life was supposed to go, gross anatomy notwithstanding.

It would be like Janet Dailey's *Big Sky Country*, or like the movie *The Blue Lagoon* with Brooke Shields and Christopher Atkins, except somehow that epic romantic setting always eluded me. I think *Big Sky Country* was set on a ranch in Montana, so that was out, and there were simply no lagoons, blue or otherwise, to speak of in Hazel Crest. And although plenty of folks lost it in Chicago at The Point on 57th Street, or Bongo Beach on 63rd, I didn't really know a lot of Chicago boys and that seemed very different anyway, so I was a virgin until I went to college. Despite the fact that from the time I was a child, I memorized the R & B songs that urged, "We can do it baby, do it tonight," or "Catfish makes my nature rise." Despite the fact that when we were fifteen, my girlfriend Alicia and I learned all the words to "Nasty Girl," by Vanity 6:

> Cuz tonight I'm living in a fantasy, my own little nasty
> world,
> Tonight don't u wanna come with me, do u think I'm a
> nasty girl?

and felt ourselves on the verge of some new power we didn't understand. Despite the fact that sex was all around me.

When I was growing up, children weren't even allowed to break the threshold of the room where grown folks were talking, but hints of sex were always in the air. Momma Susie was known to bust out with a "Well, she shoulda kept her legs closed!" on the telephone, or a "Well, she ought nota laid down with him!" in living room conversation.

Much later, she professed to be most deeply offended about the Clarence Thomas, Anita Hill hearings. "What make it so bad, he was talkin' about havin' *URRRL* sex!" she said. (I believe the word she was looking for there was *oral*, but of course everyone in the room just let that one slide.)

My Aunt Ellen and her daughter-in-law Rita were always amused by the romance novels I read during my summers in Centralia. They smiled and elbowed each other when I announced I was going to be a virgin until I got married. And although they genuinely lauded my book smarts, Aunt Ellen liked to point out that *smart in the head usually means dumb down there*. In Chicago and Centralia, where I grew up, folks loved and fought and stayed married for decades even if they lived in separate bedrooms for nearly the entire time. There was always something risqué in the air, but it was my glamorous, sexy Aunt Jackie who took things to a different level entirely.

Aunt Jackie is my father's older sister. She married and divorced five times, has two grown children, one of them a doctor, and has always been reputed to be skilled in the ways of the Kama Sutra. As a young woman (and even as an older woman, although I haven't seen her in years), she was attractive and witty with an enviably curvaceous figure. She attended my alma mater, Southern Illinois University, and was good friends with fellow student, comedian, and activist Dick Gregory. Gregory used to visit Centralia and go to my grandparents' restaurant, the Confectionary, to chat up Momma Susie. A couple of years ago, when I visited SIU, a high-ranking dean who'd gone to school with my aunt remembered how she'd take the hour train ride from Centralia to Carbondale in the morning, then catch the train back home to change outfits before returning to school later to attend afternoon classes or socialize.

Women were envious of Aunt Jackie—irked by the fact that she always commanded the most attention in the room, especially if it was a room full of men. They were irked by her confidence and self-possession and the fact that her nails were perfect and her hair was perfect and she was always dressed to the nines. Lots of folks wondered how she was able to do it, working first at the Confectionary and, thereafter, very little at all. But lots of folks didn't have parents like Momma Susie and Papa Lonnie, to lavish money and material things on their only daughter.

In the 1950s, Aunt Jackie would pay seven dollars for a pair of panties. And at a time when most white folks couldn't even afford to shop at Centralia's priciest store, the Smart Boutique, my aunt was on a first-name basis with the owners. She could call them up and they'd have a cab carry a new outfit right to her house. I still have the eight-by-ten photograph of Jackie, beautifully coiffed and wearing a black negligee, that she gave out one Christmas. And when we were young, the cousins couldn't wait to visit her house to see all the naked cherubs Aunt Jackie had had papered on her bedroom walls. Naturally, this kind of outsized living led to some keen insights. And my Aunt Jackie has always been very generous about sharing.

"Lonnae, looky here," she once began, summoning me close. "A man don't want nothin' but two things. You got to be a lady in the front room and a bitch in the bedroom, you hear what I'm saying?" I did hear her. But since I was maybe seventeen at the time, I could not fully appreciate that shimmery little pearl of wisdom. Later, it was Aunt Jackie who always told me, "Lonnae, remember, you've got to know your limitations."

My cousin Traci says that when she was about fifteen or sixteen, Aunt Jackie gave her the once-over and clucked disapprovingly that she wasn't more well endowed. Without more going on in the breast department, she worried that Traci would have precious little to offer a man. Then, just by way of example, Aunt Jackie began cupping her own ample bosom. "See, men like to take these big puppies and go up under the pillows to suck on 'em," she told Traci. That kind of freewheeling exchange was one of the things Traci loved about Centralia, she says. Like my own mother, Traci's mom, my lovely Aunt Carolyn, was a schoolteacher with strict middle-class sensibilities. "You weren't even allowed to go see a rated-R movie in Carolyn O'Neal's house, but you come to Centralia and you get X-rated without ever leaving the living room."

My sister Lisa says Aunt Jackie never shared any advice with her. Never tried to train her up in a way she ought to go. It kind of makes me wonder now if Aunt Jackie intuited something special about me. If she sized me up and singled me out as possessing some sort of extra *gitchi gitchi ya ya here* potential. She always was a shrewd judge of character. It can be tempting, in hindsight, to label those conversations as excess. To frown at all the 'hos, married and unmarried, I was privy to hearing about. But I don't think poorly of those working-class black women in my family who made bawdy references to sex. They faced a reality I cannot know. A reality circumscribed by race and gender and class, without the dimmest prospect of developing and using their range of talents to their full potential. Those women danced in the arena in which they found themselves, always searching for new moves, ways to navigate and assert their own terms on their lives—and always trying to open the door wider for the folks who came later. If they pulled me up to warn me not to be dumb *down there,* or that I had to be a lady in the front room but someone else entirely behind closed doors, from where they stood, this was good instruction. And it is a deep, bluesy tradition that black woman call things as they see them from exactly where they stand.

Charlton Heston and Harlequin Romance novels notwithstanding, they knew no one would come along to rescue you or carry you pliantly into happily ever after—so you better find a way to get there yourself, and that's what they were trying to tell me. But like most of life's hardest lessons, it's something I had to learn in my own time.

When I was young, I didn't know that vile sexual stereotypes had been applied to black people. In many ways, that was part of the cocoon of growing up in black places in the 1970s: we were buffered from some of racism's sharpest edges. It's something Nikki Giovanni writes about in her poem "Train Rides."

> . . . and you will sit near your fire and tell tales of growing up in segregated America and the tales will be so loving even the white people will feel short-changed by being privileged . . .

It wasn't until we moved from Chicago to the largely white suburb of Hazel Crest that I began to deeply understand what being black meant, *in context.* That I began to feel a pervasive sense of otherness. Still, I was in a unique historical place—that first generation born after all major civil rights legislation had been passed—and I never knew the lunch counter racism my mother experienced firsthand. It spawned in me a certain sense of entitlement, in ways good and bad. By the time I was in junior high, we had closed ranks in many instances and abruptly stopped associating with our white playmates from elementary school—and they had stopped associating with us. From a safe distance, we listened as some of the white girls talked about sex and came to school with hickeys (even one girl who was in my honors classes!). Later I watched a couple of them try to date my brother and his friends on the football team. I heard all the nasty things he and his buddies said about them. Of course, when I started hearing about young black girls doing the exact same "nasty" things, in my mind, those were individual acts and didn't have any group implications at all. The protective/repressive cover that was thrown, like a burka, around the middle-class black girls I knew growing up meant we were prone to unfair projections of our own about the deviance of whiteness. It often meant total silence about the implications of our own sexuality. And it meant I went away to college sadly, painfully, naive. And there is much to regret about the girls who are too naive far away from home.

In *Longing to Tell: Black Women Talk About Sexuality and Intimacy*, American studies professor Tricia Rose writes that despite pop culture portrayals of sexually assertive, available black women, it is the cult of silence that is the overarching feature of their sexuality. It is that cult of silence that, for instance, contributes to the horrific statistic that although black women were less than 15 percent of the U.S. female population in 2001, they made up 64 percent of the new AIDS cases among women (that figure had grown to 69 percent by 2003, according to the Center for Disease Control). Rose cautions that the vaunted sexual expressiveness of working-class blacks doesn't necessarily translate into more accurate information and better decision making. She points out that going back to working-class blues traditions and moving forward through hip-hop, whenever art is commodified, an element of excess and exaggeration automatically comes into play. We "should not imagine that working-class black women have all this access to their sexuality," she says. "They bear the burden more explicitly, which is the expectation of a certain level of sexual excess." Some women may embrace that association, because it gives them certain applause and notoriety, but that "doesn't mean they have more agency and freedom."

For me, the net effect of this personal and historical reality has meant silence and shame on one side and talk but no immediately useful information on the other. I was told not to be "fast," but never that men might tell people they had slept with you when they hadn't. I heard I needed to be a bitch in the bedroom, but never that an excessively jealous man might be inclined to hit you. I was warned about being *dumb down there,* but nobody ever said you can't take seven birth control pills in a day to make up for missing a week. So I've suffered from silence and from ignorance in the ways that women suffer. I've had a good hand, but at times, I've still managed to play myself badly. I've landed on my behind sometimes when that was not where I intended to be. And too slowly for my own good, but not too late, I learned to be more self-protective and to learn from my mistakes. This is why now, on the other side, I feel determined not to cede a healthy sexuality. Because, Lord knows, especially for black women, it's been hard to come by. "Revolution begins at home," contends Brooklyn writer Angela Ards. She imagines "Black Love Day," a new national holiday where "instead of boycotts, marches, mass-transportation shutdowns so that white folks can see how much they need us, black people would stay home and make love, as a reminder of how much we need each other."

It's why I keep the conversations with my husband creative and R-rated, except when we're talking about the kids' homework or who's going to wait for the car at Mr. Tire. And why I rarely miss

Saturday date nights with a man I like to call Dr. Feelgood In The Mornin'.

A friend and editor at the *Washington Post* teased me last election night because I complained that the desk where I was assigned didn't have a television, and I asked if he would have one brought in. "I can't even imagine the things your husband must do for you to make you so spoiled," he said. One of my girlfriends once chided me because I fussed about walking through the parking lot, since my husband usually drops me at the door. "See, Ralph's got your ass spoiled," she said. I understand the perception, that in many ways I'm pampered. But I just continue to stand by my final answer: Perhaps, I say, but then you don't know all the things I do for that man.

We met in her office, on a radiant spring morning. Like her husband, Michelle claimed to be totally frazzled, yet she looked remarkably fit, cheerful, relaxed. "I've got a job, and I'm the primary caregiver for two very bright little girls," she said. "It's crazy. It's not realistic."

I asked Michelle about being a political wife.

"It's hard," she said. She smiled slyly. "And that's why Barack is such a grateful man."

My Aunt Ellen always maintained that there was a special place in hell reserved for the women who undercut all our property values by givin' it away free. I sometimes wonder what she'd think of givin' it away for a laptop or a brand-new self-propelled vacuum. Or how about givin' it away just so you can get a little bit back. I wonder what the women on my father's side of my family, most of whom are long gone, would say if they could see that I've been married for twelve years. That I've had a number of painful experiences but I can still find much to love about a night of wine and rose petals.

That I like to bet dirty pretty things over a game of Ping-Pong in the basement.

That I've got a big house and a man who follows me around it from room to room.

My tendency is to want to romanticize, but experience has taught me the value of being clear-eyed, and I won't impose an artificial sentimentality that would dishonor these women's insights. That would suggest that things weren't exactly as they called them, from exactly where they stood. "You sure turned out to be a well paid [wife]," my Aunt Ellen might say.

But standing at a historically different place, a hard-fought place, a personal-as-political place, I would say my life is rich in sensuality and eroticism, especially after dishes, when I'm not exhausted and my two-year-old isn't in our bed. I would say something bluesy-sounding, with a Jill Scott hook, like if I want to go out on a Friday night, I'ma treat you right, daddy, startin' Sunday 'bout noon.

Either that, or I would call up my sexy Aunt Jackie—"I'm not as good as I once was, but I can be as good as I ever was, once"—let her know she always was such a shrewd judge of character.

I 0

When There's Trouble
at Home

Don't start none, won't be none

LAST NOVEMBER, I watched a nightmare sequence on the ABC television drama *Desperate Housewives*. The character Lynette is a former corporate type who gave up her high-powered job to stay home with her four children, and in the sequence, the kids were crying, beating pans together, and ratcheting up the stereo. Lynette yelled at them to *"Stop, stop, why don't you listen, why won't you stop?"* She slammed her fruit bowl to the floor and threw a jar of peanut butter out of the window. When she snapped back to reality and realized she was on the verge of a breakdown, she handed the kids off to a neighbor and sped off in her minivan.

Last year, in an op-ed column for the *Washington Post,* Ellen Goodman wrote that Lynette was a woman of her times:

It's Lynette who speaks truth to power—the power of the updated and eternal myth of momhood.

This "truth" is that even a woman who purposely chooses to be a full-time mom can be one nap away from losing it. The "truth" is that mothers who would throw their bodies in front of a truck for their children also fantasize about throwing their kids in front of a truck. Okay, a little wooden truck.

I related to that *Desperate Housewives* scene because sometimes I feel on the verge of a nightmare sequence of my own. Sometimes I wonder if I'm the only one in my house with vision powerful enough to see the socks lying on the dining room floor or the cornflake fossilizing in the corner of the kitchen. Sometimes there are so many people tugging at my hand, so many chores that require my attention, I can almost feel my body chemistry changing, telling me urgently it's time for fight or flight. There are times when my husband needs so much of my attention, he attacks even my briefest periods of quiet with a constant barrage of words. There are mornings when all three of my children call me so incessantly that I hate the sound of myself coming from their lips. *Mommy! Mommy! Mommy! Mommy! Mommy! Mommy! Mommy!* they call over and over again, until I want to scream *What? What? What? What? What? Shit! What?* Then, in my nightmare, my six-year-old cries and I want to comfort her because I know she's feeling hurt and abandoned, but in that moment, I cannot, because my margins are overrun. Because there is not enough air in my lungs for the measured softness of comforting words, there are too many programs open in my head, and patience requires more memory than I have available. Then I start to cry too, because now I know how my mother must have felt, but, my Lord, don't I know how my daughter feels as well.

The episode of *Desperate Housewives* ends with Lynette crying in the arms of her girlfriends. "Why didn't anybody tell me?" she implores as they try to soothe her. In her 1998 *Washington Post* essay "Nobody Can Tell You," writer Cecelie Berry talks about the hard, lonely parts of motherhood we're not supposed to mind. She gives voice to her depression, the "bastard child" of her affair with domesticity, she says, and rages against a slow, agonizing erosion of herself. It is true of marriage and true of motherhood as well, there are some things you don't know until you're well into it. And sometimes that feels way, way too late. Sometimes, when there's trouble at home it is run through with ache and bitter disappointment. I always swore my household would be free from fights with my husband and hollering at my kids, but too often, my very best efforts aren't nearly enough to stifle the angry words rising in my throat.

Growing up, there was weekly yelling in my house. Momma yelled at Daddy for drinking and running around and Daddy yelled at Momma because he was an alcoholic and a paranoid schizophrenic and his sickness always caused him to see her with men who weren't there. In good times, my parents bragged to relatives that I was bright and they affectionately called me Fifi because Momma says I was always such a prissy thing. But when I was reluctant with Saturday chores, or I needed Momma to listen to me when she was tired, my parents would sometimes snap angrily, cutting me with their words, accusing me of being lazy and too demanding. Still, both the yelling and the praise was secondary to the sustained periods of being largely unnoticed. Of being mostly unable to compete for attention with my father's alcohol abuse and mental illness; and my mother's depression. Of getting so little feedback that sometimes I would hurt myself, just to double-check that I had mass and took up space. I also wasn't yelled at a lot because, until adolescence, I was too timid to do anything that would get me into trouble. And I sometimes try to explain to my own kids how easy they have it—how when I was a child, there was zero tolerance for attitude or protest in the house I lived in and all the places I visited. "Mommy, what would happen if you talked back?" my ten-year-old daughter Sydney, acting as her own attorney, once wanted to know. Because she actually, sometimes, gets to enter into negotiations with her parents and often lobbies for more favorable terms.

"We didn't talk back," I told her.

"But what would happen if you did?" she persisted. And even after thinking hard, I could not come up with an answer. I didn't know what would have happened, I tried to tell her, because talking back was not something that existed in the realm of the possible when I was a child. It was not even a concept, so any violation felt beyond my capacity to fathom. That nonconcept is part of a couple of distinct schools I come from when it comes to discipline in my house now and the one I grew up in. They are schools with some parts I deeply want to keep and other parts I am yet hoping to overcome.

Although whippings are decried and sometimes even criminalized in places where methods of modern, mainstream parenting are debated, except for very recently, I've always known black families to be harsh disciplinarians. To yell and especially to spank (except in black places, the verb was to "whup" and it was usually done with a belt). Physicality was an inviolate part of the routine of families: kisses when you were good, pain when you weren't. My momma tells a story about inviting a little white girl from her neighborhood to their house for dinner when she was young, and making an exaggerated production of chewing her food and rolling her eyes at the table to make her friend laugh. "Okay, Betty Lou, that's enough," my genteel Grandma Mabel warned her. But Momma continued. "All right, that's enough," Grandma Mabel warned again, but after a brief interlude Momma was right back at it. Grandma Mabel didn't warn her a third time. She reached over and slapped Momma's face so hard that the food flew from her mouth and landed against the wall. Then they all finished dinner without further incident.

In her *Washington Post* article, "A Good Whuppin'?" my colleague and friend Deneen Brown writes about the commonality, folklore, and ritual of punishment in the houses of black folks.

Go outside and pick me a switch. And don't pick a small one either.

That command, for many, is part of being black in America—part of a cultural tradition that sought to steel black children for the world, forge their characters, help prepare them for the pure meanness that waited out there, just because of the color of their skin. Many black parents who whipped felt more was at stake if they did not scourge their children.

Don't get it wrong. The wielding of the switch and the belt and the wooden spoon is not a practice unique to black people. Most races spank their children, especially Southern whites who are fundamentalist Christians. But the stories of beatings done in the name of love, beatings that were endured by many—not all—black parents, are like a familiar song. There are some bad associations with slavery. There are some good associations with survival.

Feminist, abolitionist, and former slave Sojourner Truth had thirteen children and saw nearly all of them sold. That didn't stop her from whipping her kids in the time that she had them. When Truth became a mother, writes Paula Giddings, "she would sometimes whip her child when it cried for more bread rather than give it a piece secretly, lest it should learn to take what was not its own."

She whipped because what do you imagine they did to slaves caught stealing? Black families would whip their kids because white people might kill them. Because the streets could consume them, because the police would jail them.

> Tryin' your best to bring the
> Water to your eyes
> Thinkin' it might stop her
> From whuppin' your behind
> I wish those days could come back once more
> (Stevie Wonder,
> "I Wish")

They whipped because the stakes were high, missteps were costly, and *Stop! Don't!* and *No!* had to mean what they said the very first time since colored people couldn't rely on second chances (as true for Emmett Till as it was for Amadou Diallo). Sometimes, we kids also suspected they whipped us because it felt good to them, because they were horrible and mean and *I hate you!* and *I'm going to run away!* That's sometimes what we were thinking—we just never, ever said so.

In his essay "The Black Belt," journalist and children's book author Fred McKissack describes growing up in St. Louis on a block where his folks' black whuppin' belt had reached legendary neighborhood status. He talks about being a schoolboy and hearing a white kid say to his parent, "I don't feel like cleaning my damn room" and marveling that "all" he got was his mouth washed out with soap. "As recently as the last decade, for a black child to curse at his parent could be reasonably regarded as a suicidal act," McKissack writes. "Indeed, the daring youngster could wind up seeing a

child psychologist and facing the following question, 'Did you in-
tend to end your life when you called your mom a bitch?' "

It was one of those generalized pathologies grown folks whispered in our ears about white kids. *They talk back to their mommas
and their parents don't whup them.* Adults would get mad just thinking about those white kids, and we were made to understand that
none of that would ever be a problem with us. As a child, it was not
uncommon for me to be in a distant part of the house and be sum-
moned by my daddy to fetch a glass of ice water, even if the kitchen
was only a few feet from where he was sitting, or to change the television channel in the days before remotes. This had to be done
quickly, quietly, and most importantly, without the smallest sem-
blance of "attitude," or any physical tic that might possibly indicate
frustration. That meant there was no looking funny, twisting your
lips, or sucking your teeth, and we were not to "even think about"
rolling our eyes.

In the book *Fatherhood,* Bill Cosby writes that his wife, the elegant Camille Cosby, used to threaten to knock their kids "into next
week" and he once told his son, "When I come home Thursday, I
am going to kick your butt." *Today Show* personality Al Roker titled
his book on fatherhood *Don't Make Me Stop This Car,* after an oft-
repeated warning from his own bus driver dad. In his comedy
movie *Delirious,* Eddie Murphy recalls his mother's seemingly
bionic powers at landing a shoe upside his behind. And an unscien-
tific survey of my own close friends and family reveals certain recurrent themes in the threats leveled against us growing up. Routinely,
if an adult didn't appreciate something we were up to, we were
made to understand that they could, at any moment: Slap you silly,
slap you into tomorrow, slap your eyes out of your head, smack you
upside your head, snatch you bald-headed, smack your teeth down

your throat, smack the shit out of you, knock some sense into you, knock your neck to your knees, beat that ass, whup your ass, wipe the floor with your ass, knock your ass out. Break your neck, smack the black off of you. Leave you for dead. Said the luminous actress Debbie Morgan to her young onscreen niece Jurnee Smollet in the 1997 movie *Eve's Bayou,* "I will hurt you."

I remember times when childhood was less sentimentalized and motherhood less saccharine. My cantankerous grandmother, Momma Susie, used to hold babies while an inch of ash gathered on the end of the cigarette she was smoking, hands free, as it dangled from the side of her mouth. And if, on occasion, some bit of ash fell onto the baby's arm, and the baby started to cry, she just dusted it off, changed positions, and said loudly, "Aw, that baby's all right." And it was. A little smudged is all. There was not a soul in my family who ever read Dr. Spock or subscribed to the "Touch Points" theory by T. Berry Brazelton. Times were different and even white kids, who our parents told us got everything they wanted and never got yelled at, were deemed less fragile and more subject to a natural order of inviolate adult rule. Accounts of white schoolmasters and parochial school nuns were dense with stories of harsh corporal punishment, and don't you remember when Charmin or Northern toilet paper commercials featured a white child loading tissue down his pants, to cushion the impending spanking that was coming to his behind?

Some of those times resonate with me now, not because of the physical punishments (or cigarette ash) but despite them. From the time we were very young, we were made to understand that adults were in charge. That life had boundaries and consequences for crossing them. We learned that all eyes in the neighborhood were on us and any grown person, at any time, had the right to correct us, to chastise us, to smack our behinds and send us home crying to

Momma, who would smack us again because Mrs. Phillips had to get after us. Not long ago, I was listening to National Public Radio's *The Diane Rehm Show,* and author Cindy Post Senning, the great-granddaughter of etiquette maven Emily Post, was talking about her book *The Guide to Good Manners for Kids.* When a listener wanted to know how she should handle a neighbor's or relative's recalcitrant child, Senning advised against correcting other people's kids. I thought to myself, those women can't know how the world used to look from the South Side of Chicago or other black places, where neighbors have always relied heavily on each other. While we didn't think anything good about all the folks who could fuss or get us into trouble, even when we were small we could sense that the opposite of love has always been indifference. And all due respect to Ms. Post Senning, but don't I wonder what some of our communities would look like now if everyone was still together, trying to get to the same places, fussing at everyone else's kids.

The harsh discipline was often painful, but in most cases, all that "knocking your ass out" was hyperbole meant to make you think twice about acting up. I never knew anyone who lost facial parts as the result of a good whuppin'. Still, I understand much of that romantic lore is revisionist history and there is a darker, more disturbing side to excessive yelling and harsh physical punishments—to being mostly unnoticed at all. It has shown up in the lives of extended family members who grew up with too little kindness. It has also shown up in my own psyche, in struggles with my family and scars that never fully fade, even with the passage of time. My brother, who was always whipped more harshly and more often than my sister or me, is estranged from us now. It is unclear whether those whippings have anything to do with where he is today, which is nowhere lucid or sane—nowhere anybody who loves him can reach him—it's just clear those whippings must have hurt.

And sometimes the cumulative effect of all our hurts make us too heavy with pain to ever walk with dignity. My house was loud and sometimes unforgiving, and in many ways, that scarred me and made me promise things were going to be different when I had my own kids. I read all the *What to Expect* books, and memorized the book *I Love You This Much*. We decorated a nursery from the pages of a catalog and I told myself I wasn't ever going to spank or yell. For years, that worked just fine, until one day, my policy changed.

When Sydney was fourteen months old, I returned to the *Washington Post* to work as a reporter for the first time, and sent her to a home-based day care a few minutes away. The owner, Mrs. McCorkle, was young, but organized and self-possessed beyond her years. Frequently when I would pick Sydney up, if one of the children was misbehaving, Mrs. McCorkle would just start counting, and that child would cease and desist before she got to ten. Once, Sydney misbehaved while playing with a neighbor's child in the cul-de-sac where we used to live. I started counting and Syd chilled out before I got to six. Wow! said my neighbor, Ranae. What happens when you get to ten? I don't know, I told her. I'll have to call Mrs. McCorkle and ask. I think Sydney was about three when I stopped counting to ten and started to spank.

Since then, the threat of spanking has always loomed disproportionately large in the back of my children's minds, but while whippings are infrequent, sometimes I yell more than I care to admit. Not long ago, I cussed Sydney out on the way back from her ballet lesson. She made us late, she couldn't find her shoes, her body was stiff with attitude, and I spat vicious words until I was spent, and a little ashamed. Good thing there was nobody else in the car with me at the time or I'd have really felt out of control. When I picked her up, I was able to calmly say, "We need to help each other think of ways you can keep your stuff together and we can get out of the house in a more timely fashion," and Sydney agreed. A former neighbor once told me about a girlfriend who called talking about how she was "going to hurt that little bitch." My neighbor asked who she was talking about. Turns out, she was talking about her own six-year-old daughter. We could laugh because that was clearly venting gone over the top. (Kind of like in the old television series *The Honeymooners,* when Jackie Gleason used to tell his wife, "One of these days, Alice. Pow! Right in the kisser!" And that qualifies as classic television.) Because kids try you and cussing out the air or calling a friend to rant gives you time to calm down so sometimes you don't have to say things to your children that are hard to take back. Or frighten them by saying nothing at all.

Try as I might, I don't have the same iron-clad authority as the adults I grew up with, and in many ways I don't want to. My house has an appellate process, it has precocious kids who tell me, "Mom, I don't like it when you yell" and "You hurt my feelings." And I get to say, "Well, I didn't like it when you came downstairs naked." My house has more exchange, more compromise, more kisses, and yes, that often means a whole lot more funny looks and twisted lips; a lot more attitude than ever would have been tolerated when I was young. That's why, sometimes, I've got to get in little people's faces to let them know, "I will knock your eyeballs out of your head." Or maybe I say, "Don't make me tap that sammy," which means "Don't make me spank your butt." I got that one from Vita, in my book club, and it works especially well for the little ones who might find the idea of having their eyeballs violated a little too nightmarish. Later we make up in sentimental e-mails after we've had time to calm down or we go in the living room and try to bring back the love by playing a duet on the piano. Sometime we're too angry to do any of that, but we move on anyway because, really, that's all we can do.

"I Wish," sang Stevie Wonder, and I have wished I was a woman who never yells. Sometimes I wish I weren't a writer, so I wouldn't spend so much time in my head or find it so painful when people tried to pull me out. But mostly, instead of wishing, I find it more immediately useful to know my triggers, to be honest with myself; to work on my patience, and to have people around who can help me vent or check me when I'm tripping. My parenting is a constant calibration of the old-school lessons in accountability and respect (my kids say "yes, ma'am" and "no, ma'am" on the phone ever since I heard a lovely little white girl's impeccable phone manners when I called North Carolina once for a story), tempered by a modern emphasis on feelings and self-esteem. Jacqueline Kennedy once said it doesn't matter what else you do if you don't raise your children well, and I believe that to be true. Beauty fades and the most storied career passes into memory. I talk to my mother nearly every day now, but for a long time our relationship was strained, and it took us years to find our way back to each other. But tomorrow is not promised and I can't count on having years with my kids, so I try to find my way back to them sooner. To say I'm sorry now, in real time, which is the only time we've got, and let them know Momma doesn't always get it right, while they are still little, in the hopes that that immediacy lessens some of the sting. I try not to let our hurts fester long and grow deep between us.

It is something I've learned over long years and painful lessons. They are lessons that apply not only to kids but to husbands as well, because despite my best efforts, despite how different I said my house would be from the house I grew up in, my marriage is one more place where I've yelled more often than I care to admit. And it is one more place where my romantic fantasies don't always square with the wife that I have been. For a couple of years now, I've helped write an occasional column for *Essence* magazine called "Making Love Work." It profiles couples who have weathered hard times and offers their tips on pulling their relationship back together. Friends and relatives often recognize my name in the pages, but Tanzi, a friend of my close friend Stephanie, who sees my husband and me out on occasion, says she skips the column whenever she sees my name. I have the perfect marriage, she tells Stephanie, and who the hell wants to read an article about relationship problems by a woman who has never been through anything? I can see where she might get that. Because as a couple, our public face is always smiling. Because my husband knows my songs and likes to lead me to the dance floor; and I like to walk up and wrap my arms around him from behind. Because we play off each other well and sprinkle color in each other's stories. So I can see where she might think my marriage is perfect.

It's just, she's wrong about that.

Losing my rosebushes was what finally sent Ralph and me to seek professional help for our marriage—that and everything that happened along with the move to our new house. When my daughter Savannah was a newborn and Sydney was four years old, my friend Deneen brought me two tiny rosebushes, no more than bulbs and sticks, to plant in honor of each of them. A deep hearty red one for Sydney, and a beautiful light pink for Savannah. I tended those rosebushes and they grew like my daughters, who could each tell you which one was theirs. I'm sentimental and often try to keep living reminders to mark the times of our lives. When one of my best friends and sorority sister, Valerie Smith Reid, died of breast cancer when I was pregnant with Savannah, I took a cutting from a plant I sent her when her cancer went into remission and we all thought she would live. My Valerie plant sits in my kitchen, reminding me of my friend. I loved the joy and celebration that those rosebushes stood for, and I loved that I had a friend thoughtful enough to give them to me.

When we sold our first house in 2002, I asked to take the rose-bushes, said I wanted it put in our contract. My husband promised he would take care of it. That he would call the guy who still does our lawn before the move, but he didn't get around to it. I asked the day of the move, but things were so hectic, it wasn't a priority. I asked him for weeks after the move, but by that time, he had gotten into a $200 carpeting dispute with the people who bought our house. They were relandscaping, so they just dug up my rosebushes and threw them in the trash.

Those bushes were a part of my first house and my babies and my life as a young married woman. They were a gift of friendship, and why didn't he know how much they meant to me? Why did he leave them so bad-karma strangers could hurt me with their casual disregard. How was it that I was still so unable to make myself heard in this marriage, after so many years? Moving days are always stressful but I had a newborn, and my husband had left all the pack-ing to me and the Señora. It was a busy time for him at work, but I asked him to take a day or two off so that we could make a plan, touch bases, figure out logistics. He wouldn't—but why did I just sit there and play the victim?

By the time we began unpacking, on moving day, I began to re-alize a lot of things had gone wrong. There were the usual nicks on furniture and in the wooden frame to a tapestry from Guatemala, but it was my Grandmother Mabel's broken china that wracked my body with sobs. Dishes that were probably eighty years old had fallen to pieces. They had been passed down from my mother and after surviving so long, I had let them crumble on my watch. "You should have taken them in the car," my husband told me. "I couldn't remember every damn thing," I spat back. "You should have helped me plan. These dishes meant the world to me," I cried. "Everything means the world to you," he countered, his voice alien and ugly with sarcasm and scorn. After many, many battles, it was in those few months after the move that I finally felt empty and defeated. And my husband was as cold and withdrawn as I've ever seen him.

When I was a young bride, no one told me that marriage had seasons. That the marriage you have at year one is not the same marriage at year six or eight or eleven. That some days would feel like St. Tropez and some days would feel like the Gulag. Like my childhood friend Alicia once said, I thought we'd giggle all day and make love all night. No one ever tells you that sometimes you hold on to the institution because it means far more to you than the man. No one said that to me, or perhaps they tried to, and I just wasn't in a place where I could hear them.

Sometimes it seems like I've been married since I was seventeen. Only a few weeks after my college boyfriend and I broke up, I met my husband on Valentine's Day in 1989 at the Howard University Hospital where he was a pharmaceutical representative and I was getting a physical. I was twenty-one years old. We started talking and he mentioned he had a little brother. Said he loved kids and, right then, it flashed through my mind, "I'm going to marry this guy and we're going to have kids." And so we did. But for a while at first, there were a few other relationships he was loath to let go of. This left me jealous and angry. Still, like my momma before me, I was young, *and I had to have that boy.* I used to call my husband "The King" when he'd come visit me at work. Used to get a kick out of talking him up to everyone we met. He was smart, he had played college football, he was a Que, and I always did have a thing for the fraternal men of Omega. He left his W-2 on the table when

we were dating and I fell in love with his salary and benefits. Before
the wedding, somebody I worked with told my friend Stephanie,
"Lonnae's not ready to get married." And he was right. But that's
something else no one could have told me that at the time. I was all
packaged like the magazine and television shows instructed, and I
just wanted to be taken off the shelf. I had an engagement party,
three showers, and a bachelorette party. I had a big wedding and a
big ring on my finger. Our picture was in *Jet* magazine. After all of
that, I thought marriage would be magically delicious.

We married and Sydney came quickly. Then, I became a *Washington Post* reporter. I was meeting people and hanging out after
work, and suddenly I wasn't the little twenty-one-year-old who
liked to make brief appearances on stage before scurrying behind
the curtains, where it was safe. I had a promising career and people
who told me I was good at what I did. I was coming out from behind my shadow. I was growing, but my marriage was stagnate. My
husband grew resentful of this new wife and her bigger world. He
said I wasn't the woman he married. And I grew resentful, because
he was right, I wasn't.

> (Black Thought)
> Yeah, so what you sayin I can trust you?
> (Female Voice)
> Is you crazy, you my king for real
> (Both)
> But sometimes relationships get ill
> (Female Voice)
> No doubt
>
>   (The Roots,
>   featuring Erykah Badu, "You Got Me")

I can't detail all the arguments we had. How many times I'd walked out in my mind and how ready my body was to follow along. I couldn't talk to my husband. That had been one of our recurrent themes, but I don't know if it was because he wasn't listening or because from my daddy's house to my husband's, I had never had much of a voice. I wrote things down so I could know what I thought. I couldn't talk to my husband, so I left a message for one of his best friends asking if we could talk, and I poured all my sadness into my journal, which I carried with me always. Except the day I left it in my bedroom, which is where my husband found it. I didn't want to come home from work that night. I wanted to run away, right then and there, but it's a familiar story to a lot of women. My child was with him, and I couldn't walk away from her or take her from her daddy.

Ever practical, my sister Lisa told me I needed to decide what I was going to do and if I wanted to stay married. She said I should give it a year to try to work things out, then I'd be in a good position to know.

That summer, after a journalism convention in Chicago, I went to see my grandmother, Momma Susie, who was living with my Uncle Ronnie. My complicated, hard-cussing Momma Susie had always cautioned the women in the family to wait until they were thirty and had done some living before getting settled down. But she waited until late in life to give me advice about my own marriage. As I sat at the side of her bed rubbing her hand, she began: "Lonnae, I was married for fifty years. Some of it good, some of it bad, but I wouldn't change nothing. You stay married. There's nothing out there in the streets for you. You find somebody else, they got the same problems, or different ones. You stay married." I nodded and cried and kissed her cold, fading hand. Fifteen minutes after I left her, my Momma Susie died. And since we hadn't spoken in at least two years, she had no way of knowing that my marriage was in trouble. I decided the universe was trying to tell me something that day. And I decided to listen. With all our cards on the table, things got better between my husband and me. Then Savannah came along, then Satchel, then we moved into our new home.

Not long ago, one of my best girlfriends and I were talking about problems in marriage and she said, "You know, black people don't go for all that counseling." I took her point. I grew up seeing couples who stayed together for decades, living in separate bedrooms—couples who would be more likely to smother each other than ever see a therapist. But I'm an advocate of counseling. I've had to face down too many dark things I wouldn't have been able to look at without help. Early in our marriage, I had asked my husband if we could talk to someone, but he had always refused. If we needed to talk to someone, we didn't need to be together, he would say. Later, when he was ready, I was not, because things had gotten better. Finally, after the move, we were both ready, and we decided to go to counseling. The experience has given us better tools and a language for the times when bitter words fail us. Although black couples have the highest divorce rate in the country, says Audrey Chapman, a Washington, D.C., therapist who wrote *Getting Good Loving, Seven Ways to Find Love and Make It Last,* they have been slow to avail themselves of therapeutic remedies. Chapman, who also hosts the long-running radio call-in program *The Audrey Chapman Show,* says men, especially, are more resistant, less inclined to want to have "other people in their business." Black folks "are so hung up on that, it's taken them years and years to come around," she says. Like anything you want to last, marriage takes maintenance, tune-ups, "continual work," says Chapman. "Weekly, monthly, yearly, work."

Shortly after we moved, we were welcomed to the neighborhood by the Taylors, a few doors down, who have three children of their own. She's a psychiatrist, he's a nurse anesthetist, and they're very involved with their church. They're busy people, but they reserve one day a week as a date night for just the two of them. Ralph and I were so taken by this idea that last year we adopted the practice ourselves. For five or six years, Friday nights have been family movie night at the Parkers; now Saturday nights are date nights. Sometimes it's dinner and a movie, sometimes just a drive to a furniture showroom or even Home Depot. The point isn't where we go, just that we make time to be alone, together. As writer Angela Ards puts it:

> There are no set roles. We play to our strengths and pick up the slack. I cook the most, because it's relaxing and I enjoy feeding friends, but he burns in the kitchen most regularly. He also washes dishes, the chore I avoid like the plague, and takes the heavy lifting. At times what looks like tradition is more personal sensibility. . . . We say thanks a lot, which sounds kind of formal but is actually very nice because it's a reminder that we're choosing to love.

I'm glad Stephanie's friend Tanzi thinks I've never been through anything. Because I've never wanted my hardest times to linger on my face. If she thinks I make marriage look easy, it's because I work at it. I work at my marriage and my family when it hurts. I work at it when I fantasize about leaving it all alone. I work at it because I've had to work at everything in my life and I have no expectation that it will ever be any different, because, especially for the black women I've known, it never has been. It is true that there are some things nobody can tell you, but sometimes it is worth it to try.

The move to my new house taught me a couple of things. If you have something that would be unbearable to lose, you have to find ways to take care of it. It's as true for marriages and children as it is for china and rosebushes. I think I've always known that, but it is important and affirming to remind myself daily. We do it with rituals—family dinners, movie nights, and date nights—to sustain us. Sometimes when there's trouble at home, we circle each other warily, waiting to see how it's all going to play out. My husband has a saying for those times, a balm he likes to drop. "Bring back the love," he says. And not always, but more often than not, the love is stronger than all the angry words rising in my throat.

11

The Promises and Perils
of Keeping It Real

More than any other generation before
us, we need a feminism committed to
"keeping it real." We need a voice like
our music—one that samples and layers
many voices, injects its sensibilities into
the old and flips it into something new,
provocative and powerful.

> JOAN MORGAN,
> *When Chickenheads Come*
> *Home to Roost*

AT OUR OLD HOUSE, when my daughter Sydney was a pre-
schooler, she used to love to play with the little white kids, William
and Chrissy, who lived across the cul-de-sac. Their momma, Ranae,
and I were close. We'd swap babysitting favors and sit outside talking and watching the kids play as summer afternoons turned to dusk.

Chrissy was the youngest, so that often made her the perfect,
pliant subject for Sydney's tending. Most especially, Sydney loved to

play in her soft, fine, nearly white blonde hair. She combed it, she brushed it, sometimes she tried to shellac it with Ultra Sheen, and I'd have to pull her up, *Uh-uh, girl, that's just our special thing,* so she'd put the hair grease down. Chrissy was one of the few little white girls on our street, maybe one of the only ones in her day care as well, and one day, as Ranae combed her hair, Chrissy asked her momma if she could please style it in a dozen ponytails with colorful hairballs and matching barrettes, just like all the other little girls around her. "I need to get this child around some white kids," Ranae laughed as she relayed the story.

That's especially funny, because I remember when I had the exact same revelation about my own child.

I live in Prince George's County, Maryland—a place of vast income disparity, although with an estimated average household income of more than $68,000, it is the wealthiest majority-black county in the country. It's a place with a mixed bag of things to offer; a place I've deliberately chosen although I could live almost anywhere in the Washington area I want. I know you can't go home again, but I left the South Side of Chicago as a little girl, and in some ways, it feels like I've been trying to get back ever since.

When we moved from Chicago, the south suburbs of Chicago were mostly white. They turned black quick, but not before a profound sense of alienation settled around my shoulders and the thoughtful parts of my head. I was smart, but I had no comeback for the white girl at my grade school who stood in line and yelled that Timmy Listauskaus acted "just like a nigger." Or for when cute little Robbie Story argued me down, saying there was no way that the beautiful woman on the cover of *Jet* magazine was black. I had eyes. I knew Tina Turner was black, but Robbie was awfully insistent, and being vastly outnumbered by those white kids had a funny way of making you doubt even the things you were sure of.

When I was young, some of the popular black girls said I was a teacher's pet and they didn't want to be around me, so I made several white friends. But by late in the first year of junior high, social sets changed, hormones kicked in, and everybody got much more clannish. Interracial divisions began to surface more keenly. Culture began to assert itself more prominently. I remember one morning before school, my sister excitedly called me into her room. *Come here, you've got to hear this!* Something brand new was playing on the radio.

> to the hip hip hop, a you dont stop
> the rock it to the bang bang boogie say up jumped the
>   boogie
> to the rhythm of the boogie, the beat

The year was 1979, and although "Rapper's Delight" wasn't the first rap song, it was the first rap song to make it all the way from the South Bronx to Hazel Crest, Illinois. I was twelve years old when hip-hop came into my life and began to shape my politics and perceptions and aesthetics. It gave me a meter for my thoughts and bent my mind toward metaphor and rhyme. I couldn't sing a lick, but didn't hip-hop give me the beginnings of a voice. About the time rap music hit Hazel Crest, all the black kids sat in the front of my school bus, all the white kids sat in back, and the loudest of each often argued about what we were going to listen to on the radio or portable boom box. Music was code for turf and race in the integrated, mostly-white-but-heading-black south suburbs of Chicago; it was primal and powerful beyond our ability to understand its power. So one day, our bus driver tried to defuse tensions by doing without the radio and disallowing boom boxes. But there was something in the air in those days. A few years later it would show up in the surprise 1983 election of Harold Washington as Chicago's first black mayor, and the sustained backlash afterward. But on the front of my school bus in 1979 it showed up in a song. Left without music, one afternoon some of the black kids started singing "Rapper's Delight." Within a couple of lines we all joined in.

Now what you hear is not a test—I'm rappin to the beat

Then the white kids started in on their own: "Dis co sucks, dis co sucks, dis co sucks, dis co sucks," they chanted, although we hadn't imagined that what we were singing was disco. They got louder: DIS CO SUCKS, DIS CO SUCKS, DIS CO SUCKS.

And we got louder too:

SEE I AM WONDER MIKE AND I'D LIKE TO SAY
   HELLO
TO THE BLACK, TO THE WHITE, THE RED, AND
   THE BROWN, THE PURPLE AND YELLOW

Then the white kids started yelling, raising their voices until their faces suffused with color: DIS CO SUCKS! DIS CO SUCKS! DIS CO SUCKS! DIS CO SUCKS!

And so we started yelling the rhymes I still know to this day, some of which my kids know and, I bet, so do some of the kids of those white kids who screamed at us from the back of my junior high school bus, raging against change, raging against black people, or, who knows, maybe just not appreciating our musical stylings.

WELL I WAS COMIN HOME LATE ONE DARK
   AFTERNOON

A REPORTER STOPPED ME FOR A INTERVIEW
SHE SAID SHE'S HEARD STORIES AND SHE'S
   HEARD FABLES
THAT I'M VICIOUS ON THE MIKE AND THE
   TURNTABLES . . .

DIS CO SUCKS! the white kids yelled, but they were demateri-alizing in front of our eyes. Because "Rapper's Delight" was a tale, nearly fifteen minutes in the telling, and we were in another world, transported by the beat and the collective sound of our own raised voices. Transfixed by our newfound ability to drown out all that nullification, *She's too pretty to be black. Timmy, you act just like a nigger. DIS CO SUCKS!* When I listened to hip-hop, I couldn't hear any of that at all, because as California State professor and au-thor Tricia Rose, the first person in the country to write a disserta-tion on hip-hop, writes in her book *Black Noise*, it's a cultural expression that prioritizes black voices.

I grew older and my love affair with rap music continued. I rapped to the Sugar Hill Girls, I rapped to Kurtis Blow, I rapped to Grandmaster Flash and the Furious Five. I learned all the rhymes they played on black radio, because do you remember when MTV wouldn't touch black music at all? Then when I got to college, thanks to my boyfriend and all the folks we hung with, I started getting my beats underground, which is where I stayed to find my hip-hop treasures. The B-I-G D-A-D-D-Y K-A-N-E, Salt-N-Pepa, MC Lyte, Whodini, Eric B. & Rakim, Dana Dane, EPMD, A Tribe Called Quest, all the B sides of LL Cool J. I was young and hungry and hip-hop was smart, and like Nena Cherry said, we were raw like sushi back then, sensing we were onto something big, not real-izing how easily it could get away from us.

In college, I used to be the only Alpha Kappa Alpha sorority girl on the yard who knew all the words to the NWA song "Dopeman" ("Gold around his neck in 14K heaven . . ."). I still remember them, along with a number of cuts from their seminal, underground album, *Straight Outta Compton,* and I suspect, although I could be wrong, that may make me one of the only reporters in the country who's covered a state dinner at the White House who could make this claim. And that feels like a metaphor for all the places my head can go on any given day.

From Shogun to Raygun / Rock me Amadeus / Parsley, Sage, Rosemary and Thyme / Rebecca, Lolita, Deshawn and Dawn / On & on & on & on my cipher keeps movin' like a rolling stone . . .

I grew up, equally, a black girl in a colored world punctuated by shades of white and a colored girl in a white world sustained by black thoughts. My duality is organic, and it has served me in myriad ways. When I'm on the phone as a reporter, I can be whichever color I want (although it is possible that all those vowels in my name, L-o-n-n-a-e, might give me away). I called down to Georgia for a story once. I let all traces of black accent fall from my voice. I have no doubt the state senator thought he was talking to a young white reporter, and that's why he invited me to his house to see his granddaddy's Confederate flag. But when I'm in a long line at the Taco Bell on 14th Street in Washington, my gestures, my words, my beats all come rushing back to me: my black is perfectly pitched, and so are all my shades of gray.

In a 1997 *Washington Post* essay on Ebonics, I wrote: "At work, I can toggle between software applications in a keystroke. I am constantly reading, researching and importing text between applications with different rules, different aesthetics, different sets of assumptions. It kind of reminds me of what black people in this country do all the time. I spend my days alt-tabbing through competing realities." Like the women in Charisse Jones and Kumea

Shorter-Gooden's book *Shifting*, I code-switch constantly: "shifting White, then shifting Black again, shifting corporate, shifting cool." But in many ways my shifts are even more existential. I consider myself thoroughly bicultural, and arguably bilingual, but not because I speak passably conversational Spanish. It's because I can jog up one side of the culture and sprint down the other. "I can talk Dante, and Brontë but you know I gots to bring a lil' Ha'y Belafonte. And y'al be straight sleep on that Roxanne Shante," I wrote in that Ebonics essay. Musically, I have a deep knowledge of funk, but I've always had more than a little doobie in my funk. (*Can you imagine doobie in your funk?*) That's because when we lived in Chicago, my daddy used to keep the kitchen radio locked on lite rock. "Listen children to a story that was written long ago," I sang along to "One Tin Soldier" and The Carpenters' "Rainy Days and Mondays" always spoke to my personal melancholy.

In the decade after the civil rights movement helped lift black families to better-paying jobs and restrictive housing covenants began to fall away, we moved to the suburbs, becoming part of a mass exodus of black folks chasing the promise of better things. And there is much we gained, but it feels like we lost a lot as well. I managed to hold on to my soul after the move, although at times it almost got away from me. Because I could see the advantages of greater numbers and some great rewards on the other side. And I could see some of me. But sometimes to get to that side, you had to give up too much, and even as a girl, I sensed that the price for crossing over was too high. That if I went swimming in the deepest waters of the mainstream, I might lose my beats and history and insights. I might not be able to get back to a shore I recognized, or I might not be able to recognize myself because the waters had changed me. So when we moved, I kept my colored lenses, but sampled heavily from everything that interested me. I soaked up the added opportunities offered by the well-funded suburban schools I attended. I thrived under elementary teachers whose weekly current events competitions instilled in me a passion for news. Oh, the places my mind could go just as long as it could always find home. But for some black children, the distance, psychic and otherwise, was just too far.

In her essay "Young, Black and Too White," journalist Karen Grigby Bates talks about the unforeseen consequences of integration: "We began to notice that our kids weren't, well, as black as we had been," she writes, lamenting the irony of black children who are privileged but unmoored from the history and struggle of previous generations—children who don't have colored friends and don't date colored people, who've gained exposure and material things but who have lost some of the most soulful parts of themselves.

"At lilac evening I walked with every muscle aching among the lights of 27th and Welton in the Denver colored section, wishing I were a Negro, feeling that the best the white world had offered was not enough ecstasy for me, not enough life, joy, kicks, music, not enough night," wrote Jack Kerouac, the most famous of the early 1950s nonconformist Beat writers, in his book *On the Road.*

It kind of reminds me of a very funny essay I ran across on the Internet not long ago. Writer Ashok Mathur contends that my beloved sitcom characters, Samantha in *Bewitched* and Jeannie in *I Dream of Jeannie,* are actually "racialized others passing in white-drag," or as author Nalo Hopkinson puts it, "white stand-ins for women of color in mixed-race marriages." Instead of race, it is their magic that Darrin and Major Nelson insist on keeping under wraps so they can hold on to their good jobs and good reputations. It's their magic, Mathur says, that has to be hidden and denied to preserve their white, middle-class normality and keep them from embarrassment and possible persecution. It sounded like an implausible supposition until I thought about how familiar it all seemed. How, despite their best efforts, a little of Samantha and Jeannie's witchcraft was always breaking through, upending tables and levitating lamps. How Darrin always worried how much witch would turn up in his kids. And didn't Samantha and Jeannie both have those crazy relatives always popping up, irritated that they had chosen to pass for mortal and intent on causing trouble. I even remembered an episode where Jeannie's "master," Major Nelson, forbade her from ever using her magic again, and she slowly began to disappear—to die from sadness. And I wonder if that isn't the kind of thing that could happen to black people if we don't deliberately hold on to some magic of our own.

I used to think the saddest thing in the world was to be black and to feel uncomfortable in a room filled with black people. To be insufficiently inoculated against Miss Clairol commercials, where the model tosses her auburn highlights and dances to black music, reminding us that the Isley Brothers were once made to feature white lovers on the front of their albums; reminding us that there's always been a place for black culture in white face. The push for civil and women's rights were about choices. But now those choices are more complicated and require greater deliberation. My sister, who has always lived in largely white suburbs, has been less deliberate in her own choices, and in many ways that makes me profoundly sad. I fear sometimes my niece thinks she's the only supersmart, beautiful black girl on the planet. And my handsome twenty-year-old nephew has never had a self-professed black girlfriend in his life. They have been culturally underexposed, and so their perspectives, and their choices, are less well informed. I believe we get to find love wherever it is good for us; it's just sad that that might mean fewer people to help my daughters fashion a healthy self-concept or that some of our family traditions may wither on the vine. As Vertamae Smart-Grosvenor writes in *Vibration Cooking*, "That love of your tribe is important, and if it doesn't happen in childhood, I don't believe you can acquire it."

One of my best friends from college, Julie, an educator at a charter school, is a world traveler. I still wear the shirt she gave me from Singapore. For a little over a year I'd get postcards from Vietnam or Italy or the opera house in Sydney. She takes weekend trips to London, and a couple of years ago, she and a small group of friends celebrated her sister's thirtieth birthday by renting an apartment in Paris, along the Seine River across the bank from the Tour Eiffel. But for all the places Julie has been, she lives in a building she bought deep in the historic Bronzville neighborhood of Chicago's South Side. "I like a black world, with the option to travel," she once said to me, and that feels like the kind of healthy, love-of-self and deep-appreciation-for-others perspective I've vowed to try to give to my own kids. Which is nice. Except, affirmation and warm feelings notwithstanding, there is, of course, a dark side to all that black culture. And no matter where you live, there are some messages that can't be filtered.

Not long ago I was driving and six-year-old Savannah was in the back seat mouthing words to herself. "What are you back there talking about, Savvy?" I asked. She just continued mouthing words, rocking back and forth, baring her little teeth and looking subversive. "Savvy, what you are saying?" I asked again, and she finally got loud enough for me to hear. "E'rybody in the club gettin' tip-sy. E'rybody in the club gettin' tip-sy," she rapped. Right. "Where did you hear that song?" I asked, but I already knew. That Daddy had been listening to unauthorized radio with the girls in the car again. I made a point to remind him later not to do that. To remind him that the girls were not allowed to hear even fairly innocuous songs from nonapproved stations. Although rocking back and forth, listening to the radio is one of the most evocative memories of my childhood, I rarely let my own children listen to urban contemporary radio at all. And, increasingly, I don't bother with it much myself.

My friend Stephanie is friends with a popular local DJ in Washington. She was riding home midafternoon listening to his station once when she heard a lyric from the Terror Squad that made her call him immediately.

> She said "Daddy let me take ya home,
> Papi let me take ya home"
> And I said "Mami you can take me home if you let the
>   whole crew get on" (bitch)

"What, are you kidding me?" Stephanie asked her friend the DJ. Why, she wanted to know, was that entreaty to gang-bang a song lyric. And why would the station play that lyric midafternoon when her eleven-year-old daughter could be listening and could think this might be a way to get some guy she likes to spend time with her. "I was so disgusted," Stephanie says. I understood her outrage. I passed it a long time ago. These days, I am headed full speed toward numb.

In the October 2004 issue of *Essence* magazine, Michaela Angela Davis, an *Essence* beauty editor and one of the founding editors of *Vibe* magazine, writes about her own complicated decision to quit hip-hop. This forty-year-old mother of thirteen-year-old daughter likens it to a painful, unexpected breakup. "Many popular hip-hop CDs and videos feature a brand of violence and misogyny that is as lethal as crack and as degrading as apartheid," she writes, and she can no longer risk sacrificing her daughter's self-esteem and that of other young girls for dope beats and tight rhymes. *Essence* has since begun a comprehensive, yearlong look at the ways black women are depicted in popular music.

I've written enough stories on hip-hop to understand some of the large, powerful forces that influence the songs in play. Black culture, created in response to specific political, social, and economic conditions, is the raw material for much of what becomes American popular culture (can I get a high five anyone?). It gets appropriated and commodified, and, in the case of hip-hop, certain aspects like violence, sex, and materialism are rewarded by record companies with splashy packaging and trucks full of cash. Several years ago, for a *Washington Post* article on whites in hip-hop, I quoted Dave "Davey D" Cook, a Berkeley grad whose self-titled website is one of the most expansive hip-hop sources. He said that urban mythology gets repackaged and sold back to the black community and the larger society as the dominant reality. That in turn alters what gets produced, as blacks abandon much of their creativity and political expression to conform to what gets paid, and that changes the reality on the ground. I once heard the talented rapper Calvin Broadus, "Snoop Doggy Dogg," tell an interviewer that rap hadn't crossed over to pop, it was pop that came to the streets. I'm unclear if this was before or after I saw the photo of heiress Paris Hilton jumping into his arms.

At the 2003 MTV awards, Snoop and popular rapper 50 Cent embellished their performance of the song "P.I.M.P." by featuring black women on leashes being walked onstage. I have to say, I've been on a number of streets, but even the most trifling black places would not allow brothers to put dog collars on women's necks and walk them around the yard. It is a useful piece of fiction to say this is street, this is hard-core, this is "realer than Real Deal Holyfield," but as academic and author Mark Anthony Neal points out, it is young white men who are the primary consumers of hip-hop. In 1999, I cited a SoundScan marketing firm report that 70 percent of all R & B and rap is bought by whites, accounting for 81.3 million rap albums sold that year. In 2002, rap was the second most popular music genre, accounting for a 13.8 percent share of all music purchases. It's not streets that have had the most enduring influence on hip-hop culture, it's money, just like the most corrupt and pervasive aspects of the larger culture. Still, I wonder if the rappers who are serving up all the hos and bitches and guns are moved at all by the fact that it's not whites who are shooting up their neighborhoods, trying to be hard. According to the Sentencing Project in Washington, D.C., it's not one in three white males born today who will spend time in prison during their lifetime. And according to the Centers for Disease Control, it's not whites who were 69 percent of the HIV cases among women in 2003. I wonder, do the dozens of rappers who are better paid than their best-paid [women] ever turn around to see who it is that's pimping them, holding on to *their* leash? I wonder, don't they care about any black children other than their own? Because buying computers for schools or contributing to the Save The Music Campaign is a nice gesture, but, really, it doesn't have the same sway as rhyming about AK-47s. (And just think, [brothers] used to just shoot you with they bop guns.)

"In a community in which the influences of ghetto life permeate everyday life, embracing ghetto styles takes on different meaning for youth who are in predominantly White middle-class neighborhoods," says Mary Pattillo-McCoy. "Sometimes when you dress like a gangsta, talk like a gangsta and rap like a gangsta often enough, you are a gangsta."

My mind goes down a separate corridor for the women who help make all the shooting okay. I would say to Destiny's Child, to

Kelly, Beyonce, and Michelle, who I like and my daughters adore, ENOUGH with the soldier already. Their 2004 song featured these lyrics:

> If his status ain't street I ain't checking for him . . .
> Gotta know to get dough and he better be street . . .
> I know some soldiers in here
> Where they at, where they at
> Don't mind taking one for me

Taking one what, ladies? A bullet? Soldiers kill or they get killed, and don't you think, don't you think, don't you think, black people have had enough of all that? If I thought it would do any good, I would say to the sisters I understand your sexuality is a source of power and who among us wants to turn away from power? I would say I don't have easy answers for what could replace it, because black people don't get it easy, but together can we find ways of celebrating and empowering you without killing ourselves? I'm just asking, holla if you hear me, because I believe Tupac was smart and thoughtful and more complicated than his repeated proclamations about thug life suggest, but it doesn't really matter, he's just as dead.

I wonder about the women who further validate the most destructive aspects of the culture by signing up to be the bitch in the middle or the freak in the back on videos and awards shows. As Joan Morgan points out, "only when we've told the truth about ourselves, when we've faced the fact that we are often complicit in our oppression, will we be able to take full responsibility for our lives." There has always been a dearth of opportunities for black women in the entertainment industry, often forcing them into stereotypical, one-dimensional roles if they want to work steadily. Still, their choices have consequences. And I wonder about Megan

Good, that beautiful young woman from the movie *Eve's Bayou* who nodded vapidly in the rap video a couple of years ago when a rapper asked would she wait for him to get out of jail. I'm wondering, will she be waiting for all the black women's sons, the thirteen-, fifteen-, and seventeen-year-olds, who were watching that video and are persuaded that jail will just add to their cool, because, after all, the prison rape scenes are always deleted in videos, no? On behalf of mothers with sons, I would ask her not to use her beauty in ways that help further mainstream black boys in evil places. And on behalf of mothers with daughters, I would ask her to want more for herself and for all the little girls who daydream of being just like Megan.

If I thought it would do any good, I'd write an open letter to some of the rap stars. Because as Danyel Smith, author and former *Time* magazine editor and editor-in-chief of *Vibe* magazine, points out, "We were so happy that black men were having a chance to speak their truth," that with the exception of a handful of female rap acts, we've gone too long without challenging them on their myth-making—without consistently inserting ourselves into the conversation. And perhaps now, hip-hop is too far gone. I'd quote Smith in my letter, as well. "I understand the poetry, I do, the depression, I do, the futility, I do." I'd say I understand the need to be seen, paid, and celebrated to make up for hundreds of years of nothing much at all. I appreciate that you've come a long way and in many ways changed the world, or at least Madison Avenue, so if I start off by giving you props, would it make a difference? If I talk about how well you can rap and rhyme and point out that your budget for clothes and jewels gives a decidedly ethnic bent to millionaire style—if I acknowledge, no doubt, you've got the baddest girlies and they save all their freakiest moves for you alone—if I *genuflect* when I see you, would this be enough to ask, humbly, in the spirit of dead black teenagers, can some of you please, please rap about something else?

"I never thought we'd get here," Michaela Angela Davis says sadly, making me remember my own boundless enthusiasm at all the beats that used to run through my head. But you can't stay in something that hurts you, she says. "It's like a family member who is hooked on drugs. . . . Hip-hop is lost and it's got to find its own way back." And this is why I mostly turn from urban contemporary black radio and will myself not to care. Because I don't like men who dislike women. Because my fingers aren't quick enough to change stations and I never know what kind of madness and crude comments black folks are going to spout over the airwaves, what kind of lyrics they are going to play. And like Davis, I can't risk that for my kids. So as much as I love black voices, there is a redacted portion in the soundtrack to my own kid's lives. And in that blacked-out space, I loop Stevie Wonder, New Edition, and En Vogue. I spend money on A Tribe Called Quest CDs for Christmas, and I continue to search the aisles for Salt-N-Pepa and Heavy D; for Queen Latifah's *Ladies First* and *2Hype* by Kid 'n Play. "Mommy, is that the Ohio Players," Savannah might ask from the back seat. "No, darling, I believe that's One Way, featuring Al Hudson," I reply. I fill my kid's lives with contemporary artists I respect and the coolest, most conscious, most "bang-bang the boogie say up jump the boogie" songs from when hip-hop and I were young. It is revisionist history, I know, but sometimes, I swear, I just prefer to remember black people the way we were. Engaged, grappling, reaching for the positive, or even, you know, just trying to have a good time.

Of course, some of the same things could be said about a lot more than hip-hop. And like the music that has spun out of control, I also struggle with how much I want to expose my children to other aspects of black culture, even extending to some of our most revered institutions. Although my mother often quoted scriptures and grew up as a weekly churchgoer, I grew up attending church just enough to learn prayers and hymns and rituals. To learn the Old Testament stories of Noah, and, certainly, Shadrach, Meshach, and Abednego, delivered by God from the furnace of King Nebuchadnezzar. Enough to attend vacation Bible school, Bible camp, and to remember one of my most fervent prayers was that Momma wouldn't "get happy" in the aisles, hyperventilating and calling forth the nurses with their Dr. Martin Luther King Jr. fans, or calling attention to me. Now, with my own family, we attend church infrequently, mostly on major Christian holidays, although we try to make a search for spirituality part of our daily routine. I often think about returning to the remembered rituals of Sunday morning—the old church mothers, the young people's choir, the hats, the Word. As Patrick Henry Bass and Karen Pugh write in *In Our Own Image: Treasured African-American Traditions, Journeys, and Icons*, missing church can feel like missing one of the oldest, most resonants parts of yourself. It's just sometimes I don't recognize the black church I'd be returning to.

Few institutions are as deservedly venerated as the black church and the righteous black worshippers who sustained themselves through slavery and Jim Crow, then fueled a movement and changed the country. In *This Far by Faith,* authors Juan Williams and Quninton Dixie write:

> Black men and women used personal faith to claim a church that was founded by whites and initially antagonistic to blacks.
>
> The influence of the church on the United States' Civil Rights movement stands out for the same reasons that made the church an agent of change in Poland, South Africa, and

El Salvador. The church offered money, a protective structure for organizing, and leaders who used the skills they had honed in the pulpit to provide direction to the movement. And in time the black church produced the leaders, the structure and the vision for the greatest social movement in U.S. history.

Lord knows, we could use some of that old-time, activist religion right now.

Last year, I was at a meeting where Prince George's County officials had been invited to talk about schools. Despite the county's relative affluence and educated black leadership, the school system ranks second to last in performance standards among the twenty-four systems in Maryland. Blaming a lack of revenue, one state senator offered that at some point, citizens were going to have to consider all the new church construction that was gobbling up prime real estate and potential tax dollars. "I'm not antichurch or anything," this official said quickly, defensively, "but it's something we've got to think about." The audience remained mostly quiet. On a recent visit from Illinois, one of my cousins also observed, "There sure are a lot of churches around here," and he was right. According to a 2004 story by *Washington Post* colleague Ovetta Wiggins, Prince George's County has 1.5 religious institutions per square mile, the overwhelming majority of which are churches that seem to compete for grandness and amenities. And signs announcing new ones go up all the time. This wouldn't be a bad thing except that even with the advent of all these churches, a lot of black people don't seem to be doing that much better.

Sometimes as I ride past the county's grandest sanctuaries, I close my eyes, but I can't say I feel God in these places. I don't sense humility. "Jesus loves the little children," the song says, and many of these churches have schools, but of course all of them charge tuition. And to date, no two of the nearly eight hundred churches in the majority black county where I live have gotten together to build a free, overflow *school* open to all the ill-served, undereducated little children Jesus loves here. That might be too difficult, but they also haven't coordinated sufficiently to establish a free, weekly, county-wide tutoring night to make the resources and smarts of all those African American professionals available to the children coming behind them. Instead, many nearby churches and megachurches seem more engaged in the national phenomena of "prosperity theology," which means, according to a 2004 *Dallas Morning News* article, "many of the most prominent black churches now focus mainly on building wealth." (The churches near my house are certainly prosperous. Their lots are filled with luxury cars, and every year I get a flyer telling me how to get my fifty-dollar tickets for a Christmas program filled with the spirit.)

David Person, a race, religion, and cultural values columnist for the *Huntsville Times* in Alabama and on BlackAmericaWeb.com, says it's critical to understand the black church's evolution. It remains the singular black institution that has grown and thrived mostly outside of white influence, support, or control. It has been a proving ground for black leaders who have not traditionally had access to leadership in other venues. He cites the fact that blacks have become more prosperous as a people: According to the December 8, 2004, *Washington Post* article "A Tenuous Hold on the Middle Class," from 1967 through 2003 the median household income for blacks has increased nearly 50 percent. And not unlike other aspects of black culture, that new money has helped shape some of the church's agenda. "What's happened, I think, is that prosperity gospel has become codified and ritualized so that in the black community, it seems to be the primary driving force for what is passing for ministry. The idea that financial success and well-being is almost elevated to being a virtue; a measure of faith," Person says. "It's become nearly as important as more historically spiritual issues like how we treat other people, personal behavior and the prophetic kinds of concerns like social justice, poverty, helping orphans . . . making sure everyone has the opportunity to live in fair and just society." It is part of what scholar Cornel West decries as the lack of visionary black leadership in his 1994 treatise, "Race Matters."

I remember talking with a woman at my daughter's dance class several years ago who said she received a flyer from one of the country's largest churches inviting her family to "come worship on our marble floors." This sounded to both of us especially obscene, but it wasn't until a few years later that some of my dismay hardened. In October 2002, the Dawson family of East Baltimore, two parents and five children, were murdered in a fire set by a drug dealer the family had repeatedly reported to police. The Dawsons had been trying to hold on to their home, their community, their kids, their street, but two weeks before the fatal fire, someone had tossed two Molotov cocktails into their kitchen and the family barely escaped. After that, they were trying desperately to move somewhere safe.

Angela Dawson found a low-income house and was scrambling to try to make the down payment when the drug dealer, who was later convicted of the killings, kicked open the door and poured gasoline around the family's escape routes before lighting a match. The city of Baltimore was traumatized after these murders. So was I. And I was profoundly angry. All those grand churches, some of the largest in the country, located between Baltimore and Washington, nearly eight hundred in Prince George's County alone, and all I could think of was, Why weren't their doors open to provide sanctuary? Why couldn't it be common knowledge on the streets that the Dawsons, or any family in need, could go to any of these churches, especially the black ones, and seek shelter or the money to move out immediately? Nationally, why aren't black churches, storied institutions that worked together to help change a country, a tangible daily presence on the meanest black streets?

In Prince George's County, there is a consortium of churches that serves twelve thousand lunches a year, four days a week, to homeless individuals and families; they operate a revolving loan fund that helps prevent hundreds of families from being evicted. Other individual churches operate drug treatment facilities on part of their sprawling campuses. They run training programs for welfare mothers, and there is a partnership with the local state attorney's office to provide a safe haven for battered women. It's not that churches aren't, in many creative and inspired ways, undertaking the hard, humble work of community restoration. It's just that given their immense size, their unprecedented wealth, their deep reach, their storied history and organizational capacity (and their luxury cars, Learjets, mansions, and national television programs), it's simply "not enough to say, well, we've got a prison ministry or we feed the homeless," says Person. Because black people are hungry for so much more.

It can be a difficult proposition for people of all colors and denominations to raise concerns about the church. As that Maryland state senator's defensiveness in the school meeting I attended demonstrates, for blacks, who, as a people, have been largely sustained by black churches, this is even more painfully true. But every healthy institution requires dialogue, exchange, and self-reflection. The Bible says all have sinned and fall short of the glory of God. And doesn't it seem hollow to decry the excesses of black hip-hop and R & B artists when the black middle class worships material things just as much? In his 1957 critique, *Black Bourgeoisie*, sociologist E. Franklin Frazier maintained that the black middle class had developed the "conspicuous consumption" culture of overacquiring material possessions to compensate for second-class citizenship. According to a 2003 report, "The Buying Power of Black America" by the research firm Target Market News, "while other ethnic groups are growing in population, black consumers are still out-spending all other groups in apparel, food, beverages, cars and trucks, home furnishings, telephone service and travel."

I don't begrudge anyone nice things; it's just that the Dawson family in East Baltimore, two parents and five kids, could have been saved for the price of marble floors. It's just that in the Book of Matthew, in the New Testament of Jesus Christ, the Bible asks, "For what shall it profit a man, if he shall gain the whole world, and lose his own soul?"

Despite school overcrowding and other disappointments, I live in a majority-black county to populate my children's head with memories of all kinds of black people and counter the narrow images in media and popular culture. I live here because when my oldest daughter, who has always gone to predominantly black schools, was six, she may have cried anguished tears because her hair would never wave down her back, but when my youngest daughter was four, and the only little black girl in her preschool class, she came home one day and flat-out said, "I wish I was white." It's a little like when my former neighbor's daughter Chrissy was the only white girl in her class and she pined for twelve ponytails with matching barrettes, except without the weight of history. Because complicated times require deliberate choices, I deliberately expose my kids to a range of black voices, then correct them if their standard English slips into too much vernacular or gets too sassy. I make them repeat a sentence until it sounds good to my ear, the same as my friend Liana's mother did to her, growing up in East St. Louis, the same as my friend Stephanie's mother did to her in Washington,

D.C. "Sydney, repeat after me, the rain in Spain falls mainly in the plains," I say to her. Because there's an appropriate place for Audrey Hepburn and Pam Grier in the lives of my daughters, just as there has been in my own. And continuing in the tradition of my former neighbor Ranae, sometimes I very deliberately say to myself, *let me get these children around some white kids,* so they'll have other images and accents to draw upon as well. I want my kids to have the language of many places fully at their disposal. Because no one voice can speak for the world.

I live in a majority-black county because when my son Satchel was a year and a half, my good friend Dana took him to her mostly white office Christmas party where everyone was entertained by his precocious busyness. One ten-year-old said to Dana, "He's a big guy, what's he going to be when he grows up, a rapper?" Perhaps—or maybe he'll get an MBA from Duke like his father, I thought to myself when I heard the story. I don't think this kid meant to suggest anything untoward or circumscribed about Satchel's options at all, it's just that, so what? I don't have the time or inclination to deflect the energy even well-meaning folks will heap on my black son. It's just that I deeply understand, after so many messages, whether intentional or not, Satchel could begin to internalize other people's narrow expectations of him. And I want his world to brim with possibilities.

Sometimes it feels like we're part of a grand American experiment, where, to a greater degree than ever before, we get to pick and choose the things we want to show our kids. We can take them to the Smithsonian to hear freedom songs from the civil rights movement or go for chili dogs on Washington's historic U Street so they can hear the beauty in black working-class voices as well. We take them around black kids who are both more well off and less well off than they will ever be to reduce the psychic distance between themselves and kids who grow up in different worlds, but may have beauty and insights and talents to offer. For years, the girls have socialized with the smart, sweet, home-schooled white girls (and a handful of black ones) they see several times a week at ballet, while the hours I spend talking to their mommas has been one of the genuine highlights of my own week. And last Hanukkah, Savannah was invited over to light candles by her schoolmate and buddy, six-year-old Pearl, "Pearl Girl," who lives across the street. We returned the favor by inviting her over to light a candle for Kwanzaa and because it was Kuumba, the sixth night, a celebration of creativity, Pearl did an interpretive dance in the living room as Sydney and Savannah and I alternated playing Christmas duets on the piano. Sometimes I marvel at the breadth of experiences we've been able to bring into our lives. But sometimes it feels like such an uncharted place that I'm standing in—that I'm broadcasting from a narrow bandwidth, or, more accurately, that my parenting is as ger-rymandered as a voting district in Texas. But I am a product of my times, grounded in both culture and middle-class entitlement, driven to peel off the best parts of all the worlds I know and desper-ate to try to avoid the worst. And only time will tell what sticks with my children.

Sometimes I walk into the black bookstore near my house and one of the associates, LeRoyal, greets me, "Good morning, queen." And no matter how harried my day, his words always feel like a balm; a sweet spot of hip-hop nationalism and naiveté, when we were still delighted at the power and promise of our voices. It re-minds me of the importance of intangibles and makes me remem-ber connections. One day he asked me if I enjoyed living in our part of the county, and I turned the question back on him. "Sure," he said, "but I think some of the folks can be kind of bourgeois."

"Yeah, well some black folks are bourgeois and some of us have other problems," I told him, and we both just laughed. I used to think the saddest thing in the world was to be black but to feel like a foreign correspondent around black people. Now I'm a mother and I look at some of the other black mothers in Washington, D.C., where twice as many people under eighteen were killed in 2004 than the year before, and I think there are some things in the world that are infinitely sadder.

I could live almost anywhere in the Washington area that I want, but I have a dream deeply rooted in the American dream. There's a new development going up near my house. Its part of the "new urbanism," suburban living that's meant to resemble city neighborhoods with porches and parks and community schools. I've been talking it up to friends for years because in my fantasy, when the time comes, all the cool people I know, the best racial and class and consciousness mix I can find, will pick up and homestead in this new place, and maybe it will remind us of thirty years ago, only better. Because seems like we had something once, and in many ways we've lost it, but just perhaps we can get it back again, and this time take better care, because now we know that things fall apart. This dream is deeply contrived, potentially elitist, and perhaps even a little Stepford-sounding, I realize, but in 1967, the year I was born, Martin Luther King Jr. published his last book, *Where Do We Go From Here: Chaos or Community?* And I long for community like I hunger for old hip-hop and activist black churches. If I close my eyes, I can even hear the soundtrack to this new place. It is, of course, remix. A community that sets "Devotion" to the beat of "Ain't No Stopping Us Now," and just keeps adding in powerful, funky new voices and rhythms—a community that never sells us out, no matter who's rapping or preaching, no matter how high the price.

12

Time to Dance

To everything there is a season, and a
time to every purpose under the heaven:

A time to be born, and a time to die; a
time to plant, and a time to pluck up
that which is planted . . .

A time to weep, and a time to laugh; a
time to mourn, and a time to dance

ECCLESIASTES 3:1–2, 4

I DON'T RECALL why I was seething that first night I attended
dance class nearly five years ago. I know my foul temper had something to do with the house or the kids or the job or the groceries. It
was something my husband had done or hadn't done, or perhaps it
was the constant weight of things I had yet to do. I don't remember
specifics—just the sense that there was too much pressing in too
close and my margins were giving way. I felt myself under psychic
attack and very close to snapping.

I had heard about this adult dance class at the ballet school where
I had just enrolled Sydney. I had been intending to check it out for

weeks, and there it was another Thursday, but the last thing I wanted to do was dance. Still, the way I was feeling, my alternatives felt socially unacceptable, so I drove to class. The hour and a half neuromuscular integrative action class was a blend of yoga, ballet, tai chi, and modern dance and was designed to promote fitness, healing, and self-expression. Prior to that, I had taken a couple of classes in hip-hop and modern dance over the years and had been in and out of aerobics and step aerobics classes, but most of my best moves had been limited to clubs and house parties. I hadn't been a good dancer growing up. I didn't have a natural kinesthetic ability, and when I was very young, I was too painfully self-conscious to let go and move.

> I used to go out to paaartays
> and stand around

As I got older, started liking boys and wanting to go to parties, I started dancing more. I lost myself in the joy of the floor. I had all the enthusiasm and abandon in the world—I just had no rhythm to speak of. When you are young and black, this is akin to a moral failing, or at least a fairly serious ethnic flaw. Especially when you don't have the good sense to just sit it out or do an inoffensive two-step. And I wanted to shine like a ghetto drag queen in a gospel revival of *Fame*.

> And my boooday yearned to be free

Still in college, when my sorority sisters would participate in the energetic step competitions that were a hallmark of black Greek life, I couldn't muster up the confidence to join them until my last year. Until I was about to graduate and I could feel myself starting to spill over my self-imposed limits.

No more standin' (along the side walls) upside the wall

After college, when I moved Washington, D.C., to attend graduate school at Howard University, I began the hard work of inventing and reinventing parts of myself. One of the areas I worked on was dancing. This was aided by meeting my husband, who had the most sublime moves I had ever seen. He taught me steps and I learned to settle myself and listen to the bass. After that, for years when we were dating, we would hang out on the dance floor and sometimes even draw a crowd of partygoers around us.

Now I('ve) got myself together, babay
(Marvin Gaye,
"Got to Give It Up")

By the time I was driving to dance class, much of that was behind me. With two kids, we rarely went to parties, and although I'd let my hair down at annual journalism conventions, it wasn't enough to carry me more than a couple of months. By the time I went to dance class, it had probably been years since I had been to the gym with any regularity, although that had always been part of my routine, and my avowed devotion to physicality had dwindled to nothing.

I didn't know if that NIA class—low impact and kind of new age—would be my cup of tea. Turns out, it was revelatory. I kicked my legs, opened my arms, and felt my mood crawl up from the basement, where it had been digging shallow graves, to rejoin humanity. For the rest of the night I was calm, patient, and available; I felt like myself on a very good day. I was no longer ready to snap. And I think that's when I first consciously recognized the linear connection between moving my body and changing my mind—

when it crystallized that taking time for me could be one of the best ways to promote the well-being of my family. That may have been my first conscious connection, but of course I had been moving that way for quite a while. When Sydney was born, I asked my obstetrician, the late Dr. Richard Peters, a Heathcliff Huxtable type straight out of central casting, if he would discharge me early because I couldn't wait to get home and spend time with my new baby. He refused, keeping my in the hospital the maximum number of days insurance allowed so I could rest. "If you're lucky you'll get to spend eighteen years at home with your baby," he told me. "If you're unlucky, it'll be thirty-five." When I got home I didn't leave the house without Sydney for six months, and the first time I did, it was only to attend an infant CPR class with my husband. We left detailed instructions with my friend Dana and still called several times. Four years later, when I had Savannah, I no longer wanted to leave the hospital early. I was a full-time reporter, my husband had been working and commuting four hours to weekend graduate school, and we had been through trying times both personally and professionally. He had just accepted a job that would require him to commute to Philadelphia for two years, and I had imported Cousin Kim from Illinois to help out because I knew things were about to get tough. When Savannah was two months old, I decided I needed something I had never had: a spa weekend alone.

I left a refrigerator filled with milk. I left my baby, my four-year-old, my nineteen-year-old cousin, and my husband waving at a gas station as I flew up Interstate 95 like the Red Baron. I don't remember what I was reading, but I had rented *The Defiant Ones,* with Tony Curtis and Sydney Poitier. I signed up for healthy meals, daily workouts, and all the wellness treatments I could afford. According to the spa staff, I made it just in time. A class on polarity showed that my chakras were out of alignment and apparently my third eye wasn't seeing straight. A session of reflexology revealed that my toes were "crunchy" from carrying as much stress as the therapist had ever seen. All weekend I enjoyed my solitude and worked out my kinks. About two years later, I went on another spa weekend to the same place with good friends Deneen and Lisa, colleagues from the *Washington Post*. This time the workout was both physical and emotional as we had long, intimate, cathartic conversations about our lives and our hurts. We decided there was a god especially for black women who was stirring all our pots, and we settled on words we wanted to write.

Before I went to that dance class, it had been too long since I had taken any kind of consistent and deliberate time for myself. And my important parts were worn. Afterward, dance became a metaphor for release and reconnection and restoration. I wonder if there's a word for the lessons we learn over and over again. Lessons whose central assertions we know abstractly, but we don't feel until the very instant their truth quiets our distress and calms the hackles rising on our neck. Lessons that can't sit still in our head, but have to be practiced or lost. I hadn't imagined there would be such lessons all those years ago when my friends and I confidently, naively, swore allegiance to our essential selves, vowing not to let the demands of work and family grind us to dust. Now I'm a true believer, and I like to preach and practice the word. Shortly after my second child, Savannah, was born (or was it my third child, Satchel? Whatever, they know who they are), I struck up a conversation with a woman in a restaurant bathroom. We bonded instantly, and upon hearing I had young kids, the woman gushed, telling me I looked good. I had had a glass or two of wine, so I thanked her and then held forth. "You've got to stay in roll-out condition," I told her, reminding myself of my Aunt Jackie. "Because you never know when you've got to (Tina Turner–Proud Mary hands here) roll out on a man." We both cackled.

When my girlfriends and I talk about roll-out condition, it's only a little bit about hair or makeup or the latest fit-for-life diet. It is more about self-preservation, about maintaining a certain intactness. In our construct, it is a deep truth that radiates outward, culled from the cautionary tales of women who let themselves go in slow, painful stages, then watched the people around them leave. Who sacrificed their ambitions or let their interests shrivel. Who gave away so much of their good stuff to people who gladly took it all that there wasn't enough vitality left to cover a whole woman. And over time, large parts of them oozed out through the gaps in their skin. Because I have a dramatic bent, it reminds me of an exchange between Eowyn and Aragorn that stayed with me from the movie *The Lord of the Rings*.

EOWYN: Women of this country learned long ago: Those without swords can still die upon them. I fear neither death nor pain.
ARAGORN: What do you fear, my lady?
EOWYN: A cage. To stay behind bars until use and old age accept them. And all chance of valour has gone beyond recall and desire.

I was reminded in more pedestrian terms of a similar fear expressed by my former colleague Tracy Thompson.

My first ambition, after the ballerina dream got ditched, was to avoid becoming the heroine of *Marjorie Morningstar*, a 1955 bestseller I read as an adolescent, in which Marjorie dreams of becoming a Broadway actress but instead winds up living a mundane life on Long Island as Mrs. Milton Schwartz, housewife and mother of three. Please, God, I thought when I was 16, don't let that happen to me.

This speaks to me as well, but it's not the housewife part, it's not the mother of three, it's not even life on Long Island, which I've never sensed as being particularly ghastly. Rather, it is the intending all along to do something else until one day you look up and you're all out of time. It is that deep-seated fear of becoming a woman who has let herself get so far away that she can never be reacquired and so she tells herself she's merely grown in a different direction. My friends and I hadn't known all the ways that life could rear up on you when we took our pledges of allegiance. We hadn't realized that cares and complicating factors can consume the days that easily turn to years that double and flip end over end. That sorrows come unbidden, but you must be deliberate about your joy. And please tell me where's the women's studies professor to correct our fuzzy math? I'm looking for the professor with some funky new remixed math that says there is a law of diminishing returns, and if you give everything you have without ever replenishing yourself, restocking the well, taking good care, there will naturally be less of you to go around, and that's not a balanced equation for anyone. This is why the airline stewardess instructs you to put your mask on first before assisting your child. It is the recognition that you are of no use to anyone if you're gasping for air. I talk about roll-out condition because it bespeaks a certain self-containment, a keeping all your vital parts vital and growing as a deliberate exercise of choice. And most assuredly as a hedge when things fall apart.

A woman's got to stay in roll-out condition, because you never know when you might have to roll out on a man. I don't ever plan on leaving my husband, but it won't be because I don't have other options.

You would think that, between the vow to my friends to always rock it and my devotion to the doctrine of roll-out condition, I would be the ultimate glamour mom. That with my own momma and my Aunt Jackie as guides I'd be *done, yo,* every time I left the house. But you would be wrong. Deep beliefs not withstanding, I live in the material world. I consider myself an able woman, but I do not defy the laws of physics. I cannot conjure time where there is none to spare. I have to chauffeur kids to afterschool activities. I have to braid hair and shop for snacks. I have to write freelance magazine pieces on and off deadline, and rub my husband's back. I am constantly prioritizing, and personal glamour, or even just curling my hair, usually falls to the bottom of my list, making black and brown banana clips among my most prized possessions. This often prompts critical comments from my daughters, who don't fully appreciate the subtleties of my big picture. Who don't realize that I'm just *playing* low-key and Wal-Martish for months on end, or longer, waiting for my time to shine. For many years, I volunteered in my daughter Sydney's class. This typically embarrassed her, but it didn't start getting bad until she was in about third grade. She would ask about the outfit I was wearing to the school, if I had any different shoes, and especially, if I was going to let my hair down because that helped to hide, "you know, that thing on your neck." That thing was a mole I had never had the good sense to be self-conscious about until my daughter made it sound like one of those goiters on the necks of the old black women that we used to giggle about when I was little.

In kindergarten Savannah used to be delighted when I would volunteer in her class, but in first grade, she changed her tune a bit. "Are you coming up to the school, Mommy," she'd ask. "Maybe if you wear some cute pants, some cute boots, a different shirt—maybe one of Sydney's shirts that fits you—and wear your hair down, then when you meet with Mrs. Brennan that would be better." Yes it probably would be better, I thought to myself, but as I've said before, I can have it all, just not on the same day. And as a practical matter, that means daily decisions about how best to spend fifteen- and twenty- and forty-five-minute blocks of time.

I smile when I see the moms coming from storytime at the library with cute leather backpacks or maybe a toe ring peeking from their sandals. I give them my tacit approval, a silent high five for their small displays of individuality. My own, slightly more involved, individualized strategy requires keeping my mind and body in a state of latent fabulousness, so that at a moment's notice (actually three to five days is best because it allows time for hair and nail appointments, eyebrow waxing, and maybe a doubling-up of my birth control patch to deepen my cleavage), I can get brand new. I can change into a different person to attend the White House Correspondents Dinner, an interview with singer Maxwell or actress Halle Berry, or even just happy hour with friends. I can climb into what Momma and I call "the attitude."

My husband first noticed it one day years ago when I was getting dressed. When I was all in the mirror and deep in the zone. "There's something different about you," Ralph said. "It's like you've got an attitude or something." For years the term, actually coined by Momma, has been our shorthand for feeling confident and pulled together and "layin' on full." For having the best physical and mental aspects of yourself fully at your disposal. I don't whip out my attitude often, because, let's face it, there's only so much attitude you need to change diapers and interview people over the telephone, and anyway, they say unkind things about women who have an attitude all the time. My goal is just to keep "the attitude" tucked in a nearby psychic recess. To have it handy enough to sustain me as I negotiate the minutiae of my days; for the times when I say to myself, Okay, Lonnae, let's make a deal. How about I'll be the ballet and grocery store and elementary school field trip mom Monday through Friday, if I get to play like Vanity 6 at the National Association of Black Journalists parties and sometimes on Saturday date nights with my husband. When I remind myself I don't have to be *fierce* all the time, just as long as I can be, whenever I want. It's a psychological out that helps me to both hold fast to my convictions and compromise with my life. It's highly effective, and so I've learned to give myself other outs as well.

In 2000, I took an extended leave of absence from the *Washington Post* to travel and freelance and read. To catch up with myself, I said, because I had to put some stuff back in my head if I was going to continue making withdrawals. In 2001, as I prepared to return to the *Post*, I had to reconsider my child-care options—and I knew just what I wanted: a woman who would come in every day to watch the kids and do light housekeeping. Ralph was against the idea at first. How much money could we save if we just stayed with day care, he asked. I don't know, I said, how much is it worth to have a wife who doesn't hate you? My husband was momentarily nonplussed. Hate me? he asked. I didn't even flinch. My husband is the best man I know at sharing in the chores. He probably does dinner dishes three times as often as I do. He'll wash clothes and bathe kids; he'll fold towels *and* put them in the linen closet. He vacuums, irons, and empties trash cans full of loaded diapers. But for all the considerable good-natured work he does, he barely comes close to touching my responsibilities around the house. I see things that other people in my family cannot. Socks, lint balls, the underside of beds; drawers full of clothes that have to be separated seasonally and packed by age to save for Savannah and my goddaughter Kendall or

carted off to Goodwill. I see the hundreds of family photos that
need to be framed or scrapbooked, the Christmas ornaments that
need to be wrapped in newspaper before they are packed away to
ensure they won't break, baseboards I've cleaned with a toothbrush,
toilet bowls I've scrubbed, and every electrical outlet that should
have either a nightlight or an air freshener. And that's just for
starters. I see everything in my house that needs to be done, and I
know I can't possibly do it all. But I still feel like I should. My husband said we didn't need someone to come in because we could do
everything ourselves; but "we" wouldn't do everything. And I'd be
the only one who felt bad about it. Over time, that's the kind of
thing that can make you resent the people around you and fall short
of the glory you're trying to reach. I saw all of this clearly, so I hired
the Señora to transform my vision, help maintain my Spanish, and
give my kids the best possible shot at being bilingual. We always call
her "Señora" or "Doña Patti," we use the honorific, although she's a
few years younger than me and by now we're comfortable and familiar. I remember the little girl who called Mrs. Breedlove "Polly"
in Toni Morrison's novel *The Bluest Eye*. When that girl's momma
doesn't pay "Polly" right, it feels like a clear extension of the casual
regard she's held in. Doña Patti has been with me three and a half
years, although I've now put my youngest in day care so he can be
around other kids. Still, she continues to come in part-time and I'd
do just about anything to keep her, which includes a whole lot of
things I'm doing without. When you walk into the front of my
house and look to your left, there is no furniture. It's a big empty
room, save for the piano against the wall, and I see that open space
as a reminder of my open-ended choices. I could have new living
room furniture, a new car, and all sorts of fancy gadgets like a cell
phone that won't drop calls if you don't death-grip the headset. I

just can't have all that and have the Señora as well. And when it comes to choosing, there simply is no contest. There is nothing like coming home to a clean house. On a daily basis, it does more for my peace of mind, for my good mood, my joy around my family, to realize somebody else has remembered to change the kid's sheets than having the most well crafted living room furniture in the world. And I positively get a runner's high when she cleans out the pantry or has dinner ready. The Señora gives me less to worry about, less to obsess over, one more caring mind applied to the details of my home. There are some things that only I can do for my family and other things where it doesn't matter who does them, only that they get done. The Señora helps me figure out the difference between those two. She extends my options, and so I treat her like one of the most important people in my life.

I haven't had many concrete models in establishing my relationship with the Señora. I grew up watching reruns of episodic television, and of course I realized that Carol Brady had a nanny-housekeeper. But unlike Carol Brady, I've known and loved and prayed to black women before I sleep, and they require I see the full humanity of all working women. The long history of black women as domestics prior to the gains of the civil rights movement (60 percent of employed black women were domestics in 1940, and domestic work or some derivative thereof—health aides, cleaning in commercial or industrial environments, laundresses, et cetera—continued to comprise a plurality of black women's work for decades) informs my perspective and grants me the ability to see in three full dimensions.

Last year, a controversial article about professional women's use of domestic workers appeared in the *Atlantic Monthly;* a dispatch from the "nanny wars" entitled, "How Serfdom Saved the Women's

Movement," in which writer Caitlin Flanagan derided middle-class women, typically champions of equality movements, as having come to rely on what she calls exploited immigrant labor.

How so many middle-class American women went from not wanting to oppress other women to viewing that oppression as a central part of their own liberation—that is a complicated and sorry story. In it you will find the seeds of things we don't like to discuss much.

Like how "educated, professional class women with booming careers who needed their children looked after and their houses cleaned" no longer have a moral compunction about getting immigrant women to perform their "shit work," writes Flanagan.

I find myself in an interesting historical position to consider the philosophical underpinnings of that piece. Continued exploitation by all types of women toward other women exists. But as Jacqueline Jones makes clear in *Labor of Love, Labor of Sorrow*, white women, who have been on the front lines of racism and oppression when it comes to the women who have labored in their homes, must be especially mindful of their history.

The history of domestic service in the 1930s provides a fascinating case study of the lengths to which whites would go in exploiting a captive labor force. Those who employed live-in servants in some cases cut their wages, charged extra for room and board, or lengthened on duty hours. But it was in the area of day work that housewives elevated labor-expanding and money-saving methods to a fine art. General speedups were common in private homes throughout the North and South.

Among the best bargains were children and teenagers: in Indianola, Mississippi, a 16-year-old black girl worked from 6 A.M. to 7 P.M. daily for $1.50 a week. In the same town a maid could be instructed to do her regular chores, plus those of the recently fired cook, for less pay than she had received previously. (A survey of Mississippi's domestics revealed that the average weekly pay was less than $2.00) Some women received only carfare, clothing or lunch for a day's work. Northern white women also lowered wages drastically. In 1932 Philadelphia, domestics earned $5.00 to $12.00 for a forty-eight- to sixty-seven-hour work week. Three years later they took home the same amount of money for ninety hours worth of scrubbing, washing, and cooking (an hourly wage of 15 cents).

As a black woman who has listened to stories of black women who have always worked, I understand that fair wages contribute a lot more to justice for poor women than the most profound sense of white guilt. All my colored mothers tell me that there is dignity in the most humble job where you are well respected and well paid. I would rather incur a loss myself than exploit anyone who works in my house—that makes me an honest broker. And that is the main currency I trade in with the Señora. It is what I fall back on to navigate the dicey parts of meshing our different schedules and priorities. I imagine that as a working woman with a family, she is like me. So I give her the latitude to take off early or call in sick, even when it is inconvenient, much the same as I take for myself. I say thank you often and back up that appreciation with bonus money every time a little extra comes into my hands, which it never would if I constantly had to worry about home. I give her money that gives her agency in her life, the same as it does in my own. In this climate, she is free to love my children without the psychological negation of embracing the tools of her own oppression. I understand the racial baggage and the day-to-day challenges that cause some women to snipe and try to police one another over the appropriateness of their motives and the discharge of their responsibilities. I simply possess a different historical perspective, one that is often more simple and in some ways more creative. It is a perspective that finds comfort, succor, and solidarity in the collective, we're-all-in-this-together aspects of women's work. It is, for black women, a very old concept.

For example, in Southern tobacco factories before World War I and the Great Migration north, an oversupply of labor meant black women were forced to accept the most tenuous, perilous working conditions. Forced to find creative ways to endure and to reach for heaven.

Prevented from talking to one another or sitting in the workplace—foremen apparently believed that both conversation and chairs cause the pace to slacken—female rehandlers sang together. In this way they established a rhythm to make the repetitious tasks more bearable even as they collectively expressed a hope and a protest: "Oh, by an' by I'm goin' to lay down this heavy load." Ironically, this form of resistance to the monotony of industrial labor (apparently unique to black tobacco workers during this period in American history) convinced manufacturers that their employees were happy and content. Domestic and foreign visitors alike professed to be deeply affected by the sight and sound of stemmers moving back and forth in unison, "bodies swaying an fingers flying," their voices lifted in sorrowful lament. The novelty of the scene apparently distracted most observers from remarking upon the heat, dust, and dirt that the singers were trying to transcend. And few whites at the time would have been able to recognize the similarity between these workers and their slave foremothers who sang as they wove cloth or hoed the cotton fields together.

Alice Walker painfully laments the black women writers and painters and sculptors historically denied outlet; she asks us to consider the fate of Bessie Smith (Aretha Franklin, Billie Holiday, Nina Simone) if singing had been outlawed, as, say, reading and writing were, or if it had been unthinkable, like painting. While Virginia Woolf wrote that women writers needed money and inviolate space, it is only in recent history that anything about black women has been inviolate at all. Walker's own mother worked in fields alongside her father.

> Her day began before sunup, and did not end until late at night. There was never a moment for her to sit down, undisturbed, to unravel her own private thoughts; never a time free from interruption—by work or the noisy inquiries of her many children. And yet, it is to my mother—and all our mothers who were not famous—that I went in search of the secret of what has fed that muzzled and often mutilated, but vibrant, creative spirit that the black woman has inherited, and that pops out in wild and unlikely places to this day.

For Walker's mother, it came out in the beautiful, growing things that colored even memories of poverty with roses and dahlias and petunias. That made her mother radiant and caused strangers to stop and marvel at her art.

For her, so hindered and intruded upon in so many ways, being an artist has still been a daily part of her life. This ability to hold on, even in very simple ways is work black women have done for a very long time.

Two years ago for Mother's Day, my family and I visited *The Quilts of Gee's Bend* at the Corcoran Gallery of Art in Washington. The exhibit of about seventy years of handcrafted quilts made by generations of poor, isolated black women in southwestern Alabama had gotten critical praise as high examples of complex, artistic abstraction. But for the black women, who sang and stitched dress tails and pant legs and sacks, whatever they had available, they were something else; warmth for the night and the onliest thing they had to look forward to. A way to ease the long labors of black time. The women were "lovely people," unself-conscious artists, the pretensions of the art world in which they are now celebrated having little to do with them. On video at the exhibit, Annie Mae Young talks about how she never could "piece too much of fancy quilts. I just do my way, you know. Uh-huh." "What that quilt name?" people ask her. "A quilt," she says. "Quilt. That's what it name, quilt."

My sister's former mother-in-law, Lois, crochets the most beautiful, intricate blankets and throws. She perfected her technique during those times her ex-husband would sit her in the "hot seat" at four in the afternoon and berate her until four in the morning. Now she uses it, to keep herself from obsessing over her son, who's a military policeman in Iraq. Even those women who didn't necessarily make art certainly found outlets. There were good Christian women like the mother-in-law of a friend who raised six kids but reserved every Friday for quality time at the racetrack. Some women holler in church, some whoop it up at the clubs. I may not thin gin at the juke joint, like Sofia from *The Color Purple*, or let it all ride at the track, but I'm not mad at those who do. A woman's got to take care of home, and then has got to carve out her own in-violate space. And when you find that thing that keeps you sane, that piece of something that's yours alone, you don't sacrifice it. Not even on the altar of motherhood. I've rarely known any woman, any mother, not to find something that sustains her interest to en-gage around. But this has been most gospel true with the black women I've known. And, certainly, with all my good friends. I once heard Halle Berry describe herself as a woman's woman, and I felt an instant affinity. I love men, sho' I do, but I am happiest, most connected, and most profoundly comforted by a roomful of women—all kinds of women, but especially black women, the old-est women to walk this earth—than just about anything else I know. Long ago my friends and I realized the need for our own brain trust, a sister-girl circle, a kitchen cabinet, stocked with fruity drinks, and long ago we made tacit promises to be among the most enduring parts of one another's lives. More reliably there than the men who stay or leave and the children who grow and go away. We "date" each other, meeting regularly every two weeks at the Star-bucks for coffee, flying into town for one another's showers and parties. Sending cards, cooking dinners, and running errands. Giv-ing according to our talents. In addition to regularly leaning on "the therapy of good friends," as Halle Berry says, I am a member of our homeowner's association social butterfly committee; we eat, we plan, we drink, we talk. Last year we went Christmas-caroling, al-though few of us could sing and I couldn't help feeling that we vic-timized many of our neighbors. For years, my Sojourners book club meetings have been among my most important must-do dates. We're professionals and our readings reflect our deep hunger to fashion our own intellectual space. We focused on the Middle East after September 11 and when there was daily news about incursions in the West Bank. We read *From Beirut to Jerusalem* and *The Ques-*

tion of Palestine. Later, we switched to Africa, where some of our members have worked as aid officers, and read *King Leopold's Ghost,* about the largely forgotten Belgian colonial slaughter of millions of Congolese in the late nineteenth and early twentieth centuries. We hadn't known that Joseph Conrad's *Heart of Darkness,* which was the basis for the Francis Ford Coppola film *Apocalypse Now,* was based on a true story of African colonialization, and we spent deeply engaged hours making historical connections. We read of colonial histories, the changing race politics in South Africa, and a horrific account of the Rwandan genocide. The book club fuses our love of words with our constant hunger to know as much as we can about the places around us. It is deep, rewarding, ponderous stuff, which is real good, because I do have an outlet that's much less weighty. It's my nearly twenty-year addiction to the soap opera *The Young and the Restless,* which connects me to my mother, who also watches soap operas, and to the women in the television room of the *Washington Post,* at lunchtime, when we all look forward to watching together.

My husband left the house once to run errands, and took all three of the kids. He called later and asked what I was doing. I told him I was doing nothing. Was I watching television? he asked. And I said no. Was I listening to the radio? he continued. And I said no again. Was I reading? he wanted to know. The answer was still none of the above. I was sitting, by myself, enjoying the low tones and whisper half-notes of enveloping silence. I was in the bathroom one day and Savannah called me, said she wanted to show me how she wanted her hair for the next day. When I said hang on, she knocked again, pleading. When I told her I'd be with her in a minute, she got down on the floor and threaded her small, fuzzy braid through the narrow crack of the bathroom door. "Do you see this braid, Mommy?" she asked. "This is the braid I'm talking about." Not long ago, I was in the bathroom and Sydney knocked on the door. I didn't answer and she knocked again. I didn't answer and she knocked again. I said nothing and she continued to knock until my husband came out from wherever he was and got her what she needed. Later he chided me. "Didn't you hear Sydney knocking," he asked. I met his look with an unflinching gaze of my own. "Yes, I heard her," I said, "but there are some times when I am just unavailable and everybody in this house has to learn to be okay with that." My husband said he understood. But I don't know that he did. . . .

In the fable about the frog and the scorpion, the scorpion convinces the frog to give him a ride across the pond. The frog demurs, accusing the scorpion of wanting to sting him, but the scorpion convinces him, saying, "if I sting you, we will both die." The frog crosses the pond with the scorpion on his back, and halfway across, the scorpion stings him. As they are both about to drown, the frog asks why he did it and the scorpion replies, "It's in my nature."

It feels like that story is something of a metaphor for husbands and kids and jobs, with women as the frogs. I no longer ask the people around me to give me time. I do not know if it is fair to ask them to go against their most basic nature, which is to want me there, available for everything they need me for, for as long as they can have me. Instead, I do the hard work of being completely clear about what I need. Then they don't have to give me anything. They just have to respect the boundaries I insist on maintaining. It can still be a tough sell, but at least I've got half the battle won.

I'm a woman who pays attention to voices in her daily life—ancient and spectral, contemporary and heavy with accents. They connect me to other women, chiding me or giving me pep talks and instructions about how to keep it all going, stepping in the positive.

And although this is the busy season of my life, sometimes they tell me to put my heavy load down to read, visit with friends, watch my "stories," or just be still. Sometimes they tell me it's time to dance. Not long ago, I found out African dance classes were set to resume at the place where I had had my first NIA lesson and had been so moved. After that NIA class, I began taking regular African dance classes, along with the girls, on and off for years.

When the classes were discontinued, I lobbied the women at the ballet academy where my daughters attend classes, and they agreed to bring my instructor, Oyamiwa, into their studio. It is a delightful piece of diversity and creative energy, and I can't wait to do like Sonia Sanchez, and shake loose my skin, and the cares of my day.

Sometimes I let go and move to the sound of ancient drums. My moves are not perfect, but my attempts feel like homage to black women, a recognition that you've got to keep stepping, and in that dance there is beauty. It is there in all your days, interspersed with all your work. And if you listen, the oldest voices in your head whisper affirmations, because that's what they've been trying to tell you all along.

13

Lessons for Daughters

My Umi said shine your light on the
world
Shine your light for the world to see

Mos Def,
"Umi Says"

I am watching the 2000 movie *Love and Basketball* with Sydney and Savannah. This is no easy feat. The film is rated PG-13 and has a number of risqué parts, so I'm constantly ordering them to close their eyes and cover their ears, in between ordering them to pay attention.

"Do you see her? Monica isn't standing on the side. She's a player. She's got her own story. You must never sit around waiting for people to pay attention to you! Do you hear what I'm saying?" I ask the girls passionately. They do not understand my intensity. Sometimes I lack the words to explain it myself. I've got to do a better job with my pacing, I think—just giving them a little bit at a time. Didn't my husband caution me about being the weird mother on the block? It's just there's so much ground for us to cover, I want to say. And always there is more time than life, my Spanish professor told me.

I wonder if they'll hear the voices as clearly as I do.

Interruption from Savannah: *Rub my back, Mommy.*

Or I wonder if the voices are only clear in the hardest times, times I hope my daughters never know. How much do you have to cry before the oldest women to walk the world whisper, "You might as well get up, because no one else is going to save you"? How tired do you have to be? And if you don't hear that first part, will you still hear the part about how you've got to find a way to be joyous by proxy, just on GP, for all the bowed and disappeared who could not make the trip—who've waited the ages to clap their hands as they watch you do your thing? And for those women, my Lord, don't you want to be one of the ones who gives it all up on stage?

(Interruption to change Satchel's diaper: *Don't put that truck in your stinky stuff! Yes, I know it's your truck. I lub you too.*)

Now my daughters have gone downstairs with their dad and their brother. It's quiet in my room and I am alone with my thoughts.

(Surprise interruption from Sydney: *You're going to eat all of them,* she accuses. *Where are the Kit-Kats? Let me get some now because you're going to eat every last one of them. I know you, Mommy.*)

There is so much history that is hidden from us, I want to tell my daughters, which is why you have to seek out the stories of other women and make them your own. They let you know you have everything you need. That there is nothing new under the sun and you are just, most appropriately, customizing your beats, because that will make your remix strong.

(Interruption because everyone is coming back upstairs: *This means I will get no more alone time for the rest of the night. My husband shepherds everyone into the bathroom and then gives me the thumbs-up. I wonder if that means he will want to kiss me tonight.*)

"We just use what our mothers gave us," said the old black quilting woman from Gee's Bend, and I feel her simple truth order some of my apprehension away. I do not have to have all the words I will ever need to make it all all right tonight. I just have to have faith that the words will come in time, because I am a good listener. A mindful daughter of the god of black women.

As a matter of fact, I'm every woman. It's all in me.

It's all in us all.

Notes

INTRODUCTION

xvi "Especially in cities, a majority of black women have worked outside the home and raised families for more than one hundred years": Elizabeth H. Place, "A Mother's Wages: Income Earning Among Married Italian and Black Women, 1896–1911," pp. 490–510 in Michael Gordon, ed., *The American Family in Social-Historical Perspective,* 2nd ed. (New York: St. Martin's Press, 1978), p. 496, Table 1.

xvi "Nationally, a majority of married, middle-class black women have been in the labor force since the mid-1950s," Landry, *Black Working Wives,* Appendix B. pp. 198–199.

xx "I'm going to have babies and be a star," Chaka Khan, *Chaka! Through the Fire,* page 71.

CHAPTER I

11 "An excerpt from the 1903 publication": Quoted in Ellen M. Plante, ed., *Women at Home in Victorian America: A Social History*, New York: Facts on File, 1997, p. 108.

CHAPTER 2

18   "I finds a biscuit and I's so hungry I et it, 'cause we nev'r see sich a thing as a biscuit": Jenny Proctor, quoted in Donna Wyant Howell, ed., *I Was a Slave: True Life Stories Dictated by Former American Slaves in the 1930's*. Book 1: *Descriptions of Plantation Life*, pp. 54–55.

20   "No'm, I nebbah knowed whut it wah t' rest": Sarah Gudger, quoted in *Unchained Memories, Readings from the Slave Narratives*, p. 52. This is the companion book to the HBO documentary of the same title.

22   "it is a well-known fact that you can't starve a negro": White woman slaveholder, quoted in Jacqueline Jones, *Labor of Love, Labor of Sorrow*, p. 65.

22   " 'a healthy sexual equality' " Jacqueline Jones, *Labor of Love, Labor of Sorrow*, p. 41, quoting Eugene D. Genovese, *Roll, Jordan, Roll: The World the Slaves Made*. New York: Vintage, 1976, p. 500

22   "The contrasting contexts of black and white women's lives": Bart Landry, *Black Working Wives: Pioneers of the American Family Revolution*, p. 58.

23   "All across the South, planters complained about the refusal of black wives to work": Landry, *Black Working Wives*, Chap. 2, n. 35.

24   "Thus in 1870, when over 40 percent of Black married women reported jobs": Landry, *Black Working Wives*, p. 45.

24   "But the majority of black women were locked out of clerical work": In *Black Working Wives*, Landry talks about the differences in work strategies between black and white working-class women; see pp. 46 and 48.

25   "It was not until the end of the day that she had any time to spend with her own children": Jones, *Labor of Love, Labor of Sorrow*, pp. 129–130.

27   "The black community's appreciation for and development of the feminine intellect": S. J. Carlson, "Black Ideals of Womanhood in the Late Victorian Era," *Journal of Negro History*, 77(2): 61–73 (1992); quoted in Landry, *Black Working Wives*, p. 70.

28   "While 14 percent of working black women . . .": See Ellis Cose with Allison Samuels, "The Black Gender Gap," *Newsweek*, March 3, 2003. "According to a spring 2005 Census report, college-educated black women actually earned slightly more," "College-educated white women earn less than blacks, Asians," CNN website. Viewed at http://www.cnn.com/2005/EDUCATION/03/28/education.income.ap/ on March 29, 2005. For statistics on black married women in the labor force, see Landry, *Black Working Wives*, pp. 198–199. Figures for 2002

are from the U.S. Census, "Household Data Annual Averages, Employed Persons by Occupation, Race and Sex."

31   "Wells' pen name, Iola, was spelled out in electric lights across the dais": Paula Giddings, *When and Where I Enter: The Impact of Black Women on Race and Sex in America*, p. 30.

31   "he alleged that the Negroes in this country were wholly devoid of morality": Landry, *Black Working Wives*, p. 59.

32   "According to Fields, Terrell spoke not only about the modern woman . . .": Deborah Gray White, *Too Heavy a Load: Black Women in Defense of Themselves, 1894–1994*, pp. 21–22.

33   "torn between the financial contribution she felt she should make . . .": Terrell and Wells both struggled with ways to balance career and family; see White, *Too Heavy a Load*, pp. 91–92.

33   "club work and anti-lynching race work tugged at her . . .": Ibid.

CHAPTER 3

49   "And so our mothers and grandmothers": Alice Walker, *In Search of Our Mothers' Gardens*, p. 729, quoted in Deirdre Mullane, ed., *Crossing the Danger Water, Three Hundred Years of African American Writing*. San Diego: Harcourt, 1983, p. 240.

CHAPTER 4

51   "A black woman is the mother to the world": Martha Southgate, "An Unnatural Woman," in Cecelie Berry, ed., *Rise Up Singing: Black Women Writers on Motherhood*, p. 115.

54   "black actresses still face piles of scripts filled with prostitutes": Kelly Carter, "Berry Widens Window for Black Actresses," *USA Today*, March 19, 2003.

55   "a warm and winning hefty, full-figured, and good-hearted 'colored gal' ": Donald Bogle, *Primetime Blues: African Americans on Network Television*. New York: Farrar, Straus and Giroux, 2001, p. 19.

56   " 'No Negro performers allowed' ": "Amos 'N' Andy Show: U.S. Domestic Comedy," Museum of Broadcast Communications website. Viewed at http://www.museum.tv/archives/etv/A/htmlA/amosnandy/amosnandy.htm on July 12, 2004.

59 "the people who in all literature were always peripheral": bell hooks, *Bone Black: Memories of Girlhood*, Foreword, p. xii.

68 "I would like to cast an unpopular vote": Erin J. Aubry, "Homeboys from Outer Space and Other Transgressions," *LA Weekly*, August 6, 1999, p. 49.

CHAPTER 5

81 "The husband of Margaret fired several shots": "Margaret Garner," African American Literature Book Club website. Viewed at http://aalbc.com/authors/margaret.htm on July 30, 2004.

81 "Mamma, did you ever love us?" Toni Morrison, *Sula*, pp. 67–69.

90 "adamantly refused to compete": Position paper on Mocha Moms website. Viewed at http://www.mochamoms.org/positionpaper.html on August 3, 2004.

91 "It's amusing to see the 'opting out' trend treated as news": Cathy Young, "Opting Out: The Press Discovers the Mommy Wars, Again," Reason online. Viewed at http://www.reason.com/0406/co.cy.opting.shtml on July 1, 2004.

95 "If we run ourselves ragged taking care of everyone else's needs": Rita Coburn Whack, "Elementary Lessons," in Cecelia Berry, ed., *Rise Up Singing*, p. 246.

CHAPTER 7

118 "It's a tradition that stretched into the time": Earnings statistics for black women are taken from the Bureau of Labor Statistics website: "Usual Weekly Earnings of Wage and Salary Workers: Fourth Quarter 2004." Viewed at http://www.bls.gov/news.release/wkyeng.nr0.htm on January 26, 2005.

121 "I got my start as a writer": Joan Morgan, *When Chickenheads Come Home to Roost*, p. 56.

122 "African Americans making more than $50,000": Michelle Singletary, *7 Money Mantras for a Richer Life*, p. 129.

125 "Take the average working-woman of to-day": Alice Moore Dunbar-Nelson, "The Woman," reprinted in *Violets and Other Tales*. Boston: Monthly Review, 1895, pp. 22–25. Viewed online at the Digital

Schomburg, http://digilib.nypl.org/dynaweb/digs/wwm977/@Generic_
BookTextView/410;t= 252 on August 15, 2004.

125   "Rather than be destroyed": A'Lelia Bundles, *On Her Own Ground: The
       Life and Times of Madame C.J. Walker*, p. 35.

126   "They used to not let colored people go out there": Sharon Wertz,
       "Oseola McCarty Donates $150,000 to Southern Miss," Southern
       Miss Home website. Viewed at http://www.usm.edu/pr/oola1.htm on
       August 15, 2004.

CHAPTER 8

135   "Grits in Louisiana are stirred with butter": Donna Brazile, *Cooking
       with Grease: Stirring the Pots in American Politics*, p. 75.

136   "It is true that domestic life took on an exaggerated importance": An-
       gela Davis, *Women, Race and Class*, pp. 16–17.

146   "Food is sexy": Verta Smart-Grosvenor, *Vibration Cooking, or, The
       Travel Notes of a Geechee Girl*, p. 5.

CHAPTER 9

154   "Her large derriere": John Short, "Lecture Notes: Imperialism in Popu-
       lar Culture and Everyday Life in Germany," Cooper Union website.
       Viewed at http://www.cooper.edu/humanities/core/hss3/LEC_new_
       imperialism.html on November 11, 2004.

154   "African women didn't cover their breasts": Gail Elizabeth Wyatt, *Stolen
       Women: Reclaiming Our Sexuality, Taking Back Our Lives*, p. 5.

155   "Resistance could bring severe physical punishment": Zora Neale
       Hurston, *Their Eyes Were Watching God*, pp. 33–34.

156   "Celia was 14 years old in 1850": For an account of Celia's story, see
       Darlene Clark Hine et al., *Black Women in America: An Historical Ency-
       clopedia*, 2. vols. Bloomington: Indiana University Press, 1993, p. 703,
       vol. 2.

156   "James Roberts, a freed slave": G. W. Wyatt, *Stolen Women: Reclaiming
       Our Sexuality, Taking Back Our Lives*, p. 13.

157   "Black men were thought capable of these sexual crimes": Giddings,
       "The Last Taboo," In Toni Morrison, ed., *Race-ing Justice, En-gendering
       Power*, p. 443.

157   "This is supported by one study": John D'Emilio and Estelle Freed-

man, *Intimate Matters: A History of Sexuality in America*. Chicago: University of Chicago Press, 1997, p. 107.

159　"In women's blues": Angela Davis, *Blues Legacies and Black Feminism: Gertrude "Ma" Rainey, Bessie Smith and Billie Holiday*, p. 11.

167　"it is the cult of silence that is the overarching feature": Tricia Rose, *Longing to Tell: Black Women Talk About Sexuality and Intimacy*, p. 4, 396–97.

168　"Revolution begins at home": Angela Ards, "Where Is the (Black) Love?" *Ms. Magazine*. Viewed at http://www.alternet.org/story/11355 on November 12, 2004.

169　"We met in her office": William Finnegan, "The Candidate," *The New Yorker*, May 31, 2004, p. 37.

CHAPTER 10

171　"It's Lynette who speaks truth to power": Ellen Goodman, "Enjoying 'Desperate Housewives'" *Washington Post*, November 20, 2004, p. A19.

175　"Go outside and pick me a switch": Deneen Brown, "A Good Whuppin"? Many Who Survived Childhood Spankings Now Endorse Them, Renewing Debate Over a Peculiar Institution," *Washington Post*, September 13, 1998, p. F01.

175　"When Truth became a mother": Giddings, *When and Where I Enter*, p. 44.

176　"for a black child to curse his parents could reasonably be regarded as a suicidal act": Fred McKissack, "The Black Belt," in Jabari Asim, ed., *Not Guilty: Twelve Black Men Speak Out on Law, Justice and Life*, p. 75.

189　"There are no set roles": Ards, "Where Is the (Black) Love?" op. cit.

CHAPTER 11

198　"We began to notice our kids weren't, well, as black as we had been": Karen Grigsby Bates, "Young, Black and Too White," in *Salon* magazine's *Mothers Who Think* series, May 15, 1998. Viewed at http://dir.salon.com/mwt/feature/1998/05/15feature.html on date tk.

198　"At lilac evening, I walked with every muscle": Jack Kerouac, *On the Road*, 40th Anniversary Edition, Viking Books, Sept. 1, 1997, p. 180.

198　"racialized others passing in white-drag": Ashok Mathur, "Brown Girl in the Ring and White Witches on TV (and how magic is just too racy)," Viewed at *era21* website http://geog.queensu.ca/era21/papers/mathur.htm on January 10, 2004.

200 "That love of your tribe is important": Smart-Grosvenor, *Vibration Cooking*, p. 5.

202 At the 2003 MTV awards: Carla Thompson, "Commercial Hip Hop Trafficks Sex," *Women's eNews*, November 13, 2003; viewed at http://www.alternet.org/mediaculture/17181/on December 16, 2004.

203 it is young white men who are the primary consumers of hip-hop: Mark Anthony Neal, "Critical Noir: Hip Hop's Gender Problem," Africana.com, May 26, 2004. Viewed at http://archive.blackvoices.com/articles/daily/mu20040526hipgender.asp on December 16, 2004.

203 "In a community in which the influences of ghetto life permeate everyday life": Mary Pattillo-McCoy *Black Picket Fences: Privilege and Peril Among the Black Middle Class*. Chicago: University of Chicago Press, 1999, p. 123. Quoted in Patricia Hill Collins, *Black Sexual Politics: African Americans, Gender, and the New Racism*, p. 78. "According to the Sentencing Project": Stat is from Ryan King, research associate, the Sentencing Project, a nonprofit agency that researches sentencing and correction issues. The study, conducted in 2003, said 32.4 blacks born today would spend time in prison (not merely jail) and assumed if current trends continued so it remains true today.

204 "only when we've told the truth about ourselves": Morgan, *When Chickenheads Come Home to Roost*, p. 23.

207 "Black men and women used personal faith to claim a church that was founded by whites": Juan Williams and Quinton Dixie, *This Far by Faith: Stories from the African American Religious Experience*, Introduction, p. 2.

209 "many of the most prominent black churches": "Some Black Chicks Shun Politics," *Dallas Morning News*, 2004, "Many of the most prominent black churches," July 31, 2004, by Ira J. Hadnot, page 1G.

CHAPTER 12

221 "My first ambition," Tracy Thompson, "A War Inside Your Head," *Washington Post Magazine*, 1998, p. 12.

228 "How so many middle-class American women went from not wanting to oppress other women": Caitlin Flanagan, "How Serfdom Saved the

Women's Movement: Dispatches from the Mommy Wars," *Atlantic Monthly*, March 2004, p. 111.

228 "The history of domestic service in the 1930s": Jones, *Labor of Love, Labor of Sorrow*, pp. 206–207.

230 "Prevented from talking to one another": Ibid., p. 140.

231 "Her day began before sunup": Walker, *In Search of Our Mothers' Gardens*, p. 238. Quoted in Deirdre Mullane, ed., *Crossing the Danger Water: Three Hundred Years of African-American Writing*. New York: Anchor, 1993, pp. 722–731.

Bibliography

Asim, J., ed. (2001). *Not Guilty: Twelve Black Men Speak Out on Law, Justice and Life.* New York: HarperCollins

Bass, P. H., and Pugh, K. (2001). *In Our Own Image: Treasured African-American Traditions, Journeys, and Icons.* Philadelphia: Running Press.

Bart-Schwartz, S., & Bart-Schwartz, A. (2001). *In Praise of Black Women: Ancient African Queens.* Madison, WI: University of Wisconsin Press.

Berry, C. S., ed. (2004). *Rise Up Singing: Black Women on Motherhood.* New York: Doubleday.

Bogle, D., (2001) *Primetime Blues, African Americans on Network Television,* New York: Farrar Straus Giroux.

Brazile, D. (2004). *Cooking with Grease: Stirring the Pots in American Politics.* New York: Simon & Schuster.

Bundles, A.: (2002). *On Her Own Ground: The Life and Times of Madame C.J. Walker.* New York: Washington Square Press.

Busby, M., ed. (1992). *Daughters of Africa.* New York: Ballantine Books

Byrd, A. D., & Tharps, L. L. (2001). *Hair Story: Untangling the Roots of Black Hair in America.* New York: St. Martin's Press.

Campbell, B. M. (2000). *Successful Women, Angry Men.* New York: Berkley Books.

Carter, C. J. (2003). *Africana Women: Her Story Through Time*. Washington, D.C.: National Geographic Society.

Chafe, W. H., Gavins, R., & Korstad, R., eds. (2001). *Remembering Jim Crow: African Americans Tell About Life in the Segregated South*. New York: New Press

Chambers, V. (2003). *Having It All? Black Women and Success*. New York: Doubleday.

Clark-Lewis, E. (1994). *Living in, Living Out: African American Domestics and the Great Migration*. Smithsonian Institute.

Collins, P. H. (2004). *Black Sexual Politics: African Americans, Gender, and the New Racism*. New York: Routledge.

Collison, M. N-K. (2002). *It's All Good Hair: The Guide to Styling and Grooming Black Children's Hair*. New York: HarperCollins.

Cosby, B. (1986). *Fatherhood*. Garden City, NY: Doubleday.

Davis, A. Y. (1998). *Blues Legacies and Black Feminism: Gertrude "Ma" Rainey, Bessie Smith, and Billie Holiday*. New York: Pantheon Books.

———. (1983). *Women, Race and Class*. New York: Vintage Books.

Douglas, S. J., & Michaels, M. W. (2004). *The Mommy Myth: The Idealization of Motherhood and How It Has Undermined Women*. New York: Free Press.

Dunaway, W. A. (2003). *The African American Family in Slavery and Emancipation*. New York: Cambridge University Press.

Foner, E. (1990). *A Short History of Reconstruction, 1863–1877*. New York: Harper & Row.

Fulwood, S. (1996). *Waking from the Dream: My Life in the Black Middle Class*. New York: Doubleday.

Giddings, P. (1984). *When and Where I Enter: The Impact of Black Women on Race and Sex in America*. New York: HarperCollins.

Greenwood, M. (2001). *Having What Matters: The Black Women's Guide to Creating the Life You Really Want*. New York: HarperCollins.

Guy-Sheftall, B., ed. (1995). *Words of Fire: An Anthology of African-American Feminist Thought*. New York: New Press.

Hine, D. C., Brown, E. B., and Terborg-Pen, R. (1993). *Black Women in America: An Historical Encyclopedia*, 2. vols. Bloomington: Indiana University Press.

Hooks, B. (1996). *Bone Black: Memories of Girlhood*. New York: Henry Holt.

———. (2000). *Feminist Theory: From Margin to Center*, 2d. ed. Cambridge, MA: South End Press.

Howell, D. W., ed. (1995). *I Was a Slave: True Life Stories Dictated by Former American Slaves in the 1930's*. Books 1–6. Washington, D.C.: American Legacy Books.

Hurston, Z. N. (1937/1978). *Their Eyes Were Watching God*. Chicago: University of Illinois Press.

Jones, C., & Shorter-Gooden, K. (2003). *Shifting: The Double Lives of Black Women in America*. New York: HarperCollins.

Jones, J. (1986). *Labor of Love, Labor of Sorrow*. New York: Vintage.

Keogh, P. C. (1999). *Audrey Style*. New York: HarperCollins.

Khan, C., & Bolden, T. (2003). *Chaka: Through the Fire*. New York: Rodale.

Ladner, J. A. (1998). *Timeless Values for African American Families: The Ties That Bind*. New York: John Wiley & Sons.

Landry, Bart. (2000). *Black Working Wives: Pioneers of the American Family Revolution*. Berkley and Los Angeles: University of California Press.

Lemert, C., & Bhan, E., eds. (1998). *The Voice of Anna Julia Cooper: Including a Voice from the South and Other Important Essays, Papers, and Letters*. Lanham, MD: Rowan & Littlefield Publishers.

Morgan, J. (1999). *When Chickenheads Come Home to Roost: My Life as a Hip-Hop Feminist*. New York: Simon & Schuster.

Morrison, T. (1987). *Beloved*. New York: Penguin Group.

——. (1970). *The Bluest Eye*. New York: Penguin Group.

——. (1973). *Sula*. New York: Penguin Group.

Mullane, D., ed. (1993). *Crossing the Danger Water: Three Hundred Years of African American Writing*. New York, Anchor Books.

Peri, C., & Moses, K., eds. (1999). *Mothers Who Think: Tales of Real-Life Parenthood*. New York: Villard Books.

Pleck, E. H. (1978). *A Mother's Wages: Income Earning Among Married Italian and Black Women, 1896–1911*. Michael Gordon, ed., "The American Family in Social-Historical Perspective," 2nd ed. New York: St. Martin's Press.

Rose, T. (1994). *Black Noise: Rap Music and Black Culture in Contemporary America*. Hanover, NH: University of New England Press.

Rose, T., ed. (2003). *Longing to Tell: Black Women Talk About Sexuality and Intimacy*. New York: Farrar, Straus & Giroux.

Singletary, M. (2004). *7 Money Mantras for a Richer Life: How to Live Well with the Money You Have*. New York: Random House.

Smart-Grosvenor, V. (1970/1992). *Vibration Cooking, or, The Travel Notes of a Geechee Girl*. New York: Ballantine Books. Smith, B. (1999). *B. Smith: Rituals & Celebrations*. New York: Random House.

This Far by Faith. (2003), New York: Amistad.

Unchained Memories: Readings from the Slave Narratives. (2002). Introduction by Henry Louis Gates. New York: Bulfinch Press.

Vaz, K., ed. (1995). *Black Women in America*. Thousand Oaks, CA: Sage.

Walker, A. (1983). *In Search of Our Mother's Gardens: Womanist Prose*. San Diego: Harcourt Brace.

White, D. G. (1999). *Ar'n't I a Woman? Female Slaves in the Plantation South*, rev. ed. New York: W. W. Norton.

———. (1999). *Too Heavy a Load: Black Women in Defense of Themselves, 1894–1994*. New York: W. W. Norton.

White, J. (1998). *Soul Food: Recipes and Reflections from African-American Churches*. New York: HarperCollins.

Williams, J., and Dixie, Q. (2004). *This Far by Faith: Stories from the African American Religious Experience*. New York: HarperCollins/Amistad.

Wyatt, G. E. (1997). *Stolen Women: Reclaiming Our Sexuality, Taking Back Our Lives*. New York: John Wiley & Sons.